Fifty Tales for a Wet Weekend in Tighnabruaich

Fifty Tales for a Wet Weekend in Tighnabruaich

Tom Carbery

Kennedy & Boyd
an imprint of
Zeticula
57 St Vincent Crescent
Glasgow
G3 8NQ
Scotland.

http://www.kennedyandboyd.co.uk
admin@kennedyandboyd.co.uk

First published in 2010
Copyright © Thomas F. Carbery 2010
Cover photograph © Richard M. Orr 2010

ISBN 978-1-84921-008-9

Acknowledgements

Most of these stories have been told, told verbally, for ten, twenty, thirty, forty, aye and in some cases fifty or sixty years. I know because it was I who told them. Then again, I have to concede that things had reached the pitch wherein members of my family would protest and squirm when I was about to embark on yet another re-telling, but would correct me or prompt me if I were to falter.

That the stories now appear in book form is due to a small select band of relatives and friends.

The initiative was suggested and then advocated by two men. The first was Stephen Donnelly, a brother-in-law of a cousin of mine, the other being John McIntyre, a former academic colleague.

The word processing was improved upon by Mrs Susan McCourt, a former student of mine, and by our eldest grand-daughter, Jennifer Carbery. My son, another Thomas Carbery, helped in many important ways.

The quest for a publisher was greatly assisted by Mr Ronnie Renton, the former Deputy Headmaster of St. Aloysius College in Garnethill in Glasgow, and editorial support came from John McIntyre. I am indebted to them and readily record my gratitude.

The accuracy and validity of the stories are variables. Most of them arose from actual incidents, though in some cases names, dates, locations and other factors have been altered to protect the identity of individuals. Death much diminished the need for such action.

In short, I have tried to ensure that no-one will be slighted or peeved, far less wounded, by what appears in these pages. For any such wounding I am extremely sorry.

It is my hope that those who read this book will experience many a chuckle or smile and even an occasional laugh. At the same time I can foresee a very occasional tear.

T. F. Carbery.
Glasgow
March, 2010

Contents

Uncle Willie's Favourite Tie

Our crowd came into being in the days and years of the middle and late thirties. We were a bunch of boys ranging from ten plus to just under fourteen living in our street and two adjoining side streets. The houses in which we lived were Council housing but as we were in Glasgow everyone referred to them as Corporation houses.

We did what boys did in those days. On the good days and in the long summer evenings we played football, some cricket and occasionally rounders. We ran races and in season played marbles, which to us were jauries, and in the brown days of autumn, conkers. We got shots on bikes and on Public Holiday Mondays we went long walks to Eaglesham and East Kilbride. On wet and windy days we would gather in knots of five, sitting in draughty closes, reading *The Hotspur, The Adventure, The Wizard, The Rover* and *The Skipper* - the five magazines for boys published by the D.C. Thomson Press of Dundee. Each of us bought one and every copy was passed round the other four members of the group. So for tuppence we each had five magazines to read and so it was we helped keep Scotland a literate nation for at least one more generation.

Then came the War! We all enlisted. There was no shirking, there was no hiding in engineering works or aircraft factories, no finding a job on the Govan Ferry and claiming to be in the Merchant Navy. This was particularly difficult for James Beattie. His parents were pacifists and members of the I.L.P. His father was active in the Peace Pledge Union while his mother was president of the local branch of the Co-op Women's Guild. She lustily sang *The Mothers' International* with its strong anti-war lines. To his credit, James thought it through. One Sunday night he spoke to his parents. He explained that he understood their position and respected it but he took the view that Nazi Germany was inherently evil. He believed the reports on what they were doing to the Jews and that while he would not volunteer he would not resist being drafted. So it was that he found himself in the King's Own Scottish Borderers.

Fourteen of us went to war. Twelve of us came home. Tom Auchencloss was killed in an obscure state in the middle of America. He was training to be a pilot in the Fleet Air Arm. One day, while flying solo in his one-engined trainer, the plane stalled. Tom tried to retrieve the situation, but failed: inevitably the plane crashed and he was killed. From the afternoon the telegram arrived his mother was a recluse. When I was on leave and then after the War I would meet Mr. Auchencloss. A Cost and Works Accountant, he was immensely proud of the fact that Tom had been training to be a Scottish CA. When we met he was always courteous and polite. He would ask after my mother and was always interested in the other lads and showed pleasure at their diverse accomplishments. Yet there was always a tear in his eye.

Joe O'Brien was a big, awkwardly-shaped lad who suffered from myopia and wore glasses with lenses like the bottom of jam jars. He worked in the Post Office, started very early and seemed to work all the hours the Lord sent. Despite his eyesight he was intent on serving. He talked himself into the Medical Corps. One day in Normandy in the summer of '44 he was running with a stretcher to rescue a severely wounded driver. He stumbled and fell below a British tank. They found nothing they could bury.

Joe had been going out with Mary McCann. A neighbour was heard to say that she could never understand what that lassie saw in that big lump, O'Brien. She did not see what Mary saw. Mary saw kindness and goodness. She saw good humour in both connotations and she saw a remarkable capacity for hard work. She saw generosity of spirit. She saw humility, the foundation stone of all the virtues, and she saw devotion to his family and to her and above all to his God, to his church and to his faith.

In the late summer of '45, when the War was over, Mary took a tram to the Central Station and a train to England. She entered a convent, an enclosed Order, one with a vow of silence.

Bobby Wallace was a rear gunner in a Lancaster bomber. On what should have been the second last trip of his tour, he was very badly injured. He was in hospital for over ten months before being discharged with the rank of Warrant Officer and a very bad limp. Bobby had been a very good footballer, an elegant dancer and an energetic hiker, a hill walker and an agile rock climber. All that was behind him. Bobby lost them all.

Our wee community within a bigger community, like the nation itself, won its war. But we paid heavily for it!

It was the late forties by the time the last of our crowd, the last of the twelve survivors, was demobbed. Younger brothers and lads from other families were by then doing their National Service. We took up seeing one another, although less than hitherto. Work, developing careers, tertiary education, for some full-time, for others part-time, the early stirrings of courtship - all intruded. For all that, folk went to the pictures on occasion and to the theatre less so. Youth hostelling, camping and rock climbing were well to the fore in the better weather. Attendance at football grounds loomed large in the winter and spring. Some lads went on holiday together.

In addition to all this, there was one café and two pubs which provided casual meeting places. If one was lonely or wanted to discuss a particular topic, these establishments generally provided for the need. We became adroit at making a cup of coffee last well over an hour.

We all knew Uncle Willie. It had been Jack McNicholl who had introduced most of us. It transpired at the time of his death in the late sixties that his full name was William Simpson McLaren. Most of us addressed him as 'Mr McLaren', though Jack and his family always said

'Uncle Willie,' while a few brash characters dared to call him 'Willie', yet he did not object.

Uncle Willie was a very pleasant wee man. A widower of long-standing, he lived with a series of sisters. When one died, he moved on to another house, and through it all managed to stay in the district. For him, the main advantage was the proximity to Cathkin Park and his beloved Third Lanark football club.

What came to intrigue us about this affable, charming, courteous man was that although he was not poor and was always neatly and comfortably dressed he always wore the same tie. At least, from the early fifties he did. He even wore it to funerals. One of the lads, who had been in the RAF, had three black ties; he offered to give one to Willie, who thanked him but declined.

For our part, we tried to determine why Willie was so addicted to it, but no-one could come up with an acceptable explanation. We came back to it again and again, and found ourselves left to conclude that he liked it, and that he liked it very much.

It is, I believe, time for a revelation of some importance. Uncle Willie was not the original owner of his much-loved tie. I was the first owner!

This part of our tale starts with my two maiden aunts. In the winter of 1949-50 they gave me a very generous Christmas present in that they paid for some rather expensive textbooks which I required for a part-time course I was doing at Glasgow University. They were generous but not profligate and so they had warned me that the present for my birthday in January would be meagre. Come the day, it was the tie. It was a very fine, impressive tie - maroon with occasional twin stripes, one in bottle green and the other in pale green. In addition, there were two instances of a further stripe in cream. I liked it immensely, and proceeded to wear it with pride.

The trouble first surfaced in March, when after an evening of study in the Mitchell Library, I went with friends to a nearby restaurant of some quality which did a good line in egg and chips, with bread and butter and a pot of tea, all at a reasonable price. As I was about to enter, the Commissionaire on the door, who was normally affable, albeit gruff, grabbed me by the upper arm.

'Are you entitled to wear that tie?' he demanded.

I asserted I was so entitled, but this was clearly not acceptable. Further acrimonious exchanges at least exposed the problem. He maintained that my tie was that of the Marine Commandos, whereas by turning to the back of the tie I was able to show that it was a Tootal tie, by inference obtainable from all good retailers of menswear.

The next encounter was in the canteen of a Civil Service Club in London, where I was severely rebuked for wearing the tie of the Somerset Light Infantry.

The third and last of these incidents occurred on the train from Glasgow Queen Street via Edinburgh to Newcastle. The train stopped at Dunbar. An elderly man with a neat wee grey beard got on and sat down opposite me. Having sorted himself out and made himself comfortable, he smiled over at me.

'It's grand tae come across yin o' the lads,' he opined. 'Aye, the Royal Scots Greys! We wur great, wur we no'? Ah recognised the tie, ye see.' And with that he smiled again, looked out the window, sighed and thereupon fell asleep.

Within a week I gave the tie and some other items to two girls collecting for a jumble sale at the McCutcheon Memorial Church at the end of the street. It was reported in the café on the night of the sale that Uncle Willie had bought it. It was supposed to be a shilling, but the lady on the stall let him have it for sixpence.

So it was we progressed through the rest of the fifties and the sixties. Some of the lads married and bought houses in Kings Park, Giffnock and Clarkston. Some were moved on promotion to other parts of the country. Some applied for, and obtained posts elsewhere, but even in the early '60s a visit to the café or one of the two public houses gave one a fighting chance of encountering a face from yesteryear. In addition, there were casual meetings in the town or at football matches. All that said, it was weddings, engagement parties and funerals that resulted in us gathering in the greatest numbers. When we did meet, Uncle Willie and his tie were well-nigh certain to be one of the items for review – particularly so when Willie himself was in attendance. Throughout it all discussions on the tie were illustrations of what we called the Cathcart Circle School of Debate. You ended up where you had started.

Uncle Willie died in the late sixties.

As the Minister was in full voice at the graveside, a heavy, nasty, squally shower broke over us. The Minister judiciously cut short his already gey lengthy prayer and conferred a very short blessing on all present. The undertaker shouted that we should make for the cars and just get in any car rather than looking for the one in which we had arrived.

I found myself in a car with three men, all in their fifties and sixties. A big man with the rough hands of a manual worker remarked that he had noted with some pride that Willie had been in the Gordon Highlanders. He added you could tell that from his tie. The gentleman sitting beside him gave a polite, deprecating cough. 'I fear you are mistaken,' he observed, 'the tie was that of the Lovat Scouts. I have that on good authority; a fellow elder assured me that was the case.'

The man next to me exploded: 'Stuff and nonsense!' he roared. 'The tie was the tie of the Third Battalion of the HLI. The wife an' me know, because our Sammy wiz in that Battalion and spoke tae Willie aboot it!'

The rest of the journey to the Co-op Hall for the purvey proceeded in silence.

Once in the Hall, I gathered the lads about me. I explained that I had cracked the mystery of the tie. What had annoyed me had delighted Willie. 'It suited him fine,' I asserted. 'About half the British Army acclaimed him and treated him as a comrade-in-arms. I bet he had many a drink on the strength of it, and many a half-crown or even the odd ten-bob note slipped to him on the strength of that tie.'

But the others would not buy it. So far as they were concerned, Willie just liked that tie. Glenn Duncan, who was a late entrant to the ministry, said a loud 'Amen!' and that was the end of that.

It was not the end, however, of Uncle Willie, who remained in our conversation, and who still does.

Hector

Incredulity and scepticism were the two main reactions to Hector – to Dr Hector Sykes Fletcher, to give him his full form of address. The incredulity was experienced by those who actually encountered him, particularly those who had to work alongside him. The scepticism came from those who merely heard about him and who could not readily accept that such an outré figure actually existed. But he did.

There was no doubt that he was clever. As a boy he had been runner-up to the dux of his Scottish senior secondary or grammar school. He would have been dux but for the fact that he had no real affinity with languages: the quantitative was his world and he revelled in it.

On leaving school he went up to the University of Glasgow where he took a First Class Honours degree in Mathematics. He then went to Cambridge where he took a second degree and from there he went to Cambridge, Massachusetts where he took a doctorate from Harvard. Following his return to the UK he did further specialist work in Statistics under the auspices of the Royal Statistical Society.

One could readily see why the University Appointments Committee had been interested in him, though the members should have realised that his high-pitched, squeaky voice would not inspire confidence. On the contrary, it gave rise to disdain and ridicule.

Within three days of meeting him you knew he would never be promoted beyond the Lecturers' grade. Yet this was not the end of his eccentricity. He was an extreme right-winger, regarding the Liberal Party and all to the left of it as Communists. He appeared to believe totally and unreservedly in the dominance of the white Anglo-Saxon tradition. He was for Britain and the Empire, the Royal Family, the Conservative and Unionist Party and all things Protestant – or rather nearly all such – for he was critical of the Church of England and its sister church in Scotland for not having purged themselves of the trappings of Popery. He had a dislike to a point of detestation of Catholicism, of Judaism and of all coloured races.

Hector was of strange, formidable appearance. He was tall and slim with long limbs. He tended to remind one of Hen Broon in the strip-cartoon in *The Sunday Post*. His hair was black; he had a centre-parting akin to those in the photographs of goalkeepers and centre-forwards which appeared on the cigarette cards of the '30s.

He shaved one side of his face on a Monday and the other side on a Tuesday. The same arrangement was deployed on Wednesday and Thursday and yet again on Friday and Saturday. On Sunday, prior to going to the kirk at eleven o'clock, he shaved his entire face, put on aftershave lotion, a clean white shirt, the Glasgow University graduate tie of black and gold, then topped it all with an expensive dark, sober, almost sombre suit.

He drove a royal blue Mini, and almost always exceeded the prescribed speed limit. He lived in Elderslie from where, in those pre-motorway days, he drove to Glasgow through Paisley, by Barshaw Park, Crookston and Cardonald. It was said that he had a secret ambition to scoop up a nun outside Nazareth House convent in Cardonald on his way home and leave her dead at Paisley Cross.

On his own admission, indeed boast, there was one morning when, driving past Barshaw Park, he became aware of a forearm alongside him. Acknowledging to himself that this was rather strange, he glanced to his right and discerned that the arm was attached to a man. Thereupon the man spoke: 'Do you know you are doing seventy miles per hour?'

Hector was both confident and resilient. 'What business is it of yours what speed I am doing?' he asked in an aggrieved tone.

There was an audible sigh from the body belonging to the arm.

'It is our business because we are police officers.'

'Well, you must be doing seventy as well,' replied Hector, 'and if you are police officers you should know better and not do that!'

And with that he roared up to eighty-five and tore away.

On one famous occasion he parked his car at an awkward angle in a lane between Hope Street and Renfield Street. A large lorry with a very heavy load tried to turn into the lane. The driver got the cabin and a few feet of the lorry into the lane, and got stuck. Moreover, he could not reverse out for the tramcars plying their way both up and down Hope Street. Within minutes chaos prevailed. After twenty minutes the tailback went down Hope Street to Central Station, while up the street it went to Cowcaddens and along Sauchiehall Street as far as Trerons.

When it was at its worst, Hector appeared, jumped into his car, reversed and was about to drive away when a big sergeant in the Police banged on the roof and started roaring at our hero. Hector calmly rolled down his window and told the sergeant that he had no right to address a member of the public in such abusive terms no matter what he had done. 'More,' he added, 'I am a lecturer and last week my briefcase with new lecture notes and work by students was stolen. I reported it to your colleagues and they have never contacted me. You should be out chasing criminals instead of abusing decent tax-paying motorists!' Whereupon he drove off and yet again got away with it.

Members of staff who worked alongside Hector readily paid tribute to the conscientious way he set about his teaching. He never missed a lecture. He was never late for a lecture. He always finished, neither too early nor too late. In addition, he invariably wiped his blackboard so that it was clean and ready for the next lecturer. The students had no complaints about his marking: he always marked both promptly and fairly. There was never any suggestion of bias. Moreover, he made himself available to the students for consultation and advice.

There was, however, a recurring debate about the objectivity of his teaching, in particular the statistical exercises that he would demonstrate on the board and those he invited students to tackle in their own time.

Thus, according to these exercises, Catholics were heavily over-represented in the criminal classes, those with Irish Catholic names were over-represented among those found guilty of having been drunk and disorderly, while Jews were over-represented in the ranks of those found guilty of arson or charges of financial chicanery. What caused even more adverse comment were the recurring exercises which led to the conclusion that all coloured races were less intelligent than whites. When confronted with the misgivings of his colleagues, Hector stoutly maintained that he could not be held responsible for the messages and lessons to emerge from an examination of the raw data. His critics, on the other hand, suggested that either the data had been doctored or that Hector had rummaged around until he found data which suited his political and socio-economic views.

One brave and possibly foolhardy student suggested they should undertake an exercise in probability theory to see whether they could come up with proof that the Glasgow Rangers football club exercised a discriminatory policy in its recruitment of players, there being a widespread belief that the Club did discriminate. Hector declined the invitation. He observed that he was aware of the foul, unfair, biased and totally unfounded allegations against the Club, but it was just not true. He had been advised of this on the highest authority.

Later it transpired that his highest authority was the Rev. James Currie, a Church of Scotland minister from Blackwaterfoot in Arran. This popular, kenspeckle figure just happened to be a fanatical Rangers supporter.

Hector was a man of habit and one of his little foibles was that, each morning after breakfast, he cut the Court Circular from the pages of his favourite newspaper, a rightwing broadsheet. Having extracted it he filed it away carefully, indeed almost reverentially, in his wallet. Knowing of this little practice, mischievous members of staff with teasing intent would sidle up to him in the coffee lounge of the Staff Club. 'Hector, dear man,' they would say, 'what is Her Royal Highness the Duchess of Gloucester doing today? I ask because I know you will know. You always know these things.'

Delighted at the enquiry, Hector would plunge into his jacket, extract the wallet, find the cutting and read it. 'She is launching a new lifeboat in Torbay,' he would beam, and with a sigh of great contentment return the wallet and the precious cutting to his jacket. Such was the nature of his disposition that it never occurred to him to question the sincerity of such enquiries, even when they came from militant socialists.

It was a Friday afternoon in mid-term that gave rise to some consternation and for some, a reassessment of Hector. Five or six of us, finding that we were free from three o'clock until four, also found ourselves meeting for coffee. As ever, the chat flowed easily. We discussed the price of flights to the States, the Public Sector Borrowing Requirement, the indiscipline of children – and then religion. Murdo Nicholson, our well-known non-believer who had shocked and saddened his Free Church family by declaring himself a humanist, poured forth his condemnation of all religion. He was taken on by Alfred Appleby, a mild-mannered man from the north of England who was known to be active in the Episcopal Cathedral in the West End, and by others of diverse religious affiliation who chipped in to support him. Then Hector burst into the debate. 'Murdo is right,' he said, 'it is all a lot of piffle. That is what it is, it's a lot of piffle. It is a lot of stories for wee boys and girls. It is a lot of bilge.'

There followed an awkward and embarrassed silence which was eventually broken by Alfred.

'Hector,' he quietly asked, 'if it is all a lot of nonsense, why do you bother to go to church every Sunday?'

An even more uncomfortable silence followed this very reasonable question. When it was broken by a lot of wriggling and twisting by Hector, it took a further ten minutes for the answer to come out with reasonable clarity.

It transpired that there were two reasons. The first was that on Sunday he was awakened before eight o'clock by a lot of noisy Papists going to their idolatrous Mass, and the second was that the Kirk was part of the fabric of the proper established order in the country and an instrument for the propagation of the Protestant Work Ethic. It was for these reasons he gave the Church, provided of course it was a spirited, Protestant Church, his support and his attendance.

Then came the most dramatic and important of all the incidents and events in the Hector story – his marriage.

Over the better part of a term he had been confiding in some male colleagues, telling them that he reckoned he should marry. It was not that he had a particular lady in mind; it was just that like a medieval monarch, he thought he should do his duty - even though he thought he might not like being married. He did, however, quite like the idea of having a son and bringing him up to acknowledge the standards and traditions to which he himself subscribed.

He did not want a youngster as a wife and certainly not a flibbertigibbet. On the contrary, he was looking for a well-educated, mature woman in her early thirties. He had recognised that a lady of such an age might prove to be unable to have children so it would be as well that she should be in receipt of a good salary. So it was that he resolved that at least initially the search should be confined to members of staff. There was, however, yet another consideration: he did not approve of dark-haired

Latin ladies. He wanted a blonde of Germanic, Nordic appearance, yet did not appear concerned whether the hair colouring had emerged naturally or out of a bottle.

His first approach was to Margaret Mary Dunning, a slim, always well-dressed lecturer in English. One day he approached her in the lounge of the Staff Club. As he did so he stumbled and threw his cup of coffee over her and her fawn-coloured Susan Small costume. A kafuffle with paper napkins and blotting paper ensued. When it was finished, he made one of the most remarkable proposals of all time.

'See you,' he said, 'I'll marry you if you renounce Rome!'

Margaret Mary graciously declined, excused herself and withdrew.

We regarded it as a lucky escape. As I remarked to her later, it had been a case of 'East, West, Rome's best!'

Hector's second or third overture was to Winifred Dunlop, a lecturer in German who very appropriately lived in Dunlop. Within weeks it was clear they were an item. Shortly thereafter an engagement was announced; they were to be married in the first week of the summer vacation. The wedding took place in Dunlop Parish Church, while the reception was held in the hall of one of the most distinguished Masonic lodges in the country. His wedding present to her was a very expensive diamond and ruby brooch, while her present to him was a rather fine gold vest-pocket watch with Masonic insignia.

The gift from the staff to the happy couple was a magnificent and expensive piece of crystal ware.

The speech and presentation were made by the only woman professor in the place. As she handed it over to Hector he fumbled and dropped it, whereupon it hit the edge of a coffee table and shattered.

'Was it insured?' roared a lecturer in Business Policy.

We learned later that it had not been insured, so 'the sheet' came round again and again we contributed. On this occasion the contributions were somewhat less generous. Another, smaller piece of glassware was purchased and it was given to our potential bride.

They bought a house in rural West Renfrewshire and travelled up to town in the famous Mini.

Some eighteen months later he took a post as Senior Statistician with an oil company in London.

Almost two decades went by, when news trickled through that Hector had died. He had been a non-smoker yet had died of lung cancer brought on, it appeared, by passive smoking in an open-plan office.

Ten weeks or so after the death, Winifred phoned me with a query about his educational pension. I was glad to be of some help to her. In the course of our pension business it became abundantly clear that she wanted to speak about Hector. 'He was a wonderful husband' she said. 'No woman could have been happier than I have been. He transformed my life and introduced me to interests of which I had no experience. I had virtually twenty years of a wonderful marriage. I loved him totally and told him so at least once every day. I worked at devising ways of expressing my love and affection for him together with my appreciation of him.'

And there it was! For all his oddity and all his quirky ways and views, and for all the scoffing and teasing and disdain of his colleagues, Hector had succeeded in winning the deepest love, affection and approval of a good woman.

All too many men foolishly believe they are equally loved and appreciated. Life tells us very, very few are.

Sadly, Hector never had a son.

Gruppenführerin Blair

It was in the late summer or early autumn of 1934 that we received notification that we had been given a Council house which, being in Glasgow, we called a Corporation house. It was not quite my mother's dream house. That was a bungalow in Boathouse Avenue in Largs, which house had magnificent, unfettered views of Arran, the larger Cumbrae, Bute and the Cowal peninsula.

What we had been allotted was a three-apartment ground floor flat in a relatively new tenement property in Govanhill. This modest castle was going to be a vast improvement on the two-apartment flat in Hutchesonton, where my parents had lived since the early twenties and where I had been born.

While we were making arrangements for the move, my mother was stopped in Cumberland Street, the great shopping street of Hutchesonton, by a well-meaning, compassionate neighbour. This lady, whom we hardly knew, delicately and with due consideration asked whether my mother was sure she was doing the right thing, taking on what she referred to as 'that big hoose', particularly as my father did not enjoy the best of health. That big house? A three-apartment! Yet we knew and knew only too well what the lady had in mind. Our existing rent was what we called 1s 9d per week, i.e. one shilling and nine pennies whereas the 'new' house was destined to cost us 'ten and six' which was half a guinea. But my parents swallowed hard and notwithstanding the over five-fold increase in the weekly rental, signed on the bottom line. Whereupon the gey modest pantechnicon rolled to Govanhill with our modest possessions.

In the morning of our first full day in the new house after the flitting, we breakfasted in the living room. We were to learn later that many families ate in the kitchenette, but we had regarded that as too cramped. Shortly after eight o'clock my father left for his work as a school attendance officer in Bridgeton: this necessitated a two mile walk, hence the relatively early departure.

Precisely at nine o'clock there was a ring on our brand new electric bell. We had not had an electric bell in our old house for the very good reason that we had not had electricity. For that matter we had not had a toilet – for that facility we shared a closet on the half landing, while within the old house we had a single cold water tap and no hot water.

When my mother opened the door she was confronted by a formidable lady. It would have been ungracious, unfair and untrue to call her obese, fat or even plump. Let us say that she was comfortably well-built. She had that well-fed look, as though she came from farming stock in Ayrshire or Angus. The lady was wearing a blue linen dress partly covered by a light brown apron.

'Good morning,' she said, 'my name is Blair. Mrs Blair! I live on the top floor. I have come to welcome you to the close and to say we all hope you will be happy in your new home, and that your family will like living in Govanhill.' Here she paused, as though expecting – hoping, perchance? – that my mother would reveal where we came from. Having received no such response, Mrs Blair continued:

'At the same time, though, I should acquaint you with our little arrangements. The close should be swept four times a week at least, twice by you and twice by Mrs Andrews on the other side. It should be washed twice a week, once by each of you. You will have noticed that we prefer white pipe clay; we do not approve of red pipe clay, which we regard as pretentious, and we certainly do not approve of twirly bits.'

She continued: 'You will have observed that there are four poles in the back green. We each have one day a week for use of that main drying area. There is no washing whatsoever on the Sabbath. Your day for the drying green will be a Thursday. As and when a family leaves the close you may aspire to inherit their washing day, but allocation is made on the precedence of length of residence.'

'There are permanent ropes from two poles to the drain pipes against the walls. These are for use by anyone at any time but are, of course, for smalls such as stockings. Being on the ground floor you are responsible for the front garden. We should be grateful were you to keep the hedge at the existing height. We would not like to see it any higher or any lower. The height is as you see well-nigh uniform the length of the street. As for flowers and the like, that can be resolved at your discretion, though we would prefer it were you to refrain from growing any vegetables.'

'We notice you have a boy. There are no ball games to be played in the back green. Finally, if you need any guidance or advice we shall all be pleased to provide it.'

It was four years later, in 1938, the year the Empire Exhibition was held in Bellahouston Park, that we experienced the second Mrs Blair incident that was fated to work its way into our family folklore. It happened on a Holiday Monday. My father was sitting by the fire reading his newspaper, while I was footering about, trying to determine whether my extremely restricted financial resources would allow me to go to the afternoon performance in one of our two local cinemas. It was not taking long to count my total funds, which no matter how often I counted did not exceed three pence.

Normally on such a day my friends and I would have gone on one of our fairly long walks to East Kilbride or Eaglesham, but it was a morning of continuous heavy rain, with no indication of any clearance.

My mother had gone out to the bin or midden or refuse area with potato peelings and other vegetable material wrapped in newspaper, in accordance with a Blair 'recommendation'. When she returned she was clearly put out.

'I'll never understand that woman!' she proclaimed.

'What's wrong?' asked my Dad, a quiet, reasonable man whatever the circumstances.

'It's that Mrs Blair,' she announced. 'She has just told me she doesn't like these Public Holidays. Imagine not liking holidays! Ridiculous!'

My father agreed that it seemed strange, very strange, and with that returned to his paper.

The years rolled by. In late 1942 my father died, a few weeks after signing the documents which gave his permission for me to volunteer for aircrew duties in the RAF. Sadly, he had less than ten years in his new home.

While I was in South Africa on my training as a navigator, my paternal grandmother, who had come to live with us, died. My mother was then on her own until I was demobbed in 1947.

By the time the seventies came round, my mother was living with my wife, me and our three children in a more spacious house in Cathcart. My wife and I were the only two who shared a bedroom, a situation which resulted in the children sympathising for, but not with, my wife.

On most evenings, while preparing for bed, I would look in on my mother, whose favourite occupation was to sit up in bed reading a responsible novel while eating tablet or a Yorkie bar. On such occasions our chat would turn again and again to our years in the old Corporation house in Govanhill. The redoubtable Mrs Blair would be a recurring topic. But by that time we had come to understand the lady more. Mrs Blair, God bless her, was a woman of order. She liked predictable normality. On normal Mondays she made breakfast as usual; her husband went to work as usual; her son and her two daughters went to work as usual. She washed the dishes as usual. She made the beds as usual and then since Monday was her day for the back-green she started on her main weekly washing. We had come to see that a holiday on a Monday would and did drive her to despair. On such days the others lay abed, rose at disparate times and breakfasts of various sizes and duration lasted until afternoon. Worst of all, she could not get on with her washing and by the arrangements which she herself proclaimed and protected, she had no alternative day to which she could turn.

All this my mother and I could see, albeit with belated understanding. But more, much more, we had come to see a great profundity: this was that every tenement close needs a Mrs Blair. A close without such a lady is truly bereft.

What The Dickens

It was Glasgow at its worst. It was a case of ten-tenths cloud at zero feet. To make matters worse, there was a thin, murky mire lying everywhere. It was on the streets, it was on the pavements and it was on one's clothing. It was filthy to the touch. As though that was not enough, there was a steady smirr which, slight though it was, penetrated one's outer clothing and went on to attack other garments.

At that time I was the Statistics Clerk in Bridgeton Employment Exchange in the South-East of the city. Important in its own way though this task was, it accounted for only 90% of my working week.

Accordingly, the management team had been obliged to find other duties for me which would take up the residual 10% of my time. What they had decided was that I should be responsible for chasing up the young men of military age who appeared not to have registered for their National Service as they had been due to do on the assigned date. My first commitment was to the Statistical returns and I was left to attend to the other duties on the days when there was little or no statistical work to be done.

This was one such day. I was feeling rather miserable, partly because it was such a dull, dreich day but partly too, because I had spent the preceding half hour or so in a very mean house in a very grim tenement in a miserable street between Nuneaton Street and Springfield Road.

The entrance to the close had been quite dreadful. The paint and plaster work had been peeling from the walls which in turn had been running with condensation. There had been four doors on each landing instead of the usual three. Very few of the doors had name plates, either metal or plastic. Some had the name scribbled on a piece of card-board which in turn was affixed to the wood by a drawing pin or a nail. Many of the doors had no name whatsoever.

With difficulty I found the appropriate house. The door was opened by a scruffy, dirty, untidy, unshaven man who in an aggressive growl wanted to know who I was and what my business was with him. I explained my business and suggested that as it was of a confidential nature it was probably better were we to conduct the business inside the house rather than on the landing, where others might overhear us. He took the point and two steps led us into the single apartment which constituted the home. An untidy, unmade bed ran along one wall. The range was entirely covered in rust. The sole window was unwashed and the sink below it was cluttered with empty, smelly milk bottles. Against the other wall was a wardrobe, the mirror on the doors no longer capable of reflection. In the middle of the room there was a wooden kitchen table, in the centre of which was a roughly cut loaf and a pot of jam, about which and stuck to which was a squadron of flies.

When I explained my business in greater detail, the householder exploded in indignation. "Naw, naw," he said. 'Ma boy widnae dae that. He'd want tae go tae the sodjers. We ur a' true-blue here. No surrender!'

I explained as carefully and as patiently as I could that I had not said the young man had not registered: it appeared he had not registered, but it was possible that there was a mistake on our side. However, the matter could easily be resolved, because if the young man had registered he would have a wee brown card which would have been given to him at the time of registration. I observed that it was evident the lad was not at home, so maybe the father could ask the lad to call at the office and let me see his card.

I was astonished at what ensued.

Below the table there was a heap of rags, largish rags, a blanket of sorts and a well-worn overcoat on the top. The man proceeded to kick this heap, whereupon there emerged from it our potential soldier of the King and defender of the Empire.

There followed an extremely bitter exchange between the father and the son. At first the boy said he had registered, but when I squeezed my way into the conversation and asked to see his card, he admitted he had not registered, because he did not want to join the Army.

This intelligence drove the father to a fury. He started to kick, punch and push the young man.

In time I persuaded him to stop. I thereupon registered the young man and took my leave. I suspect he failed the medical – to his delight and the father's chagrin.

So there I was walking in my melancholy mode through the wet, woebegone streets of Bridgeton. As I went to pass yet another close, a young man of much my own age came running out of the close. We collided violently and a briquette board which he had been carrying went slithering across the pavement towards a horse and cart standing in the roadside. The horse's breath was visible and the cart was half-laden with coal briquettes. The young man and I mumbled apologies though the incident was clearly more my fault than it was his. At that point I recognised him as Mr James McGinty of Norman Street. Mr McGinty was a frequent and recurring claimant of Unemployment Benefit at our office. Many of the staff members who dealt with him suspected him of both working and claiming benefit, but we had never been able to prove it. Now here he was clearly distributing and selling briquettes.

'Ah, Mr McGinty,' I said. 'Engaged in a little commercial activity, I see. I think you should call to see me in my room at, say, 9.30 tomorrow morning.' And with that we parted.

The next morning I pulled in my colleague, Bill McGuigan, a breezy Ulsterman. As the clock hand moved to the half hour, the door was knocked and in came the bold James.

I thanked him for coming and he took a seat. When we had settled I put it to him he had been working the day before. He shuffled and wriggled a bit in his seat, then gave voice:

'Well, aye an' naw! Aye an' naw!' he said. Then sensing our displeasure and perplexity he went on. 'Well,' he said, 'Ah wiz workin' but no' fur masel'. It was fur another bloke. Ah wiz daein' him a favour, like.'

Whereupon he stopped and looked at both of us with an expression of sweet reasonableness.

'All right,' I said, 'tell us the story.'

So he did. According to Mr McGinty the briquette business was that of an elderly gentleman, "an auld bloke" as he put it, who was his mother's boyfriend. He, the elderly beau, was ill with severe bronchitis. His mother had gone to see the patient. She had taken soup and some magazines to him and he had asked to see James. When he in turn had gone to see the indisposed, the gentleman had explained that he had a lot of good customers, mainly elderly women, and he was anxious not to let them down. He had accordingly asked Mr McGinty to do him and the customers a favour. He was to go to the coal depot, explain the situation to John McMaster, the General Manager, collect the horse and cart, uplift the briquettes and call at the houses on a list already prepared by the indisposed. If he could sell some extra briquettes to neighbours of the regular customers, that would be doubly helpful.

'Them folk cannae really afford coal,' the indisposed had observed through his bronchial coughs. 'We must dae whit we can tae keep the auld souls warm. It's a work of charity, so it is!'

When Mr McGinty had finished his passably plausible story I turned and glanced at my colleague. Our eyes met and I gleaned we were broadly at one. It was a good story, but further questioning was required.

'I see,' I said. At that he smiled, but I went on. 'Now, Mr McGinty,' I continued, 'are you really asking us to accept that you went out on a day of quite dreadful weather and worked all day, all out of sympathy for this elderly gentleman and his customers, that there was no financial consideration whatsoever?'

McGinty paused, then looked at both of us in turn. 'Well,' he said. 'He said it would be aw right tae tak' aff enough dosh tae cover ra cost of ten Woodbine an' a pint of Guinness.'

Again Bill and I looked at each other. The items James had mentioned came to within a penny of the amount claimants could earn for casual labour without impairing their entitlement to benefit. Yet we remained sceptical. Indeed, this added to our reservations.

'Mr McGinty,' I declared, 'are you seriously contending that this is all there is to it – all that hard work in dreadful conditions, all for ten cheap cigarettes, a single drink and compassion for an old man?'

Here there was an even longer pause.

17

'Well,' he started. 'Ah suppose there is Dickens.'

'Dickens?' I half shouted.

'Dickens?' queried Bill.

'Aye, Dickens,' declared the bold James, all in a tone which suggested that we were imbeciles.

'Are you talking about Dickens the author?' I asked.

'Aye,' said James.

'And what the devil has he to do with you selling briquettes?' I enquired.

'Everything,' said James. He frowned in a way that suggested that he was anxious to help, but it was not his fault that we were rather obtuse. Then he went on: 'He wrote books an' pictures an' stuff. There wiz wan oan at the Olympia a wee while ago.'

The Olympia at Bridgeton Cross was by far the most impressive of the local cinemas.

At this point Bill joined in, having latched on to the seemingly tortuous thought processes of McGinty.

'*A Tale of Two Cities*? *David Copperfield*?' he half queried.

'Naw, naw,' said James impatiently. 'It wis *Great Expectations*!'

'*Great Expectations*!' I nearly exploded.

'Aye, *Great Expectations*,' said James in somewhat more conciliatory tones. 'Efter a', the auld fella might die an' leave us ra hoarse an' cairt!'

The Two Men of Business

It was Glasgow at its best. The Good Lord had sent us a magnificent Indian Summer which lasted almost the entire month of October. It was at its most outstanding for the October Week, the week when the schools were closed, ostensibly to allow the pupils to assist with the bringing in of the harvest. This made sense in rural Aberdeenshire, in Perthshire, Angus, the Borders, Dumfriesshire and in some other parts of the land but it made no sense in the cities, particularly those in the Central Belt.

It was the early seventies. At that time I was a Senior Lecturer in the Business School of the University of Strathclyde. On the day in question I had been out attending meetings at the two teacher training colleges on the west side of the conurbation. It was now about quarter to four in the afternoon. I had parked my car in the south-east of the campus and was crossing a very small manmade parkland.

Here it should be explained that Strathclyde, the first new University in Scotland since the Reformation, had been the outcome of a shotgun marriage between two inner-city colleges. This had certain consequences. Thus for one thing we had no greenery at the time of our inception. Then again, our buildings were totally disparate. We could have stuck a notice on each building indicating that any resemblance to the building next door was purely coincidental. Furthermore, as we expanded, we bought, leased or built new accommodation. Our acquisition of buildings was remarkable.

A visitor could readily be excused for thinking our Principal and the Chairman of Court were ecclesiastically minded or had a feeling for churches. We had four churches. We bought churches with the wild abandon of a boy of twelve buying railway stations when playing Monopoly for the first time.

In all of this we were the very opposite of Stirling, which had developed in the parkland of an estate on the edge of town. Stirling had employed one architect who not only stuck to his basic design but, it was understood, had insisted on using the same stone throughout the campus. It was picturesque.

Heriot-Watt University in Edinburgh had also been a city centre establishment, but it had been afforded the opportunity to move to a large greenland site at Riccarton, and had jumped at it. We, on the other hand, had received a not dissimilar offer from the East Kilbride Development Corporation, and had turned it down. Why? The disclosure date under our equivalent of the Official Secrets Act has not yet been reached, but there were and are those who found it significant that East Kilbride lay on the south-east of the conurbation and the Principal lived in Helensburgh, very much to the west. Whatever the reasoning or the lack thereof, we declined and we stayed in the city centre.

It was against that background that we resolved to have our own small, even pathetic, yet brave area of 'instant parkland'. It was not much bigger than a football field. It had many attractive features. It had undulating mounds of fine green grass, where students could lie or sit and do what students do on sloping grassy areas, though I fear that not many were to be found reading Plato. There were trees and bushes and beds of flowers. In addition, at not a little expense, we had introduced two innovations. Firstly, we commissioned a leading Scottish sculptor in metals to create an arrangement of tall stainless steel pillars. It was claimed these represented, recreated as it were, the Standing Stanes at Callanish on Lewis in the Hebrides. This proved to be a disappointment. The creation was no doubt inspired by the Standing Stanes, but in the view of most of us bore no resemblance to them. Furthermore, the metal was not stainless, or if it had been, the Glasgow rain and our acidic, industrial smog did for it.

The other innovation was much more successful, though in some instances in quite unforeseen ways. This was a constant stream or burn or brook that ran like a large, lazy capital W on the side of a hill. The water meandered pleasantly down the slope, and then, having reached the bottom, was raised by a hidden pump to the beginning to recommence its journey of descent. To add to the flavour of this pleasant pastoral scene, we had populated the stream with goldfish and other aquatic life. This was a great success for about three weeks. Within a month or so, most of the fish, large and small, had disappeared. Most had been acquired by seagulls and local cats, and much of the rest by wee boys who arrived not only from the nearby houses but from much farther afield.

By the time of the day in question, the greenery had matured, while the stream bubbled and gurgled along. A party of five or six schoolboys had clearly had a fine day fishing for 'baggies' and ploutering about in the water. It was about quarter to four. Marvellous though the day had been, the best had gone out of it, and the lads were beginning to prepare for the journey home. One boy, a tall, red-headed lad with freckles, was drying his feet with his shirt: what else would a man use? On stopping to retie my shoelace I overhead what to me was a fascinating exchange.

A small, chunky, broad-shouldered lad with a crew-cut, a brown tee-shirt and Army surplus trousers was swinging what seemed to be a home-made skateboard. He approached the red-haired boy who was drying his feet.

'Alex,' said the chunky one. 'Would you like tae use ma skateboard?'

'Aye,' said he of the feet. 'Aye, that wid be good.'

The chunky one smiled as spiders must smile when they have entrapped some flies, and then he went on.

'An' Alex, is it a'right if Ah get a shot uv your fishin' net?'

Here was the trap shut. Alex would have difficulty in declining.

Nevertheless, he made it apparent that he was not to be hurried into responding. In keeping with which, he applied himself assiduously to drying the bits between his toes. Eventually he raised his head.

'Aw right,' he replied, 'but don't get it wet!'

I was due to go into the Business School to take an Honours year seminar. I related the incident of the skateboard and the fishing-net to the students. I invited their attention to the quite magnificent bargaining skills of the chunky lad. Here was a man that seemed destined to do well in some flint-faced and maybe not particularly ethical Marketing Department.

But I invited even more attention to the outstanding resilience of Alex. Here was a man who could conjure up a conditional clause which nullified the supposed advantage of those who mistakenly believed he had been outmanoeuvred. On the contrary, it was he who had won.

God bless the Alexs of this world! Britain could do with many, many more like him.

The Remarkable Redmonds

The actress, Siobhan Redmond, is known, admired and appreciated in many households in Britain and abroad. She comes from a talented family. I had the privilege and pleasure of working with her father, John Redmond, when we were on the teaching staff of one of Glasgow's three universities. The first of that family whom I encountered was a small, squat yet thickset man who was said to be John's uncle. We knew him as 'Mungo' because he resembled the popular illustrations or portrayals of St Mungo, the patron saint of Glasgow.

When I knew Mungo, it was the late forties or early fifties. The setting was the Men's Union of the University of Glasgow. But the story, as I received it (no doubt very substantially apocryphal), was that in the days and years prior to the outbreak of the War, Mungo had been unemployed, and had been a corner boy, that is, one of a bunch of impecunious young men who stood about a street corner in a working class, if not deprived, area of the city. The story had it that on one grim day in winter an elderly lady who lived in the same tenement as Mungo asked him to take her library books to the library, and to ask the person on the desk, almost certainly a young lady, to renew the books, thereby extending the loan for a further two weeks, so preventing a fine being applicable. It was said that Mungo was not unco keen; he had never had occasion to go to the library. But he knew that his grandmother was moderately friendly with the lady, and that they were members of the same kirk, and he reckoned it was incumbent on him to say he would do it. So it was that he took the books, went to the library and had them stamped up for an additional two weeks. To his surprise, he found that he quite liked the library. It was quiet, it was warm and it was dry. These were great advantages over the cold, draughty, windy, damp corner where he spent most of his time. He noticed, too, that it had a reading room with all the daily newspapers, including *The Daily Worker*. It had, too, a series of reference books.

There were two developments from all this. Firstly, he became the elderly lady's representative. She told him the kind of books she liked and the authors of whom she approved. He in turn would liaise with the girl on the desk. He would be allowed into the library proper to select the books and have them stamped for issue to the elderly lady. The other development was that on some inclement days he chose the library rather than the street corner. In due course he applied for tickets and so became a borrower in his own right.

Gradually his life changed. He took out fewer cowboy and detective stories and turned to more profound and demanding works.

With the approach of war the economy picked up and Mungo got a job, a heavy, demanding job, in the Parkhead Forge. This brought him into the world of the trades unions, and that in turn took him into the world of politics. Some folk said he joined the Labour Party, some said it was the ILP, while yet others said he became a Communist. Whatever the party, by the time I knew him, he was certainly a man of the Left.

In the post-war period some of his political friends pointed out to him that there was a serious shortage of teachers, and that if he could pick up some Highers he could obtain admission to University and go on to a teacher training college, for all of which grants were available.

To his great credit, he responded to all of this. During his first year as an undergraduate he continued working in the Forge. Thus he would attend the University until lunch-time, forego the afternoon lectures and skip home to Bridgeton to change. He would go out to work the two to ten o'clock shift at the Forge. On arriving back from work he would wash, eat and then study until after two in the morning. Then after about five hours sleep he would arise and after a breakfast of sorts scramble up to Gilmorehill for an early lecture. He tried to recover at the weekends. One academic year of that nearly killed him. His friends persuaded him to apply for a higher grant, which he obtained.

This remarkable man eventually became Head of the Department of Education in the Sudan. He died at a comparatively young age. He died aboard ship while returning from leave.

John Redmond, Siobhan's father, was not just a very, very good teacher. He was a brilliant teacher of English Literature. He was a living reservoir of knowledge. His love of his subject and his devotion to his profession bubbled out of him. Above all, he enthused his students, who in turn came to share his love of the subject. Such teachers are a rare breed, and yet all too often they, like John, are not promoted. What happens is that they pour all their endeavours into their teaching, with the result that they do not take post-graduate degrees and do not publish either textbooks or esoteric works on obscure aspects of their disciplines. It is their students who are the major beneficiaries of their exceptional abilities.

Then again, born teachers like John Redmond are not always appreciated by those above them. In John's case, a senior member of staff, a mean-spirited little man, was frequently to be heard complaining that marginal and sub-marginal students who should have failed and failed badly kept passing their exams when they had been entrusted to John. This success should have been applauded; instead it was condemned and almost became a matter of censure.

On one famous Saturday when John had been in Bridgeton visiting relatives he went into a second-hand goods shop in Landressy Street, a small, queer, quaint and sort of ugly street at the back of the bustling Bridgeton Cross. It was the street that contained the Library which John's uncle Mungo had visited those many years before. It had a Baptist church at one end and a pub at the other. It had both a Masonic Hall and an Orange Hall. In addition it had a miscellany of wee grubby shops almost all fated to experience economic disaster. The shop dealing in a wide variety of second-hand material which John visited was the best of a bad bunch.

In the course of his meandering through the aisles he came across a gem, a find of no little importance. It was a very large leather-bound book from the years of Victoria. It was in remarkably good condition, a shade woebegone, but there was little amiss that was not capable of being retrieved. It contained the entire works of Shakespeare, including the Sonnets.

John humped it to the counter where the man in charge of the shop was smoking and adding to a potential Munro of ashes in an ash tray while reading the racing pages of a local tabloid.

John dropped the book with a thud on the counter, whereupon the ash rose, hovered and then slowly descended, not all of it returning to the ashtray.

Somewhat peeved, the man scowled at our hero.

'Aye,' he growled. 'Aye. Whit dae ye want?'

The man was put out and as a result he was peeved, and because he was peeved he was displeased. His intense study of the racing form had been broken and that had displeased him. Had he wanted to write his name in the ash now on the counter, he could have done so, and that displeased him too. Finally, he had incorrectly surmised that he was to be confronted with rough and protracted haggling. That would take time and probably offset the likelihood of a bet on the 2.30 race at Ayr, and that certainly displeased him.

There was to be some haggling but it was gey minimalist by the standards of the shop.

'Well?' he glowered.

'How much do you want for the book?' John asked, roughing somewhat his accent lest the man gleaned that he was not of, or no longer of, the local community.

The man gave a heavy sigh. His bad and alcoholic breath swept over John. The man examined the back page of the book, found the inscription he wanted and pronounced:

'Two and six,' he said.

'Two and six?' John repeated, doing so with a hint of incredulity.

'Aye,' the man sighed again. 'Hauf a croon.'

It was now John's turn to sigh. 'It's a bit much,' he commented.

This time the man scowled. 'It is the rule of the establishment that all goods must be retailed at the prices indicated thereon' he intoned, as though he had taken pains to learn how to proclaim this provision.

'It's an auld book,' John observed with a hint that the age warranted a price reduction.

'But it is a good book,' countered the man. 'Shakespeare and a' that.'

'Ah know, ah've read it,' said John.

The man saw his chance. 'Well, then, you know it's worth hauf a croon.'

John nodded in a way that indicated he was conceding the point. He went into his pocket and laboriously produced a shilling followed by two sixpences, a threepenny bit, two pennies and finally two half-pennies. The man lifted and checked the coins and tumbled them into a desk drawer.

John lifted the heavy book and made for the door where two women – one diminutive, the other enormous, with arms like sheep hanging outside a butcher's shop – were examining a mangle.

The large lady blocked his way.

'How much did he take aff ye fur the book, son?' she asked.

'Two and six,' replied John.

The lady turned to her wee friend. 'Two and six,' she pronounced. 'Is tha' no' a dead liberty? An' ra boy hid read ra book areadies!'

Mrs Drummond's *Nachos*

I remember quite clearly that the funeral service was in Brechin, but I cannot recall in which church we gathered. I am even more uncertain whether we went to a cemetery or to a crematorium. On the other hand, I recall with perfect clarity that the reception for the soup, the sandwiches, the chocolate biscuits, the tea and the coffee and the many, many drams was in one of the two hotels in Edzell.

The deceased was a very fine man called Jim Beaton, who had been a senior member of staff in the Programmes Department of one of the television companies based in Scotland. He and I had always got on well together. We were not close, but I had always enjoyed his company, appreciated his judgement and the clarity with which he expressed it. As a youth, he had attended a second-tier public school in Yorkshire. One of his stories of those days was of his experience of their sports afternoons.

After lunch on Thursdays all the boys were taken to the rugby fields, divided into sevens and told to get on with it, all under the watchful and critical eye of the sports masters. Jim could recall that after twenty minutes on his first Thursday one of the teachers had taken him aside and then taken him over to another pitch where he threw balls to him, inviting him to kick them over the cross-bar. After some ten minutes or so of this activity, the master advised him on how to place the ball with a view to kicking over for a conversion. The teacher then told him to place ten balls in a row. After Jim had kicked all ten balls over on three successive occasions, he was to retreat five yards and start all over again. The only relief from this somewhat boring activity was the reappearance of the teacher who resumed throwing balls to the boy.

For the following four years Jim was deployed in the same activity. Through rain, hail, snow and occasional sunshine Jim would spend at least two hours of each school week kicking the balls over the bar. In his penultimate year he was placed in the Second XV, and in his final year at the school, he made it to the First team.

On leaving school Jim took a post with the BBC in London. He knew the Former Pupils played in the London area, and so he applied and was accepted for their Second XV. After two years in that team he was promoted to the First XV, where the team captain was the sports master who had initiated his training in his first year at the school.

Four minutes into the game, the ex-teacher gathered a loose ball, ran twelve yards and threw the ball to Jim. As he did so, he shouted: 'Right, Beaton, kick it over!'

Jim did just that. The distance was formidable, but the ball soared from Jim's boot and went well over the bar. The drop-kick was confirmed and as the teams rearranged themselves, one of their opponents glowered at them and snarled: 'Lucky bastard!'

The captain put his arm across Jim's shoulder. 'Luck, Beaton, luck? We know luck has nothing to do with it.'

In telling the story Jim would say, 'At that moment all the Thursday afternoons were seen as having been worthwhile.'

As I approached the hotel where the purvey was to be provided, I had three objectives in mind. The first was to speak to some members of the Beaton family, to say how much I appreciated having known Jim and how much I had enjoyed meeting him, my only regret being that our meetings had not been more numerous. The second aim had been to speak to some of the television folk who would be there, while the third was to wrap my hands round a good, strong, warm cup of coffee.

Truth to tell, I had more than half a notion to aspire towards a fourth objective, which was to have a word with David Will. David was a local solicitor whose family home was in Edzell. He had been a director of Brechin City, the local football club, and at the time in question was Vice President of FIFA, and accordingly a very important man in the world of football. I was of a mind to reintroduce myself to him, while reminding him that I was a friend of his sister and her husband, who was a senior official of the Independent Broadcasting Authority, where he and I were colleagues and indeed close associates.

It should be conceded that David's success in the corridors of power in the world of football far out-stripped that of Brechin's samurai on the field of play. At that time, the Primus of the Scottish Episcopal Church was the Bishop of Brechin. A charming and gracious man, he was known jokingly to observe that when he went to England to visit friends and relatives, some of them seemed to believe that the full and formal title of his diocese was Brechin City Nil.

I have long subscribed to the view that funerals are much to be preferred to weddings. There are two strong arguments in favour of this stance. The first is that people at funerals are much more responsible than those at weddings. To begin with, there is no best man making at best foolish, at worst banal speeches full of sexual innuendo. There are no stupid young men embarking on what they regard as merry pranks on the just-married couple. The second point is that almost always there are markedly fewer children at funerals. Here I should confess that there are occasions when I consider Herod to be my favourite peripheral Biblical character. Noisy children are a pest at any time, but are particularly troublesome at church services and at weddings.

So far as my objectives were concerned, I achieved my first, and had embarked on my second, when one of Jim's sisters descended on me. She told me there was a lady – a Mrs Drummond – who was 'just dying to meet me'. She, the sister, insisted on dragging me off to meet the lady and on being presented to her, as though I were a sacrificial victim, it soon became apparent that she had not the slightest interest in who I was. Her great desire and need was to have an audience, preferably a new, hitherto untried audience. In addition it also became clear she had one and only one topic of conversation - the achievements and success of her family.

For the ensuing forty-plus minutes (half as long as a football match) Mrs Drummond's report on the wonderful achievements of her wonderful children poured over me with the awesome ferocity of the Niagara when the snow is melting. There was no hesitation; it was clearly a well-rehearsed, oft-repeated saga. Even so, she let me know that what I was being privileged to hear was but the *Reader's Digest* account. Moreover, there was no doubt that the lady relished the telling of the tale. A smile of pleasure never left her lips, while pride radiated from her whole being.

She had six children. There were four boys and two girls. All were now fully mature. The older of the two girls, who had been the lady's third child, had trained as a nurse, rapidly been promoted to ward sister, and would have been a matron but for the stupid decision to do away with that vital grade. And so she had switched to hospital administration, and was now 'a very senior administrator in a large hospital in Yorkshire.'

The other girl who had been the last-born was a teacher. She was, as we – or rather she – spoke, now a Deputy Head of one of the largest schools in Aberdeenshire.

Ian, one of the boys, was a minister of the kirk in Edinburgh. His charge was in the West End. He wrote frequently for *Life and Work*, and did a great deal of religious broadcasting. His sermons were said to be brilliant, and he was famous for the compassionate nature of his pastoral work. He was tipped to become either a Professor of Divinity or a Chaplain to the Queen, or both.

Stewart, the second-born, had been advised by his headmaster to read Spanish at University. He had gone into the Foreign Office and was now very senior in that Department. He had been in Bolivia and was now in Mexico.

David had become a policeman and it had not taken long for him to rise to Inspector and then Chief Inspector. He had moved over to Security, and was now in MI something or other, and was frequently seconded to guard the Queen.

All of which left Guthrie, who had been her first child. Guthrie was the charge hand in the butcher's shop of the Co-op Society in Brechin. It was generally recognised in the district that his butcher meat was of an exceptionally high standard, so much so that three independent butchers had been obliged to go out of business. Guthrie was famous for the quality of his sausages while his sirloin steaks and pork chops were just out of this world. Mrs Drummond argued that it would be intolerable were I to leave the area without availing myself of such delights. She would phone Guthrie and tell him to make me up a parcel of sausages, steaks and pork chops. I could call at the shop and collect them on my way home. She would explain that I had been talking to her – I had barely spoken five words. Moreover, she would tell Guthrie that he should give me the staff discount.

'After all,' she declared, 'you are now almost one of the family!'

When Mrs Drummond was working her way towards the closing section of her narration, Jim's sister, the lady who had lured me into the Drummond web, came over with a plate with one weary, pathetic sandwich and three chocolate biscuits, two of which were broken. She also brought a cup of well-stewed tea. These she put down beside me. I inferred that this gesture was designed more to placate her conscience than it was to cater to my requirements. She smiled at me and looked at the narrator, who, with an almost regal wave of her hand, signified she had more important things to do; eating was out of the question.

When Mrs Drummond rose, thereby indicating she had finished her report, she left me to make her phone call to Guthrie. She returned to say that all was in order and to give me a scribbled note which she said consisted of a guide to finding the shop.

I left the hotel after a second word or two with members of the Beaton family. I left sans soup, sans coffee, sans television gossip and sans my word with David Will. I found the shop but did so with great difficulty. No doubt Margaret Drummond was a great wife, a wonderful mother and an excellent housewife, but as a navigator and cartographer her ratings were minus quantities. And, not being a motorist, she had not taken any cognizance of one-way streets.

On the other hand, Guthrie had everything ready for me. My three items were carefully packed, each in its own small container while all three were in a much bigger plastic bag. The sum I paid was most reasonable. We shook hands and I took my leave.

When I returned to Glasgow my wife and family were impressed by my purchases and even more so after we had eaten them. The sausages and the sirloin were testimony to Guthrie and to the Aberdeen Angus breed; the pork chops were the best we had ever tasted.

The Jewish community has a term – *nachos* – which means 'justified pride in one's children'. So that whereas pride is a sin, *nachos* is not a sin. On the contrary, it is justified.

Clearly Mrs Drummond experienced very considerable *nachos*.

Notwithstanding our enjoyment and appreciation of his wares, I found that in the weeks thereafter, I was perplexed as to why it was Guthrie who rated so highly in the eyes of the mother. I was inclined to think that by both worldly and heavenly criteria it should have been Ian and his church in Edinburgh and his writing and broadcasting that would have won the greatest approval. Then I came to realise that geography and its consequences were the pace-setters in this game of *nachos*.

What mattered in the local community was the extent to which the lives and achievements of the Drummond children impacted on the friends and neighbours of the mother. Mexico City is far away, and what went on there was of no import to the folk in Brechin. The activities of David were so secret that no one knew anything about them. As for the girls, the hospital in England and the school in Aberdeenshire never touched the local folk. In one sense, the folk in the kirk could have been expected to have been appreciative of Ian's success, but they did not have much to do with Edinburgh. If they went there to stay with friends, they were more likely to attend a church in the suburbs rather than a grand kirk in the West End. Some of the people in the church in Brechin took *Life and Work*, and some of those actually read it, but not as many as 121 George Street would have wished.

No, it was Guthrie and his excellent butcher-meat which impacted on the lives of the locals.

The ladies in the Women's Guild at the church visited his shop, as did the women of the Co-operative Guild, as did the neighbours, as did the peripheral relatives. In short, the people in the world, the small world of Mrs Drummond, knew what Guthrie had to offer. They not only gave their approval, but made sure they conveyed it to his mother, who in turn revelled therein.

If you have occasion to visit Brechin for a wedding or a funeral or other such a social event, be on the alert for Margaret Drummond and avoid her. Consider. Years have passed. Her brood will have further achievements she will be anxious to report. Nor does it end there! I hear she now has ten grandchildren… and counting.

There is, however, another aspect to this situation.

It was a wise man or woman who observed that the greatest gift we can bring to the elderly and the house-bound is our ears. In other words, it could be that when next we go to a wedding in Brechin or Forfar or be it in Dunoon, Dundee or wherever, we should look for the Mrs Drummond of the vicinity or the local equivalent thereof and give the lady an hour of our time while allowing her to pour out her story of her *nachos*.

Were we to do that, Angels of the Lord who used to run around with leaky biro pens and who now all have laptops and mobiles for texting will be punching in our brownie points, whereupon our parents can enjoy their quota of *nachos*.

A Man Of Conviction

In late May or early June of 1946, an interview took place in a college in the centre of Glasgow. The vacancy was for a Senior Lectureship in two related subjects. There had been many applicants; four had already been seen, but the Selection Panel consisting of the Principal, his Deputy and four Heads of Departments had not been impressed. Yet they were hopeful in that the man they were about to see was – on paper – the strongest of all the aspirants.

His name was Frederick Featherstone. Before the War he had been a master at Manchester Grammar School for Boys. A Yorkshire man by birth, his home was in a village near Bolton. His references were most reassuring and clearly indicated that he had been a first class teacher. There was one other attractive feature and this even before he came through the door. He had three degrees. The only members of staff to have three degrees were the Principal and his Deputy.

When he was ushered into the room and invited to take a seat, the initial impression was that he was rather shy, somewhat diffident. But when the pleasantries were over and they were into the questioning the Panel members increasingly realised they had before them an extremely talented man of resolute character, a man with a clear mind and a strong voice.

Early in the interview it had been explained to him that were he to be successful in his application the teaching with which he would be entrusted would involve him with the brightest, better-qualified students who would be working towards external degrees of the University of London. Very politely he pointed out that he had inferred that would be the case, and indeed this was one of the main factors that had prompted his application.

One of the Panel members observed that two of his referees had expanded at great length on the excellent rapport he had with the young people in his care. He was asked how he achieved this commendable situation. He explained that when he was poised to embark on his career he had met a former headmaster who had advised him to treat all his pupils as though they were the children of his own friends and relations.

'Treat them as though they were all potential government ministers or senior civil servants or editors of *The Guardian* or some other broadsheet!' he had been advised. He then added that he had come to realise that it was prudent to treat someone else's offspring in the manner you would wish that someone else to treat one's own children.

Months after the interview, individual members of the selection team revealed that by halfway through the fifty minutes of the interview they had decided that he was the man for the job. Nevertheless, the questioning had continued. A Panel member asked a totally irrelevant question about corporal punishment. The applicant dealt with it admirably and concluded by observing: 'but of course in the event of my being appointed here, I shall not be involved in corporal punishment.' Two perceptive members of the panel noticed his use of 'shall' rather than the Scottish 'will' and smiled their approval.

There came a stage when it was clear that the interview was well-nigh over. Likely salary had been determined should he be offered the post, and the Principal had made the usual chuckling noises at his desire that they should decide the matter as quickly as possible.

'Did the candidate have any questions for them?' He did. They were about possible assistance in the costs of selling and buying a house. The Principal outlined the College policy on such matters. 'Well,' he added, 'I think that is that.' He thanked Dr Featherstone for his attendance and went on to say that he was sure there were no more questions.

It was at that point that the College Secretary, a man called Middlemass, forced his way into the proceedings. 'Wait a minute,' he exclaimed, and glowering at Featherstone aggressively added: 'What denomination are you?'

Clearly taken aback and equally clearly offended at the tone and maybe the nature of the query, Featherstone answered in a mild manner, yet with a clear tone: 'I am a Methodist,' he said.

There was a moment or two of total silence.

Middlemass was clearly wrong-footed: this was not the sort of answer he had expected. But he was resilient in his own fashion.

'Don't equivocate, man,' he roared. 'Are you a Protestant?'

The Principal was flustered, confused, angry and embarrassed, yet he managed to exercise enough authority to bring the proceedings quickly to a close. It was done in an untidy manner, but he did finish it. He did it with his voice and as he did so he gestured to his Deputy doing so with the wave of his hand and the nod of his head that he wanted the Deputy to escort Featherstone to retrieve his belongings. Having conveyed his instructions by gesticulation, the Principal virtually contradicted himself by going round the other side of the table and took the applicant's arm by holding him by the elbow. He congratulated Featherstone on an impressive performance and assured him he would do all he could to see they reached an early decision. He then paused and added: 'I really must apologise for the Secretary's intervention. He was out of order.'

The applicant nodded and said 'Yes!' That was all he said, but his taut face and lack of smile conveyed a message of rebuke. Translated from the silence it said: 'Yes, he was out of order, and you should have intervened and told him that was the case.'

The man was anxious to be successful but he was letting the Principal know that he was not prepared to be a push-over. His body language was eloquent and the lowering of the Principal's head indicated he had received the message and in effect conceded its validity.

When the Principal arrived at his office the next morning he immediately sent out his PA to find the other members of the Selection committee and ascertain how each member saw the situation, and in particular which candidate each man was supporting. This was not easy. One was lecturing, another taking a seminar group, yet another was seeing a student and his father, who seemed to believe that his son and heir was being treated unfairly, and so it went on. For all that, the PA was back before eleven o'clock to report that to a man they wanted Featherstone appointed. So it was that the letter went out: 'It gives me great pleasure to tell you that the Committee was unanimously of the view that the vacancy should be offered to you. It is our hope that you will accept and agree to report for duty…'

That letter went out from the office of the Principal and not that of the College Secretary.

The Principal had another task to perform that day, one that gave rise to no pleasure whatsoever.

He disliked confrontations and particularly detested formal confrontations. So he 'arranged' accidentally to encounter Middlemass outside the executive toilet.

'That was a most unbecoming outburst at yesterday's Selection Committee,' he proclaimed.

'I was looking after your own good and that of the College,' Middlemass responded.

Perplexed, the Principal looked questioningly at him.

'What are you on about, Middlemass?' he asked.

In turn the Secretary stared at the Principal as though he was prone to naivety or stupidity or both.

'We have to keep certain folk out!' the Secretary nearly exploded.

'Who?' demanded the Principal. 'Who must be excluded?'

'Them,' said Middlemass. 'The other lot!'

'What other lot?' half-raved the Principal.

'You know fine well, Principal,' said the Secretary.

'Middlemass, I despair,' said the Principal. 'You are either incoherent or much too Delphic. I cannot discern which.'

Frederick Featherstone joined the staff of the College on the second Monday of September 1946. He was entrusted with a rather heavy teaching load, but he was not dismayed. It was less than he had experienced at the Grammar School. Then again, he was delighted to find that a local public holiday would arise before the month was out, and this would allow him and his wife, Gwendoline, to bring up more of their effects from their home in Lancashire. By early October they had bought a house in Bearsden; he joined the band of middle-class commuters who travelled by train from Bearsden and Milngavie to the city centre.

Frederick and his wife joined the large Methodist church at the eastern end of Sauchiehall Street, and in due course played a prominent part in its activities, not least many ecumenical and other interdenominational events.

More importantly, by the end of the first term, in December, the bulk of the staff had come to realise and appreciate that they had in Frederick a very valuable and acceptable member of staff. (He was destined to be for ever known as either 'Frederick' or 'Dr Featherstone' until late in his career when he became Professor Featherstone. He was never Fred or Freddy.) He was recognized as a good academic and an excellent and conscientious teacher. He was more than a little reserved. He studiously avoided those who played bridge and thereby made themselves late for lectures and seminars. He also avoided those who played table tennis and those who frequented the snooker table. He was a hill-walker but not a rock climber; he joined an informal party of academics, administrators and senior students who climbed The Cobbler, Narnain and the other Arrochar hills, those around Crianlarich and up into Glencoe.

Within the College he was seen as a man of principle. He was admired, respected and liked, but he was not popular. He was always that little bit aloof, that little bit removed, for basic popularity to prevail.

There was, too, a mystery. No one knew for certain what he had done during the War. Despite this, there were two theories. One school of thought argued that he had been a conscientious objector and had spent the war years on a farm in Norfolk where the farmer was a man called Scott, descended from the land-hungry Scottish farmers who migrated to East Anglia in the nineteenth century. In support of this argument, it was pointed out that he was friendly with Hardiman Scott, the broadcaster who was coming into prominence at the BBC.

The other camp said he had been on extremely sensitive intelligence work and that he and his colleagues had been made to swear on a stack of Bibles and copies of the Official Secrets Act never to disclose to anyone – not to a spouse or to anyone else – what they had been doing.

Truth to tell, no-one knew and no-one ever did know.

One day in January, while finishing his lunch in the staff dining room, he was joined by a rather pedestrian teacher called Gardner, who was known by all the staff to be an evangelical lay preacher, a born-again Christian with the unfortunate habit of treating with disdain all those who had not followed that route. All? Well, almost all. It appeared he approved of a few others, one of them being the College Secretary.

Having joined Frederick, Gardner engaged in what he took to be acceptable pleasantries. In due course he got to the point that was of concern to him.

'I gather,' Gardner said, 'you were rather put out at a wee incident at your interview.' It purported to be an observation, but it was really a question.

'What incident?' asked Frederick.

'The one involving Mr Middlemass.'

'What do you mean?' said Frederick.

'Oh come, come,' said Gardner, 'You must not be unduly hard on him. He is a good man, you know.'

'Is he?'

'Oh yes! He is a very good Christian and a man of great and commendable conviction.'

'If you say so,' said Featherstone, and with that he rose from the table and put his used paper napkin to the side. 'Good afternoon,' he said, and walked away.

That exchange took place in the winter of 1946-47, the winter of the deep snow when the whole of the country was covered.

Towards the end of the second term, Gardner had another attempt at having Frederick express – or at least indicate – a sympathy if not quite a rapport with Middlemass.

'As I told you, he is a God-fearing man of strong personal conviction.'

'So you said.'

'Then again, he carries a great burden which weighs heavily upon him.'

This provoked neither a reply nor a comment.

Gardner pressed on. 'You see, his name includes the word 'mass' - with all its dreadful connotations.'

'He could always change it,' said Featherstone.

'Oh, you really must try to understand him,' pleaded Gardner.

Frederick paused. 'Nonsense!' he said. 'I have no such obligation. Now, good-day to you.'

Two years later a discrepancy of a few hundred pounds was found in the College accounts. It was possible that it was a clerical error. It was equally possible that it was the Secretary to blame. The auditors made a bland comment and no more was said or made of the matter.

In the middle fifties a much greater hole came to light, this time running to quite a few thousands. The senior partner in the firm of auditors was consulted. His verdict was succinct: 'Theft!'

The Head of the Department of Accountancy was invited to examine the books. His judgement was somewhat longer: 'Embezzlement!' he pronounced.

All the available evidence pointed to Middlemass as the culprit.

'The stupid bastard dipped the till!' was the succinct but inelegant remark of the senior auditor. 'How did he expect to get away with it?' he added, but it was a rhetorical question and no answer was forthcoming.

When the Principal met the Chairman of the Board of Governors, two issues arose.

The first was what they were going to do. That one was quickly resolved. Middlemass would be invited to leave, and if he declined, he would be sacked.

The other issue was trickier. Should they call in the police? Neither man had a taste for that. They recognised that many an employer would report such a case to the authorities but they were reluctant to take that course of action. This was not out of consideration for the thief, but due to enlightened self-interest. Were the matter referred to the police there would almost certainly be a trial and that in turn would provoke coverage in the press. The Principal could see that that would almost certainly lead to his being hounded for interviews by the press, maybe even invited to appear on the local television news programmes. The idea of that appalled him: that was a scene to be avoided.

The Chairman took a different line and one that did not reflect well on the Principal in his role as CEO. The Chairman argued that if the case went to court it might reveal that the internal checks and balances of the College were not as rigorous and effective as one would have wished, and this would not reflect well on a College that taught Accountancy and Finance to Honours level. For that matter, it would not do much for the Chair who was a senior partner in a firm of accountants. The verdict, then, was not to call in the police.

Middlemass refused to go, so he was dismissed, and no reference was given to him. In due course he claimed Unemployment Benefit for which he was duly disqualified for the maximum period, this on the grounds that he had lost his employment as a result of his industrial misconduct, i.e. theft.

In due course the replacement for Middlemass arrived and took up post. He had been recruited from another college in the city. He was a small, dapper man and more particularly proved to be a man of exceptional probity and rectitude. He was fastidious. On one rather famous but most revealing occasion he replied to a letter from the President of the Staff Association and finished with a paragraph which read: 'Finally I observed that your letter to me was written on a sheet of College notepaper, and accordingly I enclose an invoice for one penny.' He was pernickety.

One day during the inter-regnum Featherstone stopped Gardner for the first and only time. 'Gardner,' he opened. 'You went to great pains to assure me your friend Middlemass was a man of conviction. I take it you acknowledge that he very nearly had another conviction of a different kind.' And with that he walked away.

Two Concepts Of Duty

Jim Crichton was a fine lad who grew up to be an exceptionally fine gentleman in all the connotations of that word.

As a boy, Jim lived with his mother, father and older brother in a mean 'two-by-two' red-brick house in a mean street in the heart of Protestant Belfast. The street and all that surrounded it was one hundred percent Protestant and Unionist. The gable walls were decorated with elaborate murals depicting the heroes and heroic episodes of that tradition. King William III and his victory at the Battle of the Boyne in 1690 were well to the fore, while the stout defenders of the Siege of Londonderry were not far behind. The kerbstones were painted red, white and blue. The ever-ready Union and Ulster flags and bunting were strung across the streets as events such as Royal Weddings and Jubilees occurred. Photographs of the Sovereign and Ulster leaders such as Lord Craigavon abounded. All four members of the Crichton family knew who they were and what they were.

Together with their relatives, their friends, their workmates and their neighbours, they knew they were descended from the men and women from Scotland, from the North of England and from the London area who were willingly transported to Ireland, particularly but not exclusively to the Province of Ulster in the early seventeenth century under the provision of King James the VI and I. In short, they were of Supplanter stock, not that they liked that emotive, albeit historically accurate nomenclature. The heart of the matter was they had been sent to Ireland to take over land and employment hitherto held by the indigenous Catholic population, which in turn was driven to marginal and sub-marginal land. Those who arrived were almost exclusively Protestant.

At the time of this massive migration, the term 'a two-way street' was not in use, but there was here a tacit, well-understood bargain. Their omnipresent task, nay duty, was to hold that land and consequently Ireland for the Crown and the Protestant succession. They were to keep the mainly Irish-speaking locals in their place and be the first instrument of thumping them were they to display any rebellious inclinations. The state and its instruments would support them and in turn they would support the state.

And almost to a man they and those who followed had done their duty and done it most satisfactorily.

The Crichtons were Presbyterians, as were most of their associates, but they looked benignly on all associated with the other strands of the Reformed tradition. Congregationalists, Methodists, Baptists, both formal and informal, Salvationists, Evangelical gatherings and even Episcopalians were treated with regard, though they let it be known they did not approve of some of the Popish practices of the Church of Ireland, with its use of Bishops. Unitarians were seen as strange, but were not to be criticised. Mormons, Jehovah's Witnesses and good, God-fearing Quakers were seen as something beyond their ken, but harmless. As for Humanists, Agnostics and Atheists they were seen as folk to be pitied. Anything and everything was acceptable as long as it was not Roman Catholic; they never failed to give voice to the adjectival qualification.

In many aspects of life it is good to know who we are, what we are and whence we came. There can, however, be a downside to this normally reassuring situation. Jim Crichton was fated to find himself in that very situation. A situation which was to hang over him like an enormous cloud for many and many a year.

The day that was to transform his life started normally. It was a Saturday. His father and his brother had gone as usual to their work in Glen & Davidson's, a local engineering firm which made component parts for a wide variety of manufacturing concerns. They had stopped work at the back of twelve and on their return to the house the family had their dinner. Like most families in the district, they liked to have the main meal at midday.

After they had eaten, the father and older son had left, each with his own set of friends, to go to Windsor Park to see Linfield play against Glentoran in a League game. Linfield was the favourite team of the vast majority of men and youths in the area. There was a tendency to see the club as the sporting arm of the spirited Reformed Tradition. The players wore royal blue jerseys and white shorts with a touch of red in their stockings. The overall acceptance of the club and all for which it stood went further. Some followers spoke of the players as though they consisted exclusively of Boys' Brigade sergeants, officers and Scripture Union prize-winners. The truth was that they were no more saintly than the players of other clubs.

Jim and his mother proceeded to clear the table and wash the dishes. She would wash and he would dry.

Mother and son tended to work well as a team; indeed, one professional friend of the family once observed he discerned more than a touch of synergy when they worked together. This Saturday was no exception. They started well, she by washing the dishes in hot soapy water, rinsing them in cold and stacking them in a draining frame. Jim, working a few items behind her, shook each dish or other item and dried it with a dish towel. Dr Summerskill would not have approved, as she regarded such towels as unhygienic, but it was Mrs Crichton who ruled this house, as Jim was about to be reminded.

The blow-up started innocently enough.

Jim paused in his work and looking up at his mother with a broad smile on his face, asked:

'Ma, Ma, can I tell you a secret?'

Never averse to a good bit of gossip, it was her turn to smile.

'Of course you can, son. Of course you can. Is it your secret or is it somebody else's?' she asked.

'Mine,' said the lad.

Mrs Crichton was disappointed. She had hoped Jim had been in a neighbour's house and had picked up some salacious, scandalous item. She managed to mask her dismay, doing so markedly better than was to occur a few seconds later.

'On you go,' she encouraged.

'Well, Ma,' he said quietly and diffidently, 'Well, Ma, I have decided what I would like to do when I am big, when I am a man.'

The mother sensed trouble.

'What would that be?' she asked coldly, the affection already having left her voice.

Jim did not notice the change in the mother's tone or her apprehension. He took a deep breath and raced on.

'I'd like to be a Minister like Mr Davis in the church!'

Many a Christian mother would have been delighted but not, certainly not, Mrs Crichton. She did not merely shout, she roared her disapproval.

'How dare you!' she screamed. 'How dare you get ideas above your station!'

Pulling the towel from his hands she proceeded to hit him with it, then realising it was a gey impotent weapon, she reached for his father's leather shaving strap and in a near-frenzy used it to hit her son on his arms, his legs and his body, all the time continuing to shout at him with a flood of rebukes.

'It is not for you to want to join your betters. Listen to me, me boyo. You will do what the Good Lord decrees for folks like us. You, you would-be upstart, you will stay at school till you are fourteen, then you will leave and get started at Glen & Davidson's beside your Da and your brother. You will start an apprenticeship when you are sixteen and finish your time when you are twenty-one. When you are 23 you can start going out with girls and you'll get married when you are 28 or 30. You'll take a house round the corner and have two or three childer and you and your wife will bring them round here every other day and twice at the weekend for me to see them. Do you understand that?'

Throughout this torrent, throughout this outburst, she kept hitting him and the weals were increasingly visible on his limbs. Jim was crying, sobbing and pleading that she should stop, while interjecting wee questions based on his inability to see what he had done that was wrong.

'Wrong!' roared the mother. 'Wrong? I'll tell you what is wrong. I've already told you what is wrong. It is not for you to question the ways of the Lord. It is for the likes of us to do our duty, not to get ideas of grandeur or whatever they call it. If it is good enough for your Da, it is good enough for you, so it is, so it is.'

The remainder of that day was a grim period in the life of the boy. Tragically it was to be but the first of many grim, unpleasant hours, days, weeks, months and years confronting him. Jim was miserable all that day. He was confused, he was bewildered and through his tears, his sobbing and his shudders he did not know what to make of what had happened. For her part, his mother, like Tam o' Shanter's wife, was nursing her wrath. She wallowed in self-righteous indignation that any son of hers would not be prepared to accept the way and standard of life which she and her man had provided at no little cost to themselves.

When her husband and her older boy returned from the match, the atmosphere took a turn for the worse. Glentoran had managed to hold their team to a draw, with the result that they were dumped. The mother reported on the ungrateful selfishness of Jim, so the father rounded on him. Although he raised his voice, he did not shout nor did he go for his belt.

When he said his prayers on the Saturday night, Jim did not merely mumble his way through the prescribed utterances, as children and all too many adults are wont to do. Through his utter dejection, Jim genuinely prayed for the first time in his life. His gentle lips said: 'Dear Lord, help me to understand what is happening to me.'

At church the next morning the atmosphere was dreadful, and at its worst when they stopped at the top of the steps to speak to the Reverend Davis. He in turn readily perceived that all was not well, but sensed this was neither the time nor place to probe.

As the weeks went by, Mrs Crichton did not mellow. She and Jim still had to work together, but now they worked in a mutual sullen silence. The synergy they had once generated went up the lum.

Mrs Crichton had never heard of Thomas Aquinas, and if she had, she would not have approved of a Popish so-called saint, yet the same lady would have endorsed his dictum: 'There is no such question as 'Why do I do my duty?'' Though there was a void between them, for the lady, her duty was not to change her life in any regard but rather to cling to the life-style she had inherited and which she treasured and held dear. Her horizons were not just limited, they were well-nigh non-existent.

She never again addressed Jim as 'dear', but then she never called anyone 'dear', not even her husband.

Mrs Crichton won, of course. Her views prevailed. She got her way! The atmosphere in the house was rather dreadful and the three males realised that were she to be thwarted it would be even worse. This had no great effect on the father and the brother, but it had a devastating effect on Jim, and was to cloud his life for years to come.

Victory did not appease the mother; rather it fortified her intransigence. She told herself that the others, including Jim, had recognised that she had the better of it. More, she found evidence to support her stance. Thus she did not really approve of the Church of Ireland with its bishops, its copes and its cassocks. As she saw it, it was not a proper Protestant church. In this matter she felt sorry for the Royal Family; though there was the consolation that when the train or plane crossed the Scottish border the Royals seemed to become Presbyterians – just like her. She was sure that made them feel more comfortable.

On the other hand she did approve of Mrs Alexander, the nineteenth century hymnist who had been the wife of a Bishop of Londonderry. She liked this lady because she, in turn, had supported the Orange Order, though an even stronger reason for endorsing the lady was the clarity of the views expressed in her hymns. For example, in her *Once in Royal David's City* there were two lines which summed up perfectly what Mrs Crichton felt about the domestic scene. They read:

'Christian children all must be
Mild, obedient, good as He.'

Mrs Crichton particularly liked the use of 'must' rather than the quasi-discretionary 'should'. And did not the same lady talk in another hymn of 'The rich man in his castle, the poor man at his gate'? There was support for her view that it was a human duty to accept dutifully and willingly the station in life assigned to one by Almighty God.

She had told her younger and disobedient son 'to do what he was telt'. She was his mother and it was her duty and right to guide him, to instruct him. It was his duty to obey. Mrs Alexander agreed and so did God and that was all there was to it.

So it came to pass that Jim left school at the end of the term following his fourteenth birthday and started as an errand boy. When he was sixteen he was registered as an apprentice and he was trained as a fitter. Jim hated every minute of it.

A few weeks after Jim's eighteenth birthday things took an unexpected turn for the better. It started with his foreman telling him he was to go through to the offices as the General Manager wanted to see him. To Jim's surprise, the manager told him to take a seat. He told Jim that a week or so before he had been to an engineering dinner in an hotel off the Bangor Road. He had found himself sitting next to a Head of Department at a college in town. It was the college that Jim and some other, keener, apprentices attended two or three nights each week. On learning who the manager was and where he worked, and the position he held, the dinner companion had been a shade indiscreet. He had told him he was fortunate to have in his employment 'that very bright lad James Crichton'. With this in mind the manager had then arranged to gain access to the marks which Jim had attained. He conceded that had been a bit improper. Anyway, he had done it and what was more important the marks had been 'most impressive'. The manager congratulated Jim and observed in an aside that considering they mainly recruited as a result of nepotism, it was gratifying to find that occasionally it worked rather well.

He then said the real issue was what were they going to do about it. This, of course, was a rhetorical question, for it became clear he knew what he wanted to see happen. Whereupon he half-suggested, half-told Jim they should think in terms of him switching from coming out as a fitter and working towards his becoming a draughtsman. This was what had happened to him as a young man. He had gone on to take a degree from the Royal Technical College in Glasgow. There was no reason why Jim should not travel a similar road. Nothing need be done at that juncture; everything that had to be done could be done in due course. For the time being he should carry on as he was.

As he walked back to the grime and noise of the shop floor, Jim thanked both his God and his lucky stars for this not insubstantial change in his fortunes, while knowing he would never travel all the road travelled by the manager. The manager had been an enthusiastic engineer whereas he was not. Jim, God help him, still had dreams of a Divinity career and of a pulpit.

In the quest for a pacific, tranquil, even if not really a happy Crichton household, each member was fated to play it each in his or her own way. In the case of the wife and mother, this was simply expressed and simply discerned. She looked for total capitulation by the other three.

In the case of Jim, there was a factor which at one and the same time was both an advantage and a handicap: he was markedly cleverer, markedly more intelligent than the others.

When he was in his mid-teens he had perceived that his mother's prime concern was not that everyone in the household should walk God's way, but that they should walk in her way, which of course she pronounced to be God's way. With this came the sad realisation that she was inordinately selfish. She did not want her world to change in any regard of which she did not approve. There was virtually no change, no innovation of which she did approve. She was terrified of her little world changing. She had neither the confidence nor the wherewithal to face and deal with change. It was, concluded Jim, worse than sad. It was tragic and they all suffered.

One night when he was about twenty or so, Jim was alone in the house. His parents had gone to the local cinema and his brother to a snooker hall. Jim was listening to Radio 3, the most cerebral of the three national stations of the BBC. One programme ended and another began. It was a religious programme consisting of three churchmen from mainstream churches discussing one's duty to God. All the participants were Oxbridge men, and it showed. It did not take them long to agree that the basic responsibility was clearly expressed in the Bible, and that was 'To love Thy Lord, Thy God with your whole soul and your whole mind and your neighbour as thyself'.

But having agreed on that they had gone on to identify other responsibilities, for example, one's duty to do a good day's work for a good day's pay, and the duty of an employer to act responsibly towards his workers though they laughingly agreed that the most unpopular parable with trade unionists was that of the labourers in the vineyard.

Then one man argued that a sadly neglected responsibility was that of using and developing the talents which we received from the Holy Spirit. This quietly but firmly expressed view made Jim wince. He knew that he had talents he had not developed and that he could and should have done so much more with them. He had, in effect, neglected to nurture and develop them, justifying this to himself by saying he had acted out of obedience to his parents and an anxiety for a façade of domestic harmony.

The decade when Jim was in his twenties could be seen in retrospect to have had four milestones of great importance in his young life.

The first of these happened gradually, but as he progressed steadily from apprentice to dark-suited draughtsman and settled confidently into his new role he found he was spending less and less time with the Boys' Brigade. He was becoming more and more disenchanted, finding it too sombre, too severe, occasionally even too funereal, too militaristic.

As that association ran down, he found himself spending more and more time at the YMCA. True, this involved travelling to the city centre, but Belfast is a compact city, so this was not expensive in either time or money. What pleased him was that he found the whole setting brighter, livelier, more open, more friendly and less severe than the BB events in the church hall. Jim readily recognized that William Smith of Thurso had been a man of vision, and had done a most commendable job in bringing the Brigade into being. It had served the young men of the Protestant community extremely well. He equally acknowledged that as a young lad in his early and middle teens he had thoroughly enjoyed the annual summer camping week on the Island of Cumbrae in the Firth of Clyde. But increasingly he recognised that the Brigade which had served him well was slowly but surely drifting out of his life. Either that, or he was drifting out of its life.

The second development occurred at a joint YMCA/ YWCA dance. For most of the young people it was no better and no worse than many another dance, but for the rest of his life Jim saw it as a wonderful dance. The explanation for this was simplicity itself; it was that night he met Avril Templeton, a young graduate of Queens who was working in the Personnel Department at the Northern Ireland base of the BBC. He had been allowed to see her home to the family house off the Antrim Road. Jim's life was never the same again.

In one sense Jim's career was settled. He had continued with his studies and had taken his AMIMechE. For all that, he felt he needed a break. He got two.

Increasingly he had become involved with the local football team. One Saturday he was so short of players he was obliged to include himself in the team. Ten minutes into the second half he was at the receiving end of a very bad tackle. His leg was broken in two places and he found himself in hospital.

While in hospital, Jim had markedly more visitors than he had expected. Most of them came in the evenings and at the weekend. Friends and colleagues from the drawing office, the shop floor and the firm's offices were well to the fore. There were, too, lads from the Y, not least the players from the football team. One night they were joined by the guy who had broken Jim's leg. Some old BB associates appeared, while Avril came twice. To have turned up only once might have been seen as slightly churlish, whereas to have appeared more than twice might have been construed as indicative of a commitment not yet attained.

One wet afternoon, his mother arrived with fresh pyjamas. Her opening gambit was: 'Yer Da was thinking of ye and sends his regards.' The rest of her discourse for the incapacitated was to tell Jim the breaks were all his own fault. Thus he should never have left the Brigade; he should never have got mixed up with that lot in the town.

'Associating with a lot of people you know next to nothing about, a lot of people who believe in anything and everything.'

Jim interposed: 'They are all Christians, Ma!' but that was swept aside as an irrelevance.

Another afternoon his only visitor was a Baptist minister, with whom he had become friendly at the Y. He had brought a pile of magazines and the like. It included three copies of *The Baptist Times*, two copies of *Life and Work*, the Church of Scotland publication, two copies of *The Listener* and one of *The Economist*.

Half way through the visit his attitude and facial expression changed. He looked almost solemn.

'You know, of course, what's wrong with you? You do know, don't you?'

'Yes,' said Jim, 'I've broken my leg.'

His friend scowled. 'Don't be facetious, Jim,' he said. 'You know fine well what I mean. You know – we all know – you want to be a minister.'

Jim heaved himself as best he could on the bed. He was overcome with embarrassment that his aspiration had been so obvious, so evident.

'That's as maybe,' he said 'but what can I do about it? Absolutely nothing! We have an all-graduate ministry and there is no way I can do anything about that, is there? Talk sense, man!'

His friend looked at him with compassion and understanding.

'Maybe not here,' he said, and then after a pause went on, 'but you could do it in Canada.'

'What are you on about?' demanded Jim.

And so it was his friend explained that the Presbyterian Church in Canada was very short of young men studying and training for the ministry. They had a scheme whereby they recruited young men from other lands, paid them a basic salary while they were the equivalent of assistant ministers at the weekend and attended University during the week. His proposal was that Jim should apply, while he personally would see to the references. It would probably involve taking a couple of 'A' levels in evening study at a local college, but Jim was no stranger to that activity.

That night Jim slept better than he had slept in years.

Within a week of being released from hospital, Jim wrote to the Church authorities in Canada. His letter was more than an expression of interest; in effect it was an application. Two days later his Baptist friend forwarded four references, one from himself and one of the others being from the Rev Davis, the minister of the church which Jim and his family attended.

Later a close friend was to ask him to what extent, if at all, he had consulted Avril before committing himself. Jim explained that he had spoken to her on the phone. In any event, she was fully aware of his dream and, though he was ashamed to admit it, his bitterness. Then he went on to observe, that if Avril could not accept it, she was not the girl for him, and so she would, of course, go along with it. His friend was frank enough to tell him his logic was rather tortuous, but no doubt near enough correct to carry the day.

A fortnight after he wrote he received a reply. The Canadians suggested he make himself available for interview by their UK representative, a Presbyterian minister based in Manchester, who had served in Canada on a three-year exchange arrangement.

The interview, when it came, was over dinner in a leading hotel in the city centre. It did not take Jim long to surmise that his host was interested not only in his intelligence and his commitment to God and the Gospel and to the principles of Presbyterianism, but to a wide range of other matters. Thus he noticed that the gentleman was pleased that Jim was teetotal, and that he had succeeded in modifying very considerably what originally had been a broad Belfast accent. Then again, the gentleman dropped in rather many extremely long words to see how Jim reacted to them. Jim noticed that the representative noted how he handled his cutlery and how he took his soup. For all that, on his way home, Jim concluded that he had done quite well.

He had done well, for the Canadians wrote to say they would take him provided he obtained two 'A' levels from a list of Liberal Arts subjects. They recommended he consider taking two academic years to obtain them.

Being Jim, he resolved to take three subjects.

There then followed two encounters, both of which could have been fraught.

The first was with his parents. He did not consult them. On the contrary, he told them what he had resolved to do. His father intimated that he was rather pleased, indeed he felt proud. Predictably the mother took a different line. The brother was talking of getting married; now Jim was talking of going away. How was she going to manage with only a single wage coming into the house? His father suggested they make a pot of tea, and that was the end of it.

The second encounter consisted of a long walk on the Cave Hill with Avril. Jim made two proposals which were interwoven, and maybe even interdependent. The first was of marriage; Avril accepted with a blush and a smile. The other was that, although he so very much wanted to marry her, he felt he had to suggest a rather long engagement – five years. Two to obtain the 'A' levels and another three to take his degree in Canada... To all of this, Avril, who was even more practical and level-headed than Jim, agreed.

There was one other matter. Avril's family were Congregationalists.

Avril observed that her father argued with his Presbyterian friends over matters of Church governance, but for her part she could not find a tram ticket's thickness of difference in the teaching and preaching of the two churches. She would be glad to be the wife of a Presbyterian minister – provided Jim was the minister.

And on that they kissed.

From thereon in, everything went extremely well.

During the week Jim worked in the drawing office and spent three nights a week at college studying English, Economics and History. Once or twice a week he and Avril went to a cinema, a theatre or a concert. Occasionally they would go dancing. There was, too, another activity. About one weekend in four they would go Youth Hostelling. They were particularly fond of Slievenaman Hostel, off a lonely road at the back of Slieve Donard. One summer the Templetons let him join them on a holiday in a rather modest hotel in St Andrew's in Scotland. Another year, the couple's holiday was hostelling in the Republic.

At the end of his two years of study, Jim sat the three 'A' levels and in due course received word from the Exam Board that he had been successful in all three. In one he had been awarded a high grading and in the others very high gradings. He sent a copy of the certificate to the Canadians. All this was in early August. The Canadians replied swiftly and said they wanted him to report to the offices of the Toronto Presbytery in the third week of September. He was to contact the American Express office in the centre of town. They would make the travel arrangements and give him a float for personal expenses in the form of travellers' cheques.

Avril and he agreed they would write once a week and he would come home to Belfast for a spell each summer. In addition, he would try to come for either Christmas/New Year or post-Easter.

When Jim reached Toronto he found arrangements had been made for him to attend University, in addition to which he had been assigned to a church some fifty or so miles to the north-west of the conurbation. This was to be in a small town called Thornhill. The minister there was a Dr Andrew Dalrymple. Originally from Fife he had taken a charge in Toronto when he was in his middle thirties and now he was in what he saw as quasi retirement, though there had proved to be more work than he had envisaged. In addition, there were three other smaller towns to be served, hence the need for a trainee, or variant on a reader.

The arrangement was that Jim would come back from University on a Friday afternoon, take a funeral on the Saturday, and take the service in one of the small towns on Sunday morning and the Sunday evening service as well. In the event of there being another funeral on the Monday morning, he would attend to that prior to leaving for Toronto and his university studies.

And so it was that James Crichton was to qualify to become a very acceptable Presbyterian minister.

Four events over a five week period in the summer of Jim's thirty-first year transformed both his life and that of Avril.

The first was that he graduated with Honours from University.

The second was that at a simple yet dignified service he was ordained as a Minister of the Presbyterian Church.

The third, a week later, was the marriage of Jim and Avril. This took place in Dr Dalrymple's church in Thornhill. The doctor himself officiated. Avril had arrived a few weeks earlier and had lodged with the Session Clerk. On the day she wore a rather fine, fairly expensive, fashionable yet practical two-piece costume which she had purchased in a very good shop near City Hall, Belfast. Mrs Dalrymple was the matron of honour and the best man was a fellow ex-trainee.

The plan for the modest honeymoon was to go to Niagara for a week. H. L. Mencken once observed that the Falls were the first of many disappointments in the lives of all too many American brides. Avril did not have all that many disappointments in her married life, but she did not respond well to the cascading water. After two days they moved to an English-type village on the western side of the river and the Canadian side of the border.

When they returned to Thornhill, it was to the grand news that Jim had been appointed as an Assistant Minister in Dr Dalrymple's church. Pleasing though this was, it put a strain on the finances of the church. Until then, Jim's modest stipend had been paid by the Church at national level. Now the local congregation was responsible and the stipend was higher than it had been.

Fortunately, due in no small measure to Jim's appeal, the membership in the smaller towns had been growing.

The couple rented a flat above a store in town and Avril was recruited as a book-keeper/accountant by the proprietor of the store.

Towards the end of Jim's second year as an Assistant, a vacancy arose at a church 17 miles nearer Toronto. The doctor persuaded Jim to apply. In due course members of their Search Committee came to hear him preach. Shortly thereafter he was invited to visit and preach in their church. When the matter was put to the vote of the members, the vast majority of those in attendance voted for him; only three voted against.

So the van rolled with their modest possessions. Jim and Avril took occupancy, if not ownership, of the seven-apartment manse. The Reverend James Crichton had his first charge. It was almost twenty years to the day since the unfortunate incident during the washing of the dishes in the pokey scullery in Belfast.

When I met Jim Crichton, he was Minister of a church on the western side of the Toronto City spread. The roll of the church fluctuated around eighteen hundred.

I had gone to Canada to visit the best teacher I ever had, who had later been my colleague and who was a treasured personal friend. A Scot from Glasgow, he and his wife had gone to Canada in the wake of their son and daughter. His name was Alex McGregor. Though raised as a Baptist, Alex had lapsed and had been a Humanist for some years. Nonetheless he and Jim were, by then, the best of friends. They played chess and bridge. They drank coffee and they debated and argued, but did so totally devoid of acrimony.

When Jim and I were together, we talked about his earlier charges and about his family in Northern Ireland, which was by then living through dreadful turmoil. His father had wanted to come to Canada on a visit, but he had a heart condition and his doctor advised him not to fly. His mother steadfastly refused to come, even when they offered to pay her fare.

Despite the heart condition his father had lived to his early seventies. When he died, Jim had gone home and conducted the funeral service. Six months after the father's death his mother had written to say she was giving up the house and going to live near some cousins in Limavady.

This news had left Jim smiling ruefully. Limavady was the town where some elements had driven a young Presbyterian minister out of the town, thereby obliging the man to seek and obtain a charge in the Antipodes. What had been the heinous crime which had provoked such action? The minister had been found to have sent a Christmas card to the local Catholic priest. Some of those who had acted did not approve of Christmas, and none of them approved of fraternising with Roman Catholic priests.

When some years later Alex McGregor died, Jim officiated at the burial.

A few months ago, the McGregor girl, the daughter of Alex, was back in Scotland visiting friends. She had lots of people to see, but we managed to have her join us for a few hours. We talked about her brother and his family, and more time was spent remembering her parents and in particular the love and affection for, and appreciation of her father. She recalled being conscious of this even when she was in her early teens. She went on to say the only other person who had been known to win such adulation was Jim Crichton.

I asked how he was.

'He is dead!' she said. She went on to say that he had fallen, but while in hospital he went down with pneumonia and died. The whole episode had lasted no more than ten days. She had not managed to the funeral but had written to Avril, who had since phoned her. Avril was taking it very well: there was there a reservoir of Christian fortitude which served her well. Moreover, while on the phone she had made it clear she was grateful to God for many blessings: for her long and extremely happy marriage, wherein genuine affection and expressions thereof had remained to the very end; for the fact that Jim had been able to qualify for the ministry and thereby achieve his dream; for their four children and eleven grandchildren, with the possibility of some more to come. She was grateful too for God allowing Jim to die as he did. The thought of his drifting into dementia was too horrid to contemplate.

Jim Crichton was held in exceptionally high regard by thousands. He was admired and loved by hundreds, not only within his own denomination but across the whole spectrum of the Christian faith, from the Opus Dei battalions of Rome to the closest of the Closed Brethren and beyond them, by those of no faith whatsoever.

Sadly, his mother remained bitter to the end, but then, regrettably, all too many in her community choose to be bitter and appear to revel in their bitterness.

Dae Ye Ken Ken?

Name-dropping is not to be encouraged – as Lord Mountbatten said a week before he was assassinated.

That said, I had the pleasure and privilege of working with and knowing the late Sir Kenneth Alexander. Ken was very smart, but it is in the interests of honesty (despite the Mountbatten dictum) that I would observe that he was not the cleverest person with whom I worked or with whom I was friendly. Lord (Lennie) Hoffman and Bernard Williams, the philosopher and first husband of Shirley of that ilk, were smarter, as were Lady Sharpe, the first woman to become the Permanent Secretary of a Government department, and Sir Robert Fraser and Sir Brian Young, both Directors General of the Independent Television Authority, the ITA, later re-named the IBA. Another person to be included in this top-drawer category was my well-nigh lifelong friend Robert Crampsey, who won Brain of Britain and was a Mastermind finalist.

But let's be clear. Ken was a very, very good academic. In addition he had a remarkable run of personal attributes which stood him in good stead throughout his life. He was able and astute, he was clever and highly intelligent. He had been very hard working when he was young and in his advanced years knew how to pace himself.

He made friends easily and having acquired them knew how to use them, and that is not said in any derogatory way. He was politically alert, yet we never knew for certain in which camp he slept. That he was of the Left there was no doubt, but to which party he belonged, that we never knew for certain.

Here, then, was a very talented individual who forged out for himself a near-brilliant career. He was the first Professor of Economics in the University of Strathclyde in Glasgow. Having that post as a base camp to which he could return, he was Chairman of the famous Upper Clyde Shipbuilders and succeeded in bringing the workers to living with the economic realities of the market place. Later, he was Chairman of the Highlands and Islands Development Board. Shortly after his return to Strathclyde he left to become the Principal of the University of Stirling.

As I keep suggesting, his portfolio of personal attributes was formidable but to some it was remarkable that his impressive academic standing was based on a single degree.

But what a degree!

Ken had a BSc Econ of the University of London, where the responsibility for that degree course lay with the internationally renowned London School of Economics. Moreover, his degree had been awarded with First Class Honours.

At a time when Universities the length of Britain are debasing the coinage, as it were, by giving ten, fifteen and occasionally nearly twenty percent of their new graduates First Class Honours, it should be noted that it has been calculated that for those who embarked on the road towards this onerous LSE degree, the percentage who ended up with a First was, wait for it, 0.1.

In other words, Ken Alexander's First from the LSE was a remarkable achievement.

This brings me to a digression, though with luck, it will be seen to be a relevant or a quasi-relevant digression.

There used to be a quite magnificent American magazine called *The Saturday Evening Post*. As the name suggests, it arrived in many an American household by the last post of a Saturday, late afternoon/early evening. It resulted in many a sombre, near funereal Sabbath being made tolerable. From its brilliant covers with drawings by Norman Rockwell, through its short stories, its serials, the feature articles, the pages for the ladies, the cartoons, the funnies, the puzzles, it provided light reading and entertainment for all the family. It was recognised that the readership far outstripped the circulation.

We received it from friends in the States, and in turn passed it on to my sister-in-law and her family. I believe they in turn gave it to their neighbours. There was only one disconcerting feature about this wonderful publication: from my point of view, it was very right-wing, if not positively reactionary.

There was another regular feature which I believe I should mention - a feature called 'The Perfect Squelch' in which they paid $25 for an example of a spirited riposte. The printed account was always supported by a cartoon-type drawing.

Two examples, both related to the world of academia, stay with me.

In one, a sophomore – second year student - with décolletage down to her big toes slides up to a lecturer and coos:

'Gee, Professor, I would do just anything to pass my examination!'

The lecturer does not even bother to look at her, but he does reply.

'Including study?' he asks.

The other example involved another young female student. Dressed in hot pants and long stockings she confronts a teacher. 'Professor,' she says, 'how come you never took your doctorate?'

In this instance the teacher glowers at her.

'And who would have examined me?' he demands.

I found myself thinking again and again of the second of these anecdotes when I heard young lecturers grumbling about Ken while they were working for their doctorates, finding it tougher and more demanding than they had foreseen.

Ken had no post-graduate degree, no text-book, no outstanding research papers, but he was Ken with his quite outstanding First.

As the sixties were giving way to the seventies, the UK was visited by a Professor Lambert. Like Agatha Christie's Poirot, he was a French-speaking Belgian. As I recall, his quite lengthy visit was sponsored by the Co-operative Union, which in those days was still a financially comfortable, if not quite wealthy, organisation. Perhaps we were more than a little uncharitable, but some of us picked up the impression that he had arranged to be invited. He stayed in good hotels and was not averse to being wined and dined in good restaurants. Those of us who were known to take an interest in the wider Co-operative Movement and in bodies which did not distribute their profits were invited to meet him and hear what he had to say. It soon transpired that Lambert had arrived as something of a missionary. We learned that he was the founder and director of an organisation which, though based in Belgium, had a world-wide membership. It was devoted to encouraging and stimulating (but not financing) research on Co-operatives of all shapes and sizes and activities, and in public sector activities.

This all happened some fifty years ago, but as I recall it, his body had a name in French which was extremely lengthy. One consequence of this was that no one, not even Lambert himself, referred to the full name. Instead, everyone used its acronym, CIRIEC. The most obvious manifestation of this organisation was a bulky magazine which came out twice a year with half the articles in French and half in English. That said, the common denominator was hard to discern. My recollection is that a typical edition would have an article on agricultural co-operatives in Slovenia, fishermen's co-operatives on a Pacific island, while others would be on the alleged success of publicly owned railways in Bulgaria and shared holiday homes in Finland.

Lambert's concern was that he had no member or branches in the UK, and so he invited us to join and to be active.

We were polite. We told him we would think about it and discuss it amongst ourselves.

The debates were protracted but two bodies came into being.

The first, the one that still exists, is the Society for Co-operative Studies. The other, which lasted for about twenty years, came into being at the instigation of Ken Alexander. Like many other powerful intellectuals of the Left, he had little interest in the Co-operative sector, though he knew I had. He was markedly more interested in the wider Public Sector, so he proposed that he and I would launch a quasi-research body and call it Public and Co-operative Enterprise, whereupon our acronym would be PACE.

Our timing was poor, in that two other bodies called PACE came into being at the same time. One, based in London, was called Patriotic Action by Conservative Electors, which we regarded as somewhat tautological.

The other was based in Northern Ireland, and was called Protestants and Catholics Ecumenical. It was not a great success. The standing jest was that they had launched a membership drive which lasted a whole year, yet produced only three new members, and all three of them were in the Trinity.

PACE, our PACE, was a success, a modest success, but a success. As has been said of the House of Lords, we did nothing in particular but did it rather well.

To be more precise, we did three things, two of them below the water line and one above it. The first of the somewhat invisible activities was that we obtained some funding, usually rather modest, for post-graduate students and others undertaking research in fields which came within our far-flung terms of interest. This money came from Co-op bodies, Trades Unions, Nationalised Industries, local authorities and similar bodies.

The other was that from time to time we helped arrange for the publication of articles by those who had completed or nearly completed their research. In both these activities, Ken was much more active and successful than I was.

The visible activity was that throughout the academic year we held monthly meetings at which our members and their friends were addressed by what proved to be a remarkable range of speakers. These tended to fall into two fairly distinct groups. The first consisted of men and women who had already proven themselves, some being household names. The other group was of younger people, in the process of coming into prominence.

Two of these nights stay in my memory. The first was on a night before an unexpected General Election. The speaker had been the late Robin Cook, and we were having a drink in the lounge of the University Staff Club. Quite suddenly Ken looked at his watch, muttered that it was later than he had thought and that he must be off.

'Never mind, Robin, you will always get my vote!' and with that he lifted his coat and left.

Robin, who was the forthcoming Labour candidate in Edinburgh Central, was clearly perplexed.

'I thought he lived in Callander,' he half-asserted, half-asked.

'He does,' I replied. I went on to explain that Ken had four residences. There was the substantial family home half way up a hill in Callander. There was, too, a holiday retreat in the wilds of Ardnamurchan on the west coast. In addition to these there were flats in both Glasgow and Edinburgh for use by the family and friends as need arose. I went on to point out that being Ken, he had chosen to register as a voter in the only marginal seat of the four.

'Never fear,' I said. 'He said he will vote for you and he will. In situations like that you can rely on him. He is always looking down the road for opportunities to help the Labour Movement, no matter how small it might be.'

The Robin Cook incident occurred after an evening meeting. The other memorable incident took place before a meeting.

We could not afford to pay a fee to our speakers, but we could give them high tea and a book token. Ken was Chairman and I was Secretary. So far as the meetings were concerned, my duties were to arrange to have a speaker (subject to Ken's power of veto), to agree a topic and a title and, of course, a date and time. Thereafter I had to book a room for the lecture and a table in the Staff Club dining room for the high tea, notify the members and arrange for publicity.

The next task was to send confirmation to the speaker together with maps of the city and the campus, and arrangements for our meeting.

On the night of the meeting, the speaker, Ken and I would meet at six o'clock for a drink and start eating at quarter past. However, from seven onwards I had to slip out to see what size of audience we had. In the event of it being poor, I would scour the Club lounge for the reasonably sober and persuade some to come through for the meeting.

On one such occasion, when I returned to our tea table, Ken swung round to address me.

'Tom,' he said. 'We are discussing the BSc Econ. In which year did you take it?'

'1956,' I replied.

'Ah,' said Ken, 'that was the year when the main Economics paper had the question about the cup of coffee.'

'It was,' I confirmed. 'It was a dreadful question in that it seemed very simple but if you knew your stuff you knew that a full answer could go on for a long time, almost certainly longer than you could afford to invest in a single answer. The astute lifted their hats, so to speak, and passed on to tackle other questions.'

Ken agreed and asked me whether I could recall how it went.

I thought for a moment and ventured: 'I reckon it was along the lines of: 'Why does a cup of coffee cost more in the grill room of the Savoy Hotel than it does at the buffet at Waterloo Station?'

Ken smiled the smile of recollection. 'That's not quite right,' he observed, 'but it will do!'

He then went on to say that he had been the External Examiner and had been sent a rather onerous pile of scripts. In one paper, the candidate had tackled that very question and had written a single sentence in the middle of an otherwise virginal page.

'Because they are rotten capitalist bastards!'

The reaction of the London examiners to this startling answer had been to give it three marks out of the possible twenty five.

Ken admitted to our guest speaker and to me that he had sat gazing into the embers of his fireplace while drumming his pencil on the cushioned arm of his chair and then found himself writing at the bottom of the page: 'While it is true that this answer is unduly succinct, indeed one might say terse, the candidate does bring out one aspect of the matter not raised by many other candidates.' Thereafter, he had thought a bit more and gave the answer seven out of the twenty five.

Come the day of the Exam Board meeting, this generosity of spirit had been of no avail. The Board took it back down to five. Worse, the candidate failed!

In due course Ken left Strathclyde to take up his post as Principal at Stirling.

I became Chairman of our PACE, and my friend and colleague Bill Stewart took over from me as Secretary. Sadly, our wee organisation went into decline, though we were slow to discern this at the time. We had lost the aura of Ken. More, our membership dropped and we came to realise that some folk had joined in order to have the identification with Ken. Without him, we had lost much of our attraction.

Notwithstanding these difficulties, we carried on for another four or five years. In due course the whole issue was discussed at an AGM. We decided to wind up our activities and transferred our limited resources to the Society for Co-operative Studies which, to its credit, still exists.

Some years later, while lecturing at the STUC Summer School at Stirling University, I had occasion to go over to the main administration building to see Ken. As I sat in the outer waiting area to his suite, a porter came through to deliver a parcel to Ken's secretarial team. As he passed me he eyed me up and asked: 'Ur ye gaun in tae see ra Principal?'

I said I was. 'Dae ye ken Ken?' he queried. I told him that I did know Ken and had worked with him in different capacities.

'Aye,' he said with pride and approval. 'Aye, there ur no' that mony like him. He's yin o' us, so he is. We ur gey lucky tae hae him, so we ur.' And with that he went on his way.

There are not many University Principals who would win an endorsement like that from their porters.

A Clash Of Cultures

I liked McCrindle; indeed, I liked him very much. So too did most of his peer group in the Ministry of Labour.

He was bright, intelligent, hard-working and extremely well-read. It was always a delight to meet him. He was always good for a piece of news, an anecdote or, God forgive us, a bit of gossip – not that his gossip was vindictive or all that uncharitable.

On one occasion many years ago, the late Monsignor Ronald Knox, he who could do *The Times* crossword without putting pen to paper, preached in Scotland at the ordination of a bishop. In the course of his address he asserted that a bishop would be judged in Heaven not on the strength of his piety, or on his fine handling of Canon Law, and certainly not on the efficiency with which he ran his diocese, but rather on the extent to which hearts leapt and eyes shone at the sight of his coming.

For my own part I have grave misgivings on the doctrinal acceptability of that argument. The door to Heaven depends on more than popularity. On the other hand, were Knox to be right and had McCrindle been a bishop, his heavenly reward would have been assured. We all loved to meet him.

There was then a great deal of delight when we heard of his promotion to Higher Executive Officer or Grade 4 in Ministry of Labour parlance. At the time he was in his middle to late thirties. This was young by the age-group composition of the Department at that time.

His mother was a Gaelic speaker so it seemed not inappropriate when he was appointed as manager of an Employment Exchange in the Hebrides.

After he had been in the post for six months he came down to Glasgow on holiday. We met for lunch and I asked how it was going. He laughed and said it was certainly 'different'. He cited two examples. The first was that since his taking over he had been allocated two new young female Clerical Officers, both from the Central Belt. On both occasions he had gone to meet them coming off the boat. In both instances the girls had subsequently enquired how he had known who they were, how had he identified his personnel from the other young women who had been disembarking? He had admitted that in each case his officer was the only girl wearing silk stockings and make-up.

His other case involved sheep. According to his returns there were remarkably few sheep on the island, and virtually none owned by his part-time crofters. However, according to the documentation held by the local office of the Department of Agriculture and Fisheries of the Scottish Office, the island was awash with sheep.

On one occasion he had been leaving his office to visit an employer just as one of his veteran claimants of Unemployment Benefit was passing with almost two hundred sheep and four sheep-dogs. The claimant greeted him warmly and added by way of explanation that he was just giving the minister a hand by taking his sheep to the boat.

When McCrindle had been in post a year or so we were all extremely shocked to learn that he was to be disciplined on a matter of great gravity.

Later he told me that the first he knew of the matter was when he received a phone call from the Staffing Section at our Scottish head office in Drumsheugh Gardens in Edinburgh. He was instructed to report the following Monday to be rebuked and cautioned by the Regional Controller, one Raymond Nightingale Campbell, whose father had been an admiral and who had given all eight of his children the initials 'RN'.

Gey worried, my friend had phoned the Scottish Secretary of our Staff Association who was every bit as concerned as McCrindle. It was agreed they would report together on Monday. The ensuing meeting with the Controller did not go easily; at best it was fraught, while at its worst it was acrimonious.

At first the Controller did not want the Association representative to be in attendance. That was given short shrift. The representative quoted from the Code on Disciplinary Procedure and handed a copy to Campbell. The Head of Staffing who was present assured the Controller that 'the accused' had the right to be represented not by a lawyer but by an Association nominee.

When the meeting – it was more of a confrontation than a meeting – started, the Controller made it abundantly clear that as he saw it this interview need not take very long. He went on to say that the situation was serious but simple and straightforward. He explained that they had received a report containing a formal complaint from the local Presbytery of one of the three smaller Presbyterian churches on the island. The report was that McCrindle had committed an act of gross indecency towards the wife of one of the ministers, in that he had directed lewd and licentious remarks to the lady, such remarks being in the form of an indecent suggestion. The minister and his wife were named. He went on to say that as he saw it the Department had to accept the findings of such a respectable and august body.

'Who would question the word of one of our churches?' he asked, but he meant it to be a rhetorical question.

He was taken aback when the Association spokesman came in very quickly with an observation:

'Well, I would for one,' he said.

Having grabbed the initiative he went on to argue that the Department in its Industrial Relations work, not least in arbitration work, advised that in situations of this kind the person criticised had to be given full details of the charge against him and an opportunity to rebut or refute the charge. He went on to say it would be quite untenable were the Department in its internal affairs not to implement the advice it gave to every other employer in the land.

The Controller was very distressed. 'But what would you have us do?' he queried.

'Do!' exploded the rep. 'What I and your own IR people would have you do is what you should have done in the first instance. Write back and ask them to report what was said.'

'We cannot do that,' said the Controller. 'Not to a church,' he added.

'All right, then,' said the rep. 'Then don't write but drop all disciplinary action against our member. The choice is yours, Mr Campbell.'

In the wake of that declaration there was an awkward, embarrassed silence. While it lasted, the Staffing Director, by body language rather than the spoken word, managed to convey to the Staff Association representative that he was not doing his career prospects any good whatsoever by his zealous defence of his member.

The representative, by a shrug and a smile that had within it the elements of a sneer, signalled that he knew what the higher-paid help was thinking. Already in his middle to late fifties he was only too aware that his career had peaked. There would be no more promotion for him. He sensed they regarded him as troublesome and that as a result they would look for grounds to oblige him to take premature retirement. On the other hand, he knew he ran a neat, tidy office. The inspectors would find the usual trivia, but they would not find anything of substance to hold against him. If the worst came to the worst and he was mistaken, and they did find something substantial with which to confront him, he would go gracefully, knowing he had fought the good fight on behalf of his colleagues. Moreover, there would be his golf and his garden, extra wee holidays with his wife... They would see more of their sun-drenched wee holiday home in Crail in the East Neuk of Fife. He would live with it whatever way the ball bounced.

All of this was conveyed in seconds.

Then the Controller coughed.

'Well now,' he said. 'Let us see if we can agree on at least some of the facts.'

'Do you admit that you know the lady in the report?' he asked, half-glowering at McCrindle.

McCrindle admitted that he knew the lady, but only slightly. He had served on a local committee with her husband and had met her on a few occasions when she came to collect him.

'And do you agree that you met her on the day in question?' the glower continued.

Yes, he had met her.

'And you had converse with the lady?'

Yes, that too.

'And what did you talk about?'

McCrindle looked thoughtful. 'As I recall it, we talked about her family and in particular about her husband who was very busy, and then about holidays and the weather – it was a very cold day.'

At that point the Association's agent forced his way into the proceedings.

'This is not taking us very far,' he argued, 'we need to know the precise nature and content of the allegation. I say again that either you obtain such information or drop all disciplinary action against my colleague. I suggest we adjourn for four weeks to let you decide what you want to do.'

And they did.

When they reconvened a month or so later it soon transpired that they were 'nae further furrit' in the Scots phrase. Against his own better judgement the Controller had written to the Presbytery and requested them to be somewhat more explicit. What had McCrindle said?

The Presbytery had replied in indignation and exasperation. It wanted to know what had happened over the last five or six weeks. Were they to take it that no action had been taken against the culprit? Had the Department no regard for the sensitivities of ladies? It was bad enough that the lady had been subjected to diabolical behaviour and had been obligated to report the matter to her husband and that he in turn had been in the embarrassing position of being obliged to relate the matter in gruesome detail to his colleagues, but now the Department appeared to be suggesting, indeed requesting, that the lady repeat the offensive words; that her husband should do the same; and, more, that another lady in the form of the typist of Presbytery correspondence should be expected to record the events on paper. The whole situation was preposterous. The Department should accept the word of a Christian church whose ministers had discussed the matter and who were entirely at one in supporting the initial report. The Department should accept the report, severely discipline the culprit and advise the Presbytery on the action that had been taken. It was impossible to contemplate any other outcome.

The Controller intimated that he thought the reply was very well argued and that he was inclined to agree with it. He suggested McCrindle should do the decent thing, which was to 'own up', accept the disciplinary action and let them all be done of it.

McCrindle repeated that he had no recollection of having done or said anything untoward. He was in effect registering a plea of 'not guilty'.

His representative went further. He strenuously argued that not a single piece of firm evidence had been produced. As he saw it, there had been no progress whatsoever. In very frank phraseology he again told the Controller that either he should produce the detailed case against his member or he should drop all disciplinary action. He suggested a second four-week adjournment and added that were the matter not resolved to his satisfaction at that meeting he would take the case to national level as he was entitled to do. He was not prepared to see his colleague hung out to dry to make life easier for the Department. The Controller was mildly apoplectic but agreed to meet again in four weeks' time.

When they met some five weeks later it soon became apparent that progress had been made by both sides.

The Controller who normally looked worried, glum, grim and miserable like photographs of Lord Reith in his BBC days (or worse, in the period after he had left the BBC and was feeling sorry for himself) had been reported as having been seen pounding the corridors with a self-satisfied smile on his face. No-one knew for certain what had happened but rumours emanated from the Staffing Directorate that he had told one of his Deputies that he had been rather clever. Months later it was being said that he had recalled that his sister, Bobby (born Roberta Noreen) was married to Ian Murchieston, a baronet with an eighty-acre estate near Tayport in Fife. When Ian had been a student at St Andrews he had been friendly on the SRC with a man from Applecross on the west coast. After graduation in Arts this lad o' pairts had gone on to take a further degree from the Divinity Faculty. Following his graduation he had become a minister in the main Kirk, but had subsequently gone over to the church involved in the McCrindle saga. Much more recently he had been Moderator of their General Assembly. The Controller, it was said, had phoned his brother-in-law and asked him to ask his friend to 'speir' on what had happened to provoke the condemnatory report from the island Presbytery.

On the staff side Jim McLean, the Association representative, had persuaded McCrindle to come down to the McLean house in Stirling where, with the help of Jim's wife, they tried a re-enactment of the fatal meeting. As this exercise proceeded McCrindle recalled the conversation about the family, about how busy the minister was, about the holidays and about the weather: it had been very, very cold. This had triggered a further recollection. As they were saying good-bye he had noticed that the wee boy was well-clad in heavy clothing and was wearing full-length tartan trews. The wee girl, who had been clinging to the mother – he had thought out of shyness and timidity, but had belatedly perceived to have been provoked by her being cold – was on the other hand wearing a thin pullover, a skimpy wee tartan kilt-like skirt and short ankle socks. His final valedictory observation had been to nod in the direction of the girl. 'You should have her in trousers as well,' he had said. Could it be that this innocuous remark had given offence and provoked the entire brouhaha?

When the meeting started the others could discern a flirtation with a smile on the face of the Controller. He seemed rather pleased with himself and announced he had instigated the most discreet of enquiries and had a matter of considerable relevance and importance to report.

But before he could enjoy his moment, McLean barged in and said his member had given great thought to the encounter with the lady and wished to make a statement. Whereupon he nudged our hero, who proceeded to give his detailed recollection of the incident with the lady. He finished by again asking, as he had done in the McLean household, could it be that his well-intentioned remark about the wee girl had been misconstrued or in some way given rise to offence?

The Controller almost beamed. This account, he proclaimed, was in accord with his own intelligence. He had learned that the lady had been greatly distressed by the suggestion that a female be dressed in men's apparel.

Again McLean barged in. He argued in forceful language that there had been a deviation from the norms of contemporary Scottish life. This had not been the innocent remark of his member, which remark had been motivated not by debauchery but by commendable compassion. It was evident, he argued, the deviation from the norm had been the extremely insular and over-sensitive reaction of the lady.

This was followed by a brief discussion on the extent it was incumbent on Central Belt Scots to accommodate to the sincerely held views of some of their fellow Scots.

Yet again McLean forced his way into the discussion. Such matters were interesting, he observed, but they were 'out of order' for them in that the only matter was whether his friend was to be censured and have his staff records noted to that effect. He concluded by saying that thanks to the Controller's discreet enquiries his member had been vindicated and should leave without blemish.

The Controller beamed and said he agreed. The Staffing Director closed his files and they all went home.

So McCrindle won?

Well, yes, but no, but then again – yes!

Let me explain! In the short run he won in that he was vindicated; he was exonerated. No critical, onerous comment was made on his staff records. However, he was removed from the Islands and transferred to a very large office in Glasgow where he was to be Deputy Manager.

The distressing development was that before a month was out, and for three, six, nine months and a year thereafter he received evidence that in offices throughout Scotland when his name was mentioned, someone almost invariably said something like: 'Oh aye, he was the guy who had the torrid affair with a minister's wife on one of the islands.' According to such gossip it had been a heavily active, full-blooded, adulterous affair of bodice-ripping proportions. Worse still, too many offices had a staff member who knew someone who had seen them on a moor, in a car, in a cheap boarding house in Edinburgh or a luxury hotel in Perthshire. It was all fabricated nonsense, of course, but a distressing number of people chose to believe it.

At that time there was no telling him he had won; on the contrary he was miserable.

Having suffered this for a year or so he put in for a transfer to London. London grabbed him. And he prospered. Before he had completed five years in London he was promoted to SEO, and after a further six to CEO. Thereafter he moved smoothly into the grades of the Administrative Class.

The last time I heard from him he was an Assistant Secretary, though I heard from a mutual friend he had been given one more promotion before he retired. He had married a Scottish lady, also based in London. On his retirement she wanted to stay in the south to be near the grandchildren. He had a boat on the Solent.

So it was that he won in the short run, suffered and to that extent lost for a while, but in the long run won by having a markedly more successful career than he would have had in Scotland.

McCrindle was so good and talented and decent that he deserved to succeed and by the Grace of God he did. Yet despite the happy ending I always saw it as a sad and distressing story.

The Reverend John R. Gray

Sadly, experience taught me that not everyone in the national church, The Church of Scotland, warmed to John R. Gray, but I liked him immensely.

John was a minister in that church, but he was no ordinary, run-of-the-mill, modest, light-under-a-bushel, undistinguished minister. *Au contraire*: he was a colourful, distinguished well-to-the-fore minister. He had a formidable range of attributes, some of them almost conflicting. For example, he could be extremely proper yet had a delightful sense of humour. Being perjink and being able to make folk laugh (with you as opposed to at you) do not often run in tandem.

He did not score high on modesty, and that seemed to be a matter of concern to those members of the kirk, the ordained and those in power who did not take to him.

He was active in the world of religious broadcasting which is where we met. I took to him at once.

I remember well some of our encounters.

'Ah, Thomas,' he would say, 'the great Caesar told us Gaul was divided into three parts, but poor Garnethill is divided into three Gauls: Bengal, Senegal and Donegal.'

On another occasion he would stroll up to me:

'Ah, Thomas,' he would say, 'we must commiserate with poor Garnethill.'

I would intervene: 'John – you've told me your story of the three Gauls'.

'No, no, Thomas,' he would counter. 'You do me a disservice. This is a quite different observation. Ah yes, poor Garnethill, from Glasgow High to Shanghai in one generation.'

Such bon mots, quips, call them what you will, poured out of him.

Whether he acquired them or made them up I never knew. I only wish I remembered more of them.

I found him to be considerate. Here I might be mistaken, attributing to him what some Christian churches call 'corporal works of mercy'. As I recall it, he took his mother each year for a week or ten-days' holiday. They would stay at the Elderslie Hotel in Largs, which became the Priory Hotel, on the Broomfields side of the town.

I was for nine years the Scottish member of the Independent Broadcasting Authority. I came off the Board in the late summer of 1979, shortly after the Thatcher victory. I had been appointed in January 1970 when our activities – and our nomenclature – were confined to television.

One Sunday evening in the winter of 1979/80 our telephone rang.

John R. was then minister of Dunblane Cathedral.

'Thomas,' he started as soon as I had identified myself, 'Thomas, I want to make a formal complaint to you. My wife and I have been watching a play! I would not say it is relatively disgusting but it is much too outré for a Sabbath evening. You do evaluate not only the content of such transmissions but include such issues as the time and suitability of the day of probable transmission, do you not?'

'John,' I intervened, or rather tried to intervene, this despite his not having introduced himself. One could recognize him and his voice immediately.

My attempted interjection was of no avail. He raged on.

'I really must object and am sure I am not alone. I am fully aware there has been a sad falling away in standards in contemporary society. What is causing it is, as you know, a matter of considerable debate, but all that said....'

'John,' I half-roared.

'Thomas,' he said, and sounded somewhat peeved, 'you surely do not disagree?'

'John,' I tried again, and this time succeeded in quietening him.

'John, dear man,' I said. 'As you know I generally do agree with you, but on this occasion it is of no great import.'

'Thomas,' he came back at me, 'you shock me. Whatever do you mean?'

'John, it is of no great import because I am no longer the Scottish member of the Authority. But John, be reassured, I am confident your complaint will receive a sympathetic response, not least as my successor is an ordained minister of the Church of Scotland.'

'A minister?'

'Yes, John. A minister but not just a minister, but a minister at a cathedral, albeit of lesser importance that that at Dunblane.'

There was a refreshing silence.

'A cathedral! Where? A minister! Who?'

'John,' I ventured. 'John, I was succeeded by Bill Morris. Your Dr William Morris of Glasgow Cathedral.'

'Bill! I didn't know that.'

'Did you not, John? Guess who is not reading *Life and Work*?'

John chose to ignore that slight barb so I pressed on.

'You will have Bill's phone number in your Kirk diary. No doubt you will phone him as you did me.'

Again there was a short silence.

'Tom,' he tried again. 'Tom, is that nice man Lindsay still the Scottish officer? No doubt you have his phone number.'

I squeezed my way in once more.

'John, if you are going to phone John Lindsay, I really do believe you should phone him at his office tomorrow. Remember your Bible, John: *'The labourer is worthy of his hire'* and I would suggest, of his rest. It is his Sabbath as well, John. Phone him tomorrow. But if you really must do something this evening while your indignation is still warm, then Dr Morris is your man.'

'You think so?'

'Yes, I do, John. Good night, dear friend.' With that I brought our exchange to a close.

We never met again. Nor did we have other telephonic conversations.

John had retired by the time of the Dunblane tragedy. I knew nothing of him in his retirement. John was lively. John was colourful. John was involved in the world around him.

As I saw it, and still see it, the Kirk and the other Christian churches could do with more of the ordained being lively, even dramatic, characters. We could all do with more folk of the verve, vitality and pawky disposition of John R. Gray.

The Cruel Game

For the purpose of this tale her name was Kate McDougall.

Truth to tell, that was not her name. I do remember her name but at one time I had a number of what I regarded as good and compelling reasons why I should avoid using her real name. Now they have all gone: not a single one of them comes to mind. But I do remember with devastating clarity that they were valid. So I say again, her name was Kate McDougall.

She was a senior councillor on the Corporation of the City of Glasgow. She was too an active and effective member of the Labour Group and she was active in her Constituency Labour Party.

It was against this background that she had been adopted as the prospective Labour candidate for the Conservative-held constituency in which she lived. The seat was regarded as a relatively safe Tory seat. No one really believed she could win it but they had to have a candidate and they had taken the view that it might as well be her. Letting her be a Parliamentary candidate was akin to the Party giving her its equivalent of an MBE.

And then disaster struck!

The sitting member died. In their own ways the Labour Party crowd had respected him rather than liked him. As they saw it he had been 'a decent old stick' or 'not such a bad soul' or 'as good a Tory as we are likely to get.' He had served in the First World War and was a stalwart of the Black Watch, the family regiment. As a Captain in the trenches he had been wounded twice: one of these wounds was a very serious one which troubled him for the rest of his life. Promoted to Major and then to Colonel he had served at Command H. Q. He had married the younger daughter of a Marquis who was known to all as Lady Dorothy. He had looked like Willie Whitelaw but politically was more in tune with Ian MacLeod: at heart he had been a One Nation Tory. He had served for a spell as a Deputy Speaker but on the advice of his Harley Street doctor had been obliged to withdraw.

Now he was dead, and there would have to be a by-election.

That was not the scenario envisaged by the ruling clique of the CLP when they had conspired to nominate what they regarded as the pleasant but nondescript Mrs. McDougall as their Parliamentary candidate.

What they had foreseen was a General Election virtually indistinguishable from those over the preceding fifteen or twenty years. When the election was announced the Chairman and Secretary would take Kate aside and explain to her that they could not realistically expect to win this seat which in historic terms was fairly safe Tory territory. They would ensure that her campaign was more than perfunctory. They would see to it that the bulk of the lads would work for her for five or six nights and an afternoon or two but, they would tell her, the lads would go off on the other nights to work in more marginal seats where Labour had a better chance of winning. What they would not tell her was that the left-wingers would go and work for folk of that militant, spirited view while their right-wing comrades would go and work for mild Fabians, for Christian Socialists and for douce, reliable trade union-sponsored candidates.

Kate would get the message. She would be left to depend on her friends in the Women's Section and the Co-op Women's Guild, on the men as and when they appeared and on able teenagers to deliver leaflets and chalk the streets.

Now all that had gone or at least gone for the time being. Now they had to fight a by-election for which they were ill-prepared.

The first problem was that their political machine was as rusty as some of the equipment in the nearby shipyards.

The second problem was even more serious: they were skint. Had Kate been sponsored by a big, affluent union or by the Co-operative Party the CLP's financial position would be less worrying, but she did not have any sponsor, far less a rich one.

A third problem was an external factor. Television was beginning to play an increasing role in all aspects of British life so the activists had to conclude that their candidate would be subjected to national scrutiny not only from the press but from the radio and television as well. Kate, who in a General Election would have been but one of over 600 Labour candidates, was about to be examined and examined carefully on a national stage. Her areas of expertise were Council Housing and the quality of school meals. Foreign Affairs, Defence Policy, the strength of Sterling and the intricacies of the Balance of Payments were beyond her ken. All in all, the leaders of the CLP looked ahead and winced. Life, they reckoned, was not going to be easy!

When relief came, as it did, it came in the form of Mr. William Miller who was the Scottish Secretary of the Party.

Miller arrived and reported he brought three assets. The first was money, not exactly bags of it but there would be enough. The second was manpower: he would see to it that samurai would pour in from all the airts and pairts. The third might prove to be the best of the three. He announced that he would be the agent and he personally would nurse Kate through the campaign.

Bill Miller was a natural commander. It was easy to tell when he was in his command mode because he was always in his command mode. Physically he looked like a General in the Confederate Army. He was always well dressed in a fairly expensive yet unostentatious way reminiscent of the style adopted by Labour front-bench spokesman in the Commons and by the more sober and conventional General Secretaries of the larger Trades Unions.

When he arrived he took Kate out to dinner. Ostensibly they had an intensive discussion on her campaign but it soon became apparent that it was his campaign.

Very early within the official three-week campaign period he announced there would be a press conference every week-day morning at 11a.m in a quality hotel in the constituency. He had booked a room which held a hundred and he never had less than eighty in attendance. The journalists soon became peeved and critical but they kept coming as interest throughout the country was intense in this and the other two by-elections to be held on the same day. The Government was going through a sticky patch and it was well known that the Member who had died had enjoyed a substantial personal vote which would not accrue to his would-be Tory successor.

Every morning every national paper was represented, some by more than one journalist. All the Scottish papers had folk in attendance and there were freelance folk working for German, French and American papers and of course both radio and television were represented.

Each morning Miller and the candidate would enter the room at five minutes to the hour. Precisely on the hour Miller would start with a short comment on the news of the day whereupon he would invite questions and very correctly insisted that those who rose confined themselves to questions and did not embark on personal observations and mini-speeches of their own.

It was a good arrangement but the candidate who was always well dressed did not say very much: indeed, there was many a morning on which she said nothing. And so they would proceed.

'Ducksworth, *Daily Telegraph*: What are the candidate's views on the Iran issue?'

It would be Miller who would reply. 'As you might expect, Mrs. McDougall is fully in accord with the line adopted by the Labour front bench and by the National Executive of the Party. We are aware that many of those present are fully aware of our policy on this tricky and difficult question but for the sake of those who are somewhat less well informed I would simply explain........'

'Bob Black, *The Times*...'

Miller interrupted! '*The Glasgow Evening Times?*'

'Naw, the' – and then after a few spluttering oaths - '*The London Times!*'

'Oh, and what is your question?'

'Thank you. Does the candidate have anything to say on the matter of the latest figures on unemployment?'

Miller rose in an imposing manner.

'Does the candidate have anything to say on the latest figures on unemployment? She most certainly has; indeed she has a great deal to say.

It so happens she and I were talking about this matter only the other day. For my part, I was most impressed by her knowledge on this important matter. I was particularly impressed by her knowledge not just of the situation here in Glasgow but throughout the whole of Scotland and across the whole of Britain. She was and is very much in command on that topic. However, as she said to me, no-one could express our concern better than our party leader in his speech of last weekend in Cardiff, so with that in mind and expecting this subject to come up today, we have arranged for copies of that speech to be ready for you all as you leave at the end of these proceedings. Who wants to ask the next question?'

The third journalist to take up the bowling was John Rankine of *The Scotsman*. He wanted to know whether Mrs. McDougall had any reservations about the Labour policy on the findings of Lord Russell's Royal Commission on the press. This was easy stuff for the seasoned Bill Miller. Patiently, he explained that the candidate had no reservations, not least as she had been one of those who determined the policy. He acknowledged this called for some explanation. Not only had the lady been a delegate to the Labour Conference which formulated the policy but she had been an active and eloquent participant in the CLP discussion and formulation of its policy with which to mandate the constituency delegation prior to their departing for the conference. At the risk of elaboration he pointed out that this illustrated her double involvement in the determination of the party's support for the findings of the Royal Commission.

Miller, however, was not only shrewd, he was crafty. Still on his feet he went on to observe that he knew many of the journalists present and many of their colleagues not in attendance would appreciate and support the Commission's observations on some of the malpractices of the newspaper barons and other proprietors who collectively and individually made life so difficult for their employees, not least the journalists.

This dig at the newspaper owners produced warm applause and some cynical laughter from the journalists who had won agreements for extraordinarily generous expenses from the maligned proprietors.

The following question was about University entrance. Again Miller rose to answer. As he was getting into his stride saying how Kate viewed the situation, there was a raucous interruption from the body o' the kirk: 'Can the wumman no' speak for herself?'

Bill Miller looked horrified. 'That is a dreadful and most ungracious interruption,' he observed and continued: 'How dare you malign a fine, capable and sensitive lady with an excellent record on Glasgow Corporation! Your unbecoming interruption ill-becomes both you and your paper. I suspect they will want to replace you.'

It was an art form in its own right. The Miller policy both protected the candidate who had little to do aside from smiling and nodding her endorsement of all he said and it used up time very effectively. Day after day it was the same and day after day the press squad was both angry and bored, all of them - that is - apart from the single lady journalist who gladly accepted all the hand-out material distributed by the young ladies.

The real stramash of the campaign came in the closing days and was about the pre-election television programme planned by the BBC. *Radio Times* had it scheduled for the late evening of the day before polling. More, the TV press material indicated that the programme was to be given national coverage.

But there was a difficulty. When the producer's assistant had telephoned Bill Miller he had insisted that Kate would not appear. The assistant explained that this would make for difficulties. 'Not for us,' said Miller and put down the phone.

The following day the young BBC assistant had a second attempt at persuading Miller to agree to produce Kate for participation in the proposed programme. Yet again she failed.

Things started coming to a head on the penultimate day of the campaign. The producer managed to get hold of Miller on the phone a quarter of an hour before the start of the press conference. He told him he would take him for lunch in the same hotel and it would be 'most injudicious' were he to decline. With a grumph and a humph Miller agreed.

They met in the cocktail bar and over the drinks and the ordering of the food things were moderately cordial. Over the soup course the producer proceeded to convey his message, doing so to the very edges of brutality. Miller thought all shades of decorum had gone.

He explained, to Miller's horror, that if he did not agree to produce his candidate the Corporation would cancel the programme but put up a card akin to the test card advising the viewers that by the provisions of the BBC, in agreement with the parties at national level, the programme needed to involve all the candidates, that the Labour candidate declined to attend and consequently the programme had to be cancelled.

He observed they would stop eating about two o'clock. He would give Bill 24 hours. If he had not received an assurance that Bill would produce his candidate, he the producer would contact the other candidates and tell them the programme was off - and why. Come the specified hour the card with the message would be transmitted. As he spoke, he told Miller, their Art Department was preparing the card. The ball was in Bill's court: all he had to do was to decide one way or the other.

And with that he rose, said good-bye and left to pay the bill.

Bill Miller was fuming. As he saw it, his position was akin to playing chicken in the middle lane of a three-lane highway. At that time Britain had a great many, indeed too many, three-lane highways and young men were too prone to race towards each other in the middle lane which was meant for over-taking and even that was dangerous enough. Hartley Shawcross, a former Labour Minister used to say: 'From three-lane highways may the Good Lord deliver us!'

For the rest of that day there was no speaking to Miller. He slept on it and after breakfast he resolved what he would do: he would let Kate attend but he would tell her not to speak.

The overall result was that they reported to Queen Margaret Drive, the Headquarters of the BBC in Scotland, doing so in good time. Kate was whipped away to the make-up room not that she needed much attention; she and her hairdresser had already done well. When she was escorted into the studio, she, like most novices, was taken aback by the brilliance of the lighting. Nevertheless, she managed to look both serene and yet a shade severe: she reminded one of a new matron in a small to middle-sized hospital.

The chairman started by welcoming the nation-wide audience to Glasgow, stressed the importance of the by-election and proceeded to introduce the five candidates.

'We have in the studio this evening the five candidates and I introduce them in alphabetical order - ... first Mr. Arthur Arnott, Conservative and Unionist.'

'Good evening.'

'Then Mr Ian Borthwick, SNP.'

'Hello.'

'Our third candidate is Doctor Campbell Crawford, Liberal.'

'Good evening.'

'Who is followed by Sandy Galt, the Communist Party candidate.'

'Hello there!'

'And finally Mrs. Kate McDougall who is representing the Labour Party in this election.'

The Chairman half-turned and nodded towards Kate who graciously acknowledged his gesture, smiled both at him and the cameras, but said nothing.

Having introduced his panel, the Chairman went on to indicate, one by one, the topics for discussion to which the four men responded readily and at times rather too readily. The Chairmen had to keep intervening, rebuking them gently for interrupting and for making snide remarks, not about one another but about each other's parties and the leaders of the other parties. In addition to that he had to pull them up for irrelevancies, to which mild discipline some of them did not respond too well.

From time to time he would turn to or glance at Kate and ask her whether she wished to come in at that point but by smile or wave of her hand or by shake of her head she would decline while at the same time by body language convey her gratitude for having been asked.

Towards the end of the allotted period they were discussing the economy and there was recurring mention of the possibility of a recession. When this was at its height the Chairman became aware that Kate was becoming agitated and excited. At that point he stopped a man who was in full flow.

'Sorry to interrupt you,' he exclaimed, 'but I believe that Mrs. McDougall would like to come in. I believe we should let her do so, after all she has not been in as often as all four of you gentlemen.' This was a gracious observation for she had not been in at all. Quick as a flash, Kate, now so wrapped up in discussion and totally oblivious to the glaring lights and Miller's injunction to adhere to a vow of silence, burst into the proceedings.

'Thank you very much, Mr. Chairman,' she said and rushed on. 'Yes, you are so right, I do want in. They are talking about a recession. I just wanted to say that is where they Tories are so awfy crafty, so they are. You see when they get in, they just create a whole lot of wee recessions just tae keep the economy gaun': that's what they dae, so they dae!' And with that she nodded her head in silent endorsement of her own point.

The Chairman stared at her in a mixture of bewilderment and amazement. 'Yes,' he said, but it was a long, slow dragged-out syllable.

Turning to the Conservative candidate he asked: 'Do you want in by way of reply to that fascinating observation?'

The poor Mr. Arnott looked nonplussed, but he did manage to say 'No, thank you' but it was little more than a whisper.

Arnott having declined, the Chairman then swept round the other three men. 'And how about you three gentlemen? Would anyone like to say anything, anything at all?'

As he asked, one man recoiled in obvious horror, one who had adroitly dropped his handkerchief stooped to retrieve it while the third lifted his notes and purported to read them, thereby pretending not to have heard the invitation to participate.

Having had no takers, the Chairman commented that it appeared no-one wanted to reply and went on to say there was insufficient time to embark on a new topic and so it was time to say good-night. He thanked the viewers for being with them and thanked the candidates for a lively and interesting discussion. He rounded it off by saying: 'And so we say 'Good night' from Glasgow. Good night!'

When Kate and Bill Miller arrived back in the Labour Party rooms Kate was given a standing ovation. The rooms were filled mainly by ladies of much her own vintage. Everyone was cheering. Some came up to her and hugged and cuddled her and some actually kissed her though that Home Counties middle-class activity had yet to bite into Glasgow working-class life. Some younger women climbed up onto chairs and tables and started singing. In due course the decibel count diminished and in a period of lull the President of the Co-op Women's Guild stepped forward, waved her hand, said 'Hush!' and then pronounced 'Katie, love, you were just marvellous, so you were. See when you made that point at the end, it was great, just great. Nane o' them knew how tae answer you, so they didnae!'

An elderly man who had played cricket for Kelburn was sitting by the dying fire with both his cough and the last of his tea. Staggering to his feet he too pronounced: 'Bowled them middle wicket, so you did, middle wicket, all four of them. I didnae understand the point you were making but it must have been good. You were just great, just great.' And thereupon the room embarked on another burst of cheering. Thereafter they did what working class ladies always do on such occasions: they proceeded to make fresh pots of tea.

The following day, starting very early, Bill Miller fought a masterly campaign. The canvass had not been complete but it was very nearly complete for the strong Labour-inclined districts. He did not concentrate on bringing out the vote but he did aim at bringing out the Labour vote, doing so by deploying his own variant on the so-called Reading system devised by Ian Mikardo. He used his troops most effectively finding tasks commensurate with the physical ability and the agility of his samurai. Ten minutes before the polling station closed he was seen half dragging folk out of cars and rushing them into vote.

The count was tense and acrimony was in the air, but between two and three in the morning after a recount the Returning Officer was making his declaration of the result.

Mrs Katherine McDougall had won by just over a thousand votes.

When Kate arrived in Westminster she was acclaimed as a heroine by the Parliamentary Labour Party. About four weeks after she took her seat and after assistance from both a helpful Scottish Whip and a compassionate Deputy Speaker she made a short, neat but very effective maiden speech. It was made during a debate on Education. She spoke about the quality of school meals and the importance of such meals to low-income families. She spoke with knowledge born out of experience and she spoke with not a little passion. In the week following her speech she received well over fifty letters and notes of congratulations, nearly half of them from members in other parties. The Commons can be a cruel place but it can also be a gracious place.

She was to speak on four other occasions. In addition she was put on a committee looking at child poverty. Here too it was apparent that when she spoke she did so from a base of knowledge and experience and genuine interest. It also became clear that she had a ready grasp of procedure.

When she had been in the House for some fourteen or fifteen months a General Election was called.

She lost her seat. The Conservatives regained it. To her credit she had realised that her circumstances were markedly different from those which had prevailed at the by-election. This time she was but one of well over six hundred Labour candidates and resources both animate and inanimate were spread more thinly. Then again Miller had to oversee all the constituencies in Scotland. This time her agent was a wee local man who did his best but who was out of his depth. Then again, all too many men in her constituency party gave her little more than perfunctory support and on the nights in the run-up to polling day sloped off to work in other constituencies, ostensibly marginal seats but in truth in support of those each man saw as his political ally.

Nationally there was a swing to Labour but it was not enough to offset the changed local circumstances which confronted Kate. She lost the seat by much the same margin as she had won it. Again the majority was above a thousand.

I felt sorry, very sorry, for Kate McDougall. When she took her Parliamentary seat she had resigned from Glasgow Corporation. She was replaced at George Square, the City Chambers H.Q. of the Local Authority, by a strident, noisy young woman called Sadie Thompson who was not just miles but leagues to the left of Kate, Kate having crept into politics not with philosophical concepts of Socialism but rather in an anxiety to alleviate the lot of those living in dire conditions.

All in all t'would have been better for Kate had the by-election never occurred. Had it not arisen she would have fought her General Election campaign: she would have lost and in the wake of dignified defeat returned to her Corporation benches and the activities which she knew so well. As the years went by she might just have become Lord Provost, doing so as a compromise candidate. Had this come to pass she would have been the first woman Lord Provost in the history of the City. Furthermore, at that time in Scotland before the Wheatley Regionalisation, the Lord Provostship of Glasgow earned a knighthood for the incumbent. By that criteria Kate could have emerged from her spell as Provost as Dame Katherine McDougall.

On three occasions she endeavoured to obtain a nomination which would have given her the chance of returning to George Square but she was unsuccessful. The Party preferred younger more militant people. The song tells us that old soldiers do not die; they just fade away. The same fate awaits all too many politicians. It was a wise man who observed that politics is a hard and cruel game and that almost all political careers end in failure if not tragedy.

As I said, I felt sorry for Kate McDougall. She paid dearly for her Andy Warhol short spell of glory.

But I felt sorrier for Ossie O'Brien. Ossie was the Deputy Principal at the Co-operative College at Stamford Hall near Loughborough. He was good at his job and he enjoyed it. He was popular with both staff and students. He was happy as he was and did not aspire to be Principal either there or elsewhere.

Then a by-election arose in a town in the north: I believe it was Doncaster but I could be mistaken. Wherever it was, it was his home town and some of his friends who were active in Labour circles twisted his arm into seeking the nomination. Foolishly he agreed and not only won the nomination but remarkably won the seat which had been Tory-held for many years.

Like Kate he was cheered to the rafters. He went to London and took his seat. He resigned from the College. Some eight, ten, twelve weeks after his arrival on the London scene they called a General Election. He lost.

As I recall it the mandarins at the Co-operative Union in Manchester found another post for him but life was never the same. The post which he accepted with appropriate gratitude had not the salary or the status or the prestige of his College post. Nor did it provide the considerable job satisfaction which he had enjoyed in his many happy years at Stamford Hall. In short his life was never the same again.

The Kate McDougall saga was a sad affair whereas the Ossie O'Brien situation was a disaster for a decent and pleasant man. As Enoch Powell said: 'All political careers end in tears.'

An Observant Customer

This is not my story. It is the story of my friend of over sixty years, the late Robert Crampsey – historian, head teacher, author of travel books, novelist, broadcaster, sports-commentator. And yet, on reflection, it is not his story either. It was the story of his cousin or rather his mother's cousin, a gentleman called Frank McNaughton who lived in the Liverpool hinterland on the road to Southport and who owned a large shop in the centre of Liverpool. The shop was on a corner and was a stationers, newsagents, confectioners, tobacconists and had a sub-post office. In normal times he had twelve members of staff and in the run-up to Christmas this went up to fifteen or sixteen.

The first dramatic incident in our story happened about two o'clock on an otherwise nondescript day. As usual the shop had been fairly busy in the early morning and, again as usual, very busy from twelve to two. By arrangement some members of staff went for a lunch break before twelve while others went for lunch after two o'clock when the spell of intense activity was over. A very small group of senior staff took a shorter lunch spell as and when they could between twelve and two.

Throughout the busy two-hour spell Frank had been manning the busiest till which was close to the main door. Having dealt with one customer he turned to acknowledge the next purchaser who was a Jewish gentleman who was one of their regulars. He was in the shop on at least three occasions every week. At the beginning of the week and in the middle of it his purchases were confined to cigarettes and occasional boxes of matches. When he called on Fridays, however, he not only bought his cigarettes but took two magazines and at least one large box of chocolates and sometimes two boxes. As Frank was starting to give the gentleman his change the man stood partly aside to let one of the staff members leave for her belated lunch period. He hesitated for a moment or two and then as he accepted his change he nodded in the direction of the departing assistant and thereupon addressed Frank. 'See that one,' he remarked. 'Sack her!'

Frank at first just gaped and then having pulled himself together started to query what he had heard while asking what the man was on about. But the Jewish gentleman would have none of it. He made it abundantly clear that he had given what he regarded as sound advice but that he was not prepared to expand on it. 'It is up to you,' he said. 'I have given you excellent advice. Accept it or reject it. It is your shop and your decision but my advice is succinct. Sack her!' And with that he lifted his purchases, then his hat in silent salute and left.

Over a week went by before Frank could catch hold of the Jewish gentleman. When he did he got short shrift. Trying to be friendly and not reveal his anxiety and his annoyance, Frank greeted him with 'Hello there! When you said the other day that I …' He was stopped in his tracks. The gentleman simply raised his hand to silence him. 'Look here,' he said. 'I have given you good advice and made it abundantly clear that I am not prepared to expand on it. Nor am I going to be harassed or annoyed by you. I like this shop and I like you and I liked your father before you. But I could go elsewhere and that is exactly what I shall do if you do not desist.'

Normally, Frank McNaughton was of a pleasant cheery disposition but the encounters with the customer had knocked him out of his stride. As a result he was tetchy: he was short and peremptory with staff and even at home was out of sorts and not his usual congenial self. His sleep was disturbed and he was not enjoying his food.

Things came to a head one day on the golf course. He was known to be a good golfer: he played off five but on the day in question his game started badly and worsened as he and his friends went round the course. Back at the club house and over a round of drinks his pals quizzed him as to what was amiss and he in a mixture of anxiety and relief blurted out the whole sad and mysterious story. Two of the friends made what they thought were sympathetic and conciliatory observations which, notwithstanding the good intentions, were absolutely useless. The third friend was more positive and helpful. First, he ascertained that Frank had watched the assistant and had not found anything amiss; she was not discourteous with customers and she gave folk the correct change. Furthermore, all purchases were correctly charged and rung up on the register. She appeared blameless. With all this in mind the friend suggested that he contact his accountants and invite them to come into the shop and submit the scene to their scrutiny. The staff should be told that he was being chased by the tax authorities for considerable tax arrears and he was counter-claiming that his expenses were heavier than they had conceded thus far. It would be a costly exercise but if it solved the problem and improved his digestion it would be worth it.

So he did it and it revealed absolutely zilch!

The one good thing to come out of the move was that the senior accountant pointed out that there was a firm of accountants in Manchester who specialised in commercial fraud. It was suggested that he should repeat the exercise with them. It would be even more expensive than his own involvement and that of his colleagues but it was as much as he could suggest.

Frank thought it over at some length and a shade reluctantly decided to go for it.

The staff members were given the same story and the Manchester team arrived. To their credit they looked the part. They all had a no-nonsense air about them.

This time it worked: on the fourth day of their inspection they let Frank know that they had cracked it. They now knew what the lady had been doing. More, they confessed to being impressed: it was quite the cleverest scam they had encountered in the last fifteen years. She had been 'doing' Frank for £30 a week and this at a time when shop assistants were earning about £20 a week.

The lady was called into the office and in the presence of the team was advised to collect her things and to leave immediately. She in turn glowered at the head of the team and at Frank and rose and left.

In one sense it was over... except for the further mystery of how it had come about that the Jewish gentleman had known that something unsavoury was afoot.

The matter of the Sales Assistant having been cleared and cleared satisfactorily, Frank was anxious to speak to his perceptive customer and ascertain how he had known of the malpractice. That said, over a week went by before he succeeded in having a word with the gentleman. When he did succeed he approached him with a smile. 'You will have noticed that she has gone,' he opened, though it was as much a question as it was a declaration. 'Has she?' the customer replied, looking around the shop as he spoke. 'Yes, she is away! She was rumbled. It was not easy but the accountants from Manchester flushed her out. But tell me this. How did you know that something was amiss and that she was the one responsible for it? Do tell me. I would love to know.'

The gentleman looked Frank straight in the eye. 'Tell me this,' he said, 'how much do you know about me?' Frank was slightly embarrassed. 'Well, not very much,' he replied. 'I know you to be a good and regular customer. I know you have been coming in for years. I know you came in when my father was here, but I suspect that is about all I know, although I have always assumed that you are in business and that you work in the vicinity'. He paused and then continued: 'I suppose I took it you are in business on your own account. You have the bearing of a man who is his own boss. Am I right?'

'Yes, you are correct,' he replied. 'I am a tailor with a small business, a very small business but it suits me. I have a small workshop in a large block nearby. But let me tell you what I do. In effect I work four and a half days a week. On Friday I stop just after lunch-time. I am Jewish, of course. You knew that but you were too diffident to say so. Anyway, my family and I are Jewish. We observe the Sabbath fairly strictly, I must say. For my own part, I am not all that religious but my wife is and I like the ritual. So we have the appropriate ceremony on the Friday evening and we observe the Sabbath itself. On your Sabbath I design two coats, coats for ladies. If I have a gift, it is for design and the use of colour. On Monday and Tuesday I make two coats of the first design and on Wednesday and Thursday two of the second design. I have a part-time assistant and on Friday we finish off the belts and the buttons and parcel them for delivery to expensive stores throughout the country. A lot of my stuff goes to Harrods and places like Jenners in Edinburgh. You will see then that my coats were and are exclusives, not just exclusive but expensive. The stores take a handsome profit: the mark-up is steep but what the stores pay me gives me a very acceptable standard of living. We are not wealthy but we are fairly comfortable. Your employee was wearing one of my coats!'

And with that he smiled knowingly, said 'Cheerio', lifted his purchases and left.

Senga

Senga was a gift from God. We knew that because her aunt, a Miss Euphemia Miller, a wages clerkess in the Finance Office of the University, told us that this was the case. Upon being given this intelligence I observed that all children were from God but this did not go down at all well. Effie, as the lady was known, let me know that her sister-in-law had experienced a most difficult and dangerous pregnancy and that the child had been saved as a result of considerable and intense prayer.

As the aunt of the child, Effie was only too aware of how her survival had necessitated Divine intervention. Moreover, while not believing in Guardian Angels, she saw herself as an extra guardian of the girl.

By the time our story starts, Senga was sixteen going on seventeen, had left school in June yet by late September had not succeeded in obtaining gainful employment. One morning while driving into work, Effie heard on the car radio that the Government was introducing a job creation scheme for unemployed school leavers. On arriving in the office she swept into the Personnel Office and 'boned' the Deputy Personnel Officer and told him that the University must participate in the new scheme and that the deserving Senga must be recruited. She was far from clear in which regards Senga was deserving, though she was of course an Act of God and was Effie's niece.

So it was that Senga arrived in my outer office as a new copy typist. She had no shorthand or word processing skills but we were assured she could type though it would be prudent not to enquire about either speed or accuracy.

Within a few weeks of her arrival in our midst Senga had established her position vis-à-vis the rest of us; perhaps that should have been her two positions.

So far as the work was concerned she had shown herself to be a moderately competent copy typist but with rather too many episodes of incompetence which tended to arise from her unworldly approach to life. The young lady was no sophisticate; she was not of this world. Anything unusual tended to throw her. Accordingly, she could not cope with long unusual words, with French idiomatic phrases, with Latin tags, with German and Russian place-names or with American spelling. She could stand up for herself and did not take long to observe that, as she saw it, it was unfair to use such language. 'We don't speak like that at home,' she would protest. We in turn had to point out that it was for her to adjust to our language and phraseology and not for us to retreat from our extensive vocabulary to her rather limited range. To this she pouted and went into a huff.

On the social front she was not slow to adopt a stance of almost total superiority to the rest of us. Here her reasoning was simplicity itself. She was a born-again Christian, she was saved and by her criteria the rest of us were destined for the fires of Hell. This was certainly true of those staff members totally devoid of religious conviction and who were not slow to scoff at all matters appertaining to religion. But Senga's contempt extended to those who with varying degrees of activity and enthusiasm saw themselves identified with a wide range of Christian denominations. To all of this there was one possible exception. Miss Renwick was a Baptist though Senga did not know whether this was subject to any adjectival qualification. On the other hand, she knew that her family members were all Evangelical Baptists and with that in mind she resolved to give the Renwick lady the benefit of the doubt and, even more remarkably, an occasional smile – an activity in which she rarely indulged.

It soon became apparent that Senga did not like being rebuked, but then virtually no-one takes well to being reprimanded. In her case almost all the mild chastisement arose from her lack of professional competence and her unworldly disposition. In the latter area her recurring defence plea was to say: 'How was I supposed to know?' All we could suggest was that most young ladies of her age did know: but we knew and she knew that most young ladies lived a worldly life that was miles beyond her ken.

On one occasion I had given her a letter to an Episcopal Bishop starting it by addressing him as 'My Lord'. Senga said she would not type it: he was not the Lord. I agreed and said that although he was not the Lord he was a Lord as were folk in the House of Lords to whom I wrote from time to time. In the case of a close personal friend I could start 'Dear Ted' or 'Dear Charlie'. But when I did not know the peer very well, protocol would have me address him as 'My Lord'. She was not convinced until the senior secretary produced a book on Office Practice.

The first real confrontation occurred during the Easter recess between the second and third terms. I had gone down the hill to attend a meeting of a Senate Committee of which I was Chairman. Before departing I entrusted a modest pile of copy typing for Senga to tackle. The senior secretary was on a short holiday.

When I reached the Court/Senate suite it soon became apparent that I did not have a quorum so I ruled that I would wait fifteen minutes during which time those who were present could help me drink the coffee and engage in University gossip but at the end of the prescribed period we were still inquorate so I declared to that effect, whereupon we went back to our Departments.

When I arrived back in the office Senga was reading an enormous book. It was very clear that it was a very large family Bible.

'What are you reading, Senga?' I asked

'The Bible,' she replied.

'But what about the work I left for you?' I asked.

'It is not important. This is the Lord's work.' She declared spiritedly.

'Indeed it is,' I observed, 'but there is a difficulty and it is this. In your case the Lord has appointed the University as His instrument and the University has appointed me as its instrument and I want the typing done and done today. So there it is – close the book and go back to that pile of typing, if indeed you ever started it.'

Senga had long suspected that I was an idolatrous infidel. This episode confirmed her worst suspicions.

As I recall it, that little scene occurred about Easter time of 1977. The rest of that year was peppered by recurring periods of sullen silence. There is an eighteenth-century tombstone in an Edinburgh graveyard which tells us of a lady of standing who did 'good works but without enthusiasm': eighteenth-century society looked unfavourably on enthusiasm which it regarded as ostentatious and consequently unbecoming. Senga did her work without enthusiasm but to her credit with increasing accuracy.

Perhaps we were unintentionally following the liturgical calendar but our next major stramash took place in the run-up to Christmas. A year earlier, being unco cautious about her sensitivity, I had given Senga an umbrella and a matching scarf. My problem was what to give her for her second Christmas in our midst. Then I had what I thought was a great idea. At the instigation of those of us on the Board of the Independent Broadcasting Authority, Lew Grade at ATV had commissioned and then transmitted Zeffirelli's magnificent film 'Jesus of Nazareth'. This had been produced in book form with a script by the popular Professor William Barclay. It was a shade expensive but I saw it as the perfect solution to my dilemma. So it was that I went into the Church of Scotland book-shop in Buchanan Street, bought a copy and asked the assistant to gift-wrap it.

The following day I called the support staff into my room, gave the senior secretary her usual and rather unimaginative bottle of gin and large box of chocolates and gave Senga the book from the Kirk's book-shop. As the ladies left and I returned to my desk, I was, I fear, feeling rather pleased with myself.

As the day progressed I became increasingly conscious of an extremely cool atmosphere in the outer office. I called in the senior lady and asked what was amiss. 'It's that book you gave her,' she replied. 'She is very doubtful about it.'

'Send her in,' I declared and when Senga appeared I invited her to take a seat. This she did with obvious reluctance whereupon I went on to explain that we all acknowledged and admired her deep Christian faith; that we would not want to do anything that offended her or caused her distress; that the television transmission had been approved by, indeed acclaimed by, the Religious Advisory Council of the Authority; and that Willie Barclay was one of the most respected churchmen in Scotland. Notwithstanding that considerable case for the book I had a suggestion to make. I would advise her to take it to her pastor of whom she thought so highly and let him see it. I was confident that he would not disapprove of it. 'Will you do that?' I asked. By way of reply, Senga had her own question. 'Can I go now?' she queried and without waiting for an answer rose and left.

In early January after I had given a long spell of dictation to the senior secretary we had a brief discussion on the flow of the work. Then she changed the subject. 'Did you hear what happened to that book you gave to Senga?' she asked and then, without waiting for a reply, went on: 'She cut out the photographs for her Sunday School class and she burned the text.'

Mid-way through the ensuing March, Senga intimated she would be leaving us. It transpired she had applied to an Evangelical Missionary Society to be trained for missionary work, probably in Africa though it was possible that she would be sent to Latin America or the Far East. She had been accepted.

Eddie Blacklaw, one of our older and more cynical members of staff, was amazed. He observed that Senga was Agnes in reverse spelling '...and that is not the only way that she is backward' he averred, and went on to suggest that the organisation must be very short of applicants if it was accepting her.

At that time I was the Chairman of our Inter-denominational Chaplaincy Centre. One day while Senga was 'serving her notice' the Catholic Chaplain called to see me about our quest for better accommodation for his Methodist and Baptist part-time colleagues. He was a Dominican, a charming and gracious man with four degrees, two of them doctorates. From time to time he would disappear to Oxford where he would lecture on Philosophy.

As he was leaving he stopped to speak to Senga, opening by saying he had heard of her brave resolve to embark on missionary work. Throughout this encounter Senga stood as though frozen.

Later I met him at the lift. 'That is a very interesting and fortunate young woman,' he observed. I expressed my surprise. 'Oh, no,' he came back at me. 'She is very fortunate, she has accepted Jesus of Nazareth as her Lord and Saviour. She strives to adhere to the Commandments. She knows her Bible and she knows and acknowledges that she has to conduct her life in a way that ensures she will see God and live with Him for eternity. In comparison to the vast majority of the University community she is extremely fortunate.' He paused, then he went on: 'Her road is not your road, nor is it my road.' He smiled: 'In doctrinal terms it is not a Roman road, but it is a straight Roman road that will take her to her heart's desire.'

And at that point the lift came and took him away leaving me alone and reflecting.

Senga never became a missionary. She met Harry, married him and had a family.

A Wonderful Prospect

As I recall it his name was Currie, but it could have been Cowie or even Cowan. Then again, it might have been either Craig or Carson, both highly revered names, at least in one section of the community, the community being Northern Ireland.

Yet in one sense his name is not and was not important. What mattered was that he was important. He was a Minister of the Presbyterian Church of Ireland and was well to the fore in that Church in its stronghold of Northern Ireland. He was the Minister in one of the largest and most important Presbyterian churches in that Province. With one exception all the Presbyterians in the Cabinet at Stormont were members of his congregation, while the exception was his brother-in-law. In addition, his fame was not confined to that section of society. He was a man of exceptional learning and this was readily acknowledged throughout the Christian Churches. He wrote extensively and appeared frequently in the world of Religious Broadcasting. He lectured regularly at Conferences both at home and abroad. He was extremely hard-working and this was recognised by his many friends, not least those who worried about his health.

One Sunday evening as midnight chimed and Monday crept in, things came to a head. In the wake of the twelve striking he had gone to his study intending to work until near two, but about quarter past twelve his son and daughter came in to speak to him, indeed to take him to task. In blunt and frank language they told him their mother was 'fair worried sick' by all the work he was doing, that they shared her anxiety and that he was committing sin in that he was flirting with suicide. They did not wait for a counter-argument. On the contrary, having made their point, they rose and left.

This wonderful man did not sleep much that night and the next morning had a very serious talk with his wife. After breakfast he left as he did every Monday morning for the National Offices of his Church, the Belfast equivalent of the famous 121 George Street in Edinburgh, where he was Convener of a Committee dealing with special vacancies.

He and his colleagues started with a prayer. He then immediately told his friends that they could remove one item from the agenda. 'About that twin-charge in the Republic, the one for which we could not find any applicants... I have found an applicant for you!' His colleagues were delighted, but one man was more cautious.

'Is he any good?' he asked.

'I believe he will do,' was the careful reply.

'Do we know him? Who is it?' they asked.

'Me!' he answered and in doing so provoked consternation.

So it was that in the fullness of time the pantechnicon drew up at the door of the manse and their bits and pieces were packed and, when loaded, it and their family car drove off in convoy.

Their new home in the Republic was a fairly large bungalow by the side of the main road between the two small towns which had the churches to which he would henceforth be Minister. It was commodious and quite well appointed, but it was rather isolated. There were no other houses near them. Their goods having been unloaded, they made tea for themselves and the porters, whereupon the men and their van departed and silence reigned. It was very, very quiet. Their daughter telephoned but no-one else contacted them. The silence continued and after a rather quiet supper his wife went to bed and cried herself to sleep.

The Minister and his wife each had a disturbed night but when he awoke to daylight he found that she was in a deep sleep so he let her sleep late. About nine o'clock he made a light breakfast and took a breakfast tray to her.

The kitchen was to the front of the house, thereby enabling the householders to see what was happening by way of passing trade. As ten was striking and he was washing the breakfast dishes he was astounded to see an Army Staff Car with the tricolour of the Republic on its bonnet draw up by the path to their front-door. As soon as it had halted the driver, a sergeant, jumped out and opened the back door holding the door with one hand and saluting with the other. From the rear of the car there emerged a full Colonel, a smart man in full dress uniform, a man of about forty years of age.

The officer strode up to the door and rang the electric bell. The new Minister had taken off the apron he had been wearing and had slipped on a jacket. When he opened the door the Colonel saluted and addressed the door opener.

'Good morning, Sir,' he said. 'Have I the privilege of addressing the Reverend Doctor William Currie?' and after receiving confirmation thereof, continued: 'I would explain, Sir, that I am the Personal Emissary of the President of the Republic. May I come in, Sir? I have for you a personal letter from the President. May I come in and give it to you?'

Having been invited into the main public room the officer produced the letter which was hand-written on high-quality note-paper. In the letter the President observed that he had been very pleased to learn that such a distinguished churchman was coming to live in the Republic; that he hoped the new arrival and his wife would be happy in his new appointment; and that if he had any problems on which he thought the President could be helpful he should not hesitate in letting him know.

The officer asked whether there was a reply and the Minister observed that he would write to the President at which point the officer asked to be excused, put on his cap, saluted again and left. Somewhat dazed for a while, the Minister pulled himself together and reported to his wife who first reacted with incredulity and read and re-read the letter.

At eleven o'clock as he was starting to make coffee, a not very grand car pulled up and two men wearing white 'dog collars' came out and walked up the path. When he opened the door to them the smaller and older of the two addressed him.

'We take it you are Bill Currie, the new Presbyterian Minister for the two towns. I am Cuthbert Pumphrey, the vicar of St. Michael and All the Angels in Castlebrae, the bigger of your two towns, and this is Sean, Sean Sweeney. He is a Donegal man and is Parish Priest of Our Holy Redeemer's church, again in Castlebrae. Our two churches, and yours too for that matter, are all in the one street. By the way, is it all right if we come in?'

Once inside and helping to drink the coffee Cuthbert went on to explain that they and the new man's predecessor had played golf every Tuesday and had gone fishing every Thursday. They hoped that he would continue with that arrangement. 'Do what you can to confine weddings and funerals to the other days of the week' was his final advice and he handed over two cards with their telephone numbers.

At twelve noon the Chairman of the District Council and the Chief Executive arrived.

No-one called over the lunch period but at two o'clock it was the turn of some of his elders and the Session Clerk while at three o'clock it was the turn of the President of the local Debating Society who was accompanied by the Chairman of the local Historic Society. At four o'clock they were visited by representatives of the Drama Society, the Castlebrae Choir, the Flower-arranging Society, the Bridge Club and the Camera Club. The afternoon was rounded off by ladies from the two Women's Guilds at his new charges.

That night the wife who had cried her way into a first restless night could not get to sleep for laughing and tears of joy.

The first week-end in their new home was eventful and demanding. On the Sunday he took four services, two in the bigger town of Castlebrae – which he found to be a misnomer since it had neither a castle nor a brae – and two in the somewhat smaller town of Thornhill. On the Sunday evening they found they were running low on provisions so it was decided that on the Monday he would drive into Castlebrae for a substantial shopping expedition. On his way into town he speculated on what sort of reception he would receive. The various delegations to the manse had been friendly but now he would be dealing with different elements in the community. He decided he would start by going to the local Co-op store.

He had difficulty in parking the car and had to walk back over a hundred yards to the shop which was bigger than he had expected. On going into the store he found it a bit bewildering. The overhead signs on the location of the goods were not as helpful as he had hoped. As he wandered, a female assistant of about eighteen came up to him.

'Excuse me, Sir,' she said 'but would you be the new Minister for one of the Protestant churches in Miller Street?' and, without waiting for an answer, she raced on: 'Because, if you are, Brendan, Mr. O'Driscoll, the manager wants tae see you. If you just hold on a minute of two I'll go and fetch him for you.'

The girl disappeared but returned shortly after with a harassed-looking man in his late thirties. While he had been waiting our man had been wondering whether this would be when he would be told to take his Northern Unionist trade somewhere else. He was to find his misgivings were totally unfounded. The young man greeted him warmly and suggested they proceeded to the back shop, a corner of which constituted his 'office'. 'Would you have a seat, Sir,' he said: it was more a statement than a question. As he had been speaking he had lifted a cloth and used it to batter the dust off the top of a keg of butter or whatever and had lifted a back copy of the *Irish Independent* and placed it on the top of the keg.

'I was havin' a mug of tae,' he went on. 'Would you care for a drop?' and before a reply could be forthcoming, handed over a large mug of very strong tea. 'The sugar and milk are on the ledge,' and with that lifted a packet of Kit-Kat off another shelf, ripped it open and gave two of the biscuits to his visitor. 'Well, now, it is good of you to give us your custom, so it is and all, but clever men of your station are too busy to come in and meander through shops like this. Your lady wife will have given you a list of what she wants. I suggest that you bring it in and give it to Dymphna or one of the other girls. In fact, put your car round the back of the shop beside me own and give the girl the car keys. We'll gather your messages and box them for you. I'll cross-check the order meself and write in the price of the items and leave it in top of the box. You don't need to pay me on the day, that way your wife can double check that all is in order like. You can pay me at the end of the month when you get your salary. Is it stipend they call it? Anyway, the box will be in the boot of your car: all you have to do is to collect your car keys from the front shop and go down the lane and drive off.'

He paused and added: 'Father Sweeney tells me that intellectual sort of men, men like yourself like, would rather go into bookshops and to the library and that sort of thing. Having to spend time in shops like this is not for the likes of you, so it's not. No way! That would never do at all, at all.'

It was the Minister himself who told me his story when we met at a Conference on Religious Broadcasting. I can still see his clever, thoughtful, twinkling eyes as he smiled and said: 'You know, Tom, we should have made the move years ago but at least it was not too late. My wife and I now have the prospect of many wonderful years in this delightful place.'

The Plus Factor

Their name is McMirren and they constitute a lovely and loving family. They tend to live in and around the Paisley airt which is appropriate as St. Mirren is the patron of Paisley, hence St. Mirren being the local football team. There always seems to be about forty of them although I think that can be misleading as the total is surely bound to vary from one generation to another. They are an attractive bunch of people and their common denominator is unusually high, not with regard to their physical appearance but concerning their attitudes and approach to life. Thus: they tend to be charitable and compassionate. They tend to see the best in others. Invariably, they are regarded as great neighbours and as reliable and dependable colleagues. They make friends easily and, having made them, keep them.

Then again, in an increasingly secular society, they tend to be visibly more religious than the broad sweep of Scottish society. There is here yet another interesting phenomenon. In broad terms half of the McMirrens are Catholic and half Presbyterian and, in keeping with their general disposition, there is no animosity or antipathy and certainly no bitterness. Each side acknowledges the sincerity and commitment of the other with the result that they go not only to one another's weddings and funerals but to Christenings, confirmations and many, many social events in one another's church halls.

It is always good to meet a McMirren.

All that said, our story starts in the very early twenties and concerns a young lady in her early twenties. She and her family lived on the west side of Paisley and she worked in the Ferguslie Mills. One evening she came home exhausted after working a full shift and doing three hours' overtime. She threw her overall behind a couch and herself onto the couch. 'I am fed up, up to the back teeth,' she declared to the family and the world at large. 'I am fed up with that mill and the conditions in which I have to work. One night a week at the pictures and an odd night at the dancing is about all the social life I have. I think I'll go to America!'

Later, while she was having her late tea, her mother poured her a second cup of tea. 'Are you serious about going to America?' the mother asked and went on: 'I wouldn't want to lose you but on the other hand, I could be doing with your bed.'

So it was that the mother contributed towards the cost of the fare; that our heroine sailed to New York and in due course settled in Pittsburg and found work as a clerkess with an energy company. Sometime later she met a small, neat, dapper Italian-American at a concert in their church hall and after a brief courtship, married him.

Almost on the day of their first wedding anniversary she gave birth to a boy. One day, when the boy was fifteen months old, the father, while hurrying back to his office after a generous lunch, took a heart attack and died on the sidewalk.

There was a strong streak of Scots realism in the young mother so she wrote letters to almost all the sub-sets of the family back home in Scotland. She explained that as things stood she had a choice, an unenviable choice but a choice. Thus, she could work but not look after the baby or she could look after the child and they could both starve to death. Such, she argued, was the background to her request: were there folk back home who would agree to take the boy and raise him?

She received a reply from a couple who lived near her family home in Paisley. They reminded her that they had been married for twelve years but were still childless. They had been thinking of adoption but rather than adopt they would be glad to raise the wee boy. And while they were Presbyterian, they readily recognised that she and her late husband were Catholic and so, with the help of the Catholic wing of the family, would bring him up in that faith.

So it was that in the middle twenties a lady from Paisley went to America and returned with a wee boy on whom she would bestow great love and affection for the rest of her days.

The boy's name was Paul. He had been named after his father but not given the Italian version.

The first August of the thirties saw him enrolled at the local Catholic Primary and from there he duly progressed to the Senior Secondary. He did fairly well at school but when he was sixteen he started to feel that he should be contributing to the adopted household so he started applying for diverse jobs both in Paisley and Glasgow. In due course he was recruited as a door-boy by a very up-market restaurant just off Buchanan Street in Glasgow. They gave him a rather fine dark blue uniform with lots of brass buttons, topped off by a small, round pill-box hat akin to that worn in the Boys' Brigade. His duties involved opening and closing the door for guests, helping them deposit their coats and umbrellas in the cloakroom and going out to find taxis for the customers who required them. By this time the war was on and he had to travel home to Paisley by the last tram, doing so in the blackout.

As he approached his eighteenth birthday the management team in the restaurant suggested that he should start training either as a waiter or as a chef and since he did not have a preference he should have a 'shot' at each of them.

One night, not all that much later, when he went home to Paisley and was approaching his home, he sensed that something was different. Normally his Uncle Jim and Aunty Beth as he called them went to bed about eleven o'clock, leaving a sandwich and a glass of milk for him on the kitchen table. On this occasion, however, he sensed that someone was up and waiting for him. The moment he put his key in the door and entered the hall-way he knew he was correct: the light was still on in the kitchen. His Aunt Beth was sitting by the last fire. She was in her dressing gown and had her curlers in place. She had been reading that week's copy of the 'People's Friend'. 'Hello, Paul,' she said. 'There is a letter from America for you,' gesturing towards the mantelpiece.

'From my Mum?' said Paul, though the remark was a half-way house between a comment and a question. His mother wrote every week. Originally she wrote to Jim and Beth and, from the time when Paul could read and write, to him as well. In peace-time they could predict when the letters would arrive but the hazards of war had made delivery more erratic.

'No, not your Mum,' said Beth. 'This one is from your Uncle Sam!' It was, too, inviting him to join the colours.

The following Sunday the three of them sat down and discussed the situation. Paul revealed that his inclination was to comply. He argued that there were three reasons for going, and doing there and then what the American Government wanted him to do. The first was that he had already been of a mind to volunteer. The second was that if he did not go the British authorities would summon him anyway and the third was that the U.S. service personnel were better paid than their British counterparts. His Uncle Jim sympathised with the first of these points and agreed with the third though he questioned the second while Aunt Beth wanted to hold onto him as long as she could, so she made it clear that she wanted him to await the summons to the U.K. forces and added that it might never come as he was an American citizen. For all her passionate eloquence she eventually succumbed to the arguments of the two men, so she cried and nodded, and Uncle Jim found a wee sherry for her and she wiped her tears and went off to make the tea.

Paul reported to the American Consul who arranged for him to report to Prestwick from where he flew to Iceland and from there to the great U.S. of A, of which he had read a great deal but had no memory whatsoever.

On arrival in the States he was enlisted in the Navy and after initial training sent to the great naval base at San Diego. After innumerable tests he was interviewed by a big, one might say enormous, N.C.O. weighing at least eighteen stone but who soon revealed that he knew his job.

'Well, boy,' he started. 'What are you going to do in this here Navy?'

'I could be a waiter in the Officer's Mess,' replied Paul.

'Only blacks are waiters in this Navy,' said the N.C.O.

'Well, I could be a chef or cook,' suggested Paul.

'Only blacks are cooks in this Navy,' came the reply.

'But look you, lad, you did very well at the math!'

I find it quite intriguing that the Americans always say 'Math' whereas we in Britain always use the 's' and say 'Maths'.

The older man went on to say that Paul's score in Mathematics had been most impressive and that they reckoned he should train to be a radar mechanic. Which he did and became an exceptionally good radar mechanic. That was in 1943. By 1945 and the end of the war he was a senior N.C.O. and was in charge of a radar station with forty-plus men working under his command.

The late autumn/early winter of 1946 found him stationed at a Release Centre on Cape Cod. His entry to the Navy had been peppered with tests, medicals and interviews and the run-up to his release proved to be not dissimilar. He fully expected to be given an Honourable Discharge, and he was. One question at issue, however, was the extent to which the 'obiter dicta' would be favourable and come the day the verdict was very favourable. For the one-to-one interview he expected another N.C.O. somewhat senior to himself but he was proved to be mistaken: it was a young lieutenant two or three years older than himself.

The officer was friendly and started by asking what he was going to do. Paul explained that his mother lived in Pittsburg, Penn., while his aunt and uncle who had raised him were residing in Paisley, a town outside Glasgow in Scotland, and that it was his immediate intention to spend some five to six weeks at each of these two residences.

At this point the officer cut him off. 'Yes, yes,' he said, 'that is highly commendable. But what are you going to do with your life? That is what matters.'

At this juncture Paul started making clucking noises about restaurants but was cut off somewhat abruptly by the lieutenant.

'No, no. Now don't be foolish. You, young man, are not going back to any restaurant. For one thing you are entitled to the G.I. Bill of Rights! In other words you are entitled to go to College at the expense of the Government in Washington. But there is more to it than that. You took naturally to the radar course and to the world of electronics. We have been talking about you in the Mess and we reckon that with a push you could get into M.I.T., the great M.I.T. It will not be easy but it is worth a try. This place will give you a very favourable report and discharge. You should know that three of us are prepared to write individually urging them to take you. Mr. Simpson is a Yale man, I was at William and Mary and Captain Docherty was at Notre Dame and they are not all quarter-backs, so there it is! Our collective advice is to give it your best shot and the fall-back is that if they do not take you, then between us we shall find some other good College which will.'

He applied. The officers wrote and M.I.T. took him.

Paul went to M.I.T. and graduated with distinction. His overall performance was so impressive they offered him a scholarship to do his Master's and when he took that degree – again with distinction – they suggested that he stay to do a Doctorate and be a teaching assistant by taking tutorials for undergraduates.

In due course, armed with his three degrees and a clutch of research papers, he took off for the world of industry and business. Later he took an M.B.A from Harvard and in further time converted it to a second Doctorate.

By the time he retired in his early sixties he was Head of Research for one of the leading I.T. firms in the States.

He was very generous and thoughtful to the three adults, to his mother and to the uncle and aunt in Paisley.

It was a wonderful career, based on four years of Mathematics in a Scottish Senior Secondary school.

Gratitude

I have long subscribed to the view that friendship and the intensity of that quality can be demonstrated or illustrated by the three-ring symbol of the Royal Air Force in which I spent nearly five years during and after the war. The smallest and central ring, the one in the middle, represents one's closest and dearest friends. Their number can be a great variable. Some folk have only two or three really close friends while others can run to over thirty and more. The origins and duration of friendship can be very varied. Some seem to start in infancy and prevail throughout life. Thus, the late Robert Crampsey, the teacher and authority on football, cricket and golf, and William Boyd, the accountant who played for Rangers and Hamilton Accies, dated their deep and intense friendship from sitting in adjacent prams in a back-green in Mount Florida in the very early Thirties.

The two outer rings indicate good and acceptable friendship which while not as deep as those of the innermost ring are visibly stronger than mere acquaintanceships.

Almost all friendships, irrespective of their intensity, are based on mutual liking. While some friendships are constant stars, others are either growing and developing or are waning and starting to wither though not infrequently this is not publicly recognised with the result that the outer manifestations of friendship remain.

Donnie Renfrew was not a close personal friend of mine but he was well into the middle of the three rings. Of the two of us he was the younger by a handful of years. At the time our friendship was developing he was a young Catholic priest. Towards the end of his short life he told me that as a young curate he had been regarded as a very strong and impressive preacher. For years he had spent Sunday evenings traversing Scotland giving a 'tour de force' sermon on 'The dignity and sanctity of Pain'. With a rueful and telling smile he added: 'I was to see in retrospect that I did not know what I was talking about.' At an early age, a very early age, he was made a bishop. It was an auxiliary bishopric but he was a bishop.

Not long thereafter, it gradually transpired he had a severe kidney condition. For years he went three days a week to the Western Infirmary in Glasgow for dialysis treatment. Diverse Catholic bodies offered to raise funds to buy him a private dialysis machine but he thanked them and declined. He reckoned it was good for the public at large to see a bishop – a gey woebegone bishop, but a bishop nonetheless – availing himself of what he invariably referred to as 'our wonderful National Health Service.'

Shortly before he died he told me a story concerning one of his great-grandfathers who in the second half of the nineteenth century had been the owner of a very successful ham and egg merchant's business in Glasgow.

This gentleman and his family had lived in a large, commodious house in Pollokshields. All in all, God had been kind to them and they had lived a very happy, tranquil life but this was to be interrupted by a Prince of the Church!

At the risk of some over-simplification it can be said that the Protestant Reformation, having started in the early to middle years of the sixteenth century, was finally consolidated in Britain in the early years of the eighteenth century. One consequence of this was that in Britain the Roman Catholic hierarchy was abolished and the Catholic community, such as it was, fairly effectively suppressed.

The situation changed slowly in the wake of the Catholic Emancipation legislation of the early nineteenth century.

In 1868 an English priest, Charles Peter Eyre, who had been born in York of a minor aristocratic family of European extraction, was appointed the Apostolic Delegate to Scotland. Some ten years later, in 1878, he was elevated to the position of Archbishop of Glasgow.

Not long after this appointment our purveyor of farm produce was presented and introduced to the now Archbishop Eyre at a concert in the City Halls.

At a subsequent meeting it transpired that His Grace of Glasgow saw himself as a 'dab hand' at billiards while our shop-keeper had a large house in Pollokshields in which the top floor consisted of a large well-equipped billiards room. The Archbishop's house was in Pollokshields and, not unnaturally, it was agreed that the prelate should 'drop in' some night to play his favourite game.

Life teaches us that things that start sweetly can turn sour.

Thus it was not long before the ordained took it upon himself to 'drop in' two, three and sometimes four nights a week to knock the balls into the pockets of the billiards table.

Initially this was pleasing to both parties but it soon became evident that this was an imposition which impinged a bit too much on the family. The situation was discussed over a family lunch and eventually it was resolved that the head of the household had to explain to His Grace that whereas they were normally delighted to see him and enjoy his company over the clicking of the billiard balls, there were other activities which demanded the attention of the householder and his wife: he had to see to his accounts, there were trade dinners he was expected to attend, his wife expected to be taken to concerts, dances and the like and on top of all that they had to give dinner parties and be guests at such events hosted by others. He explained as gently as he could that it would be ever so helpful were the Archbishop, when he was of a mind to play, to send a man-servant with this intelligence. In the event of the evening in mind being suitable then play could take place but were it to be unsuitable for whatever reason other dates would be suggested in the hope that one might suit.

It is sad to report that this most reasonable of overtures was not received with the ready understanding that one would have expected, not least by a man in holy orders.

So it was that the 'spontaneous combustion' way of doing gave way to the 'by arrangement' procedure. The shop-keeper was delighted. Viewed from his end of the telescope all was well: his social life had been restored, his accounts were up to date, his wife was smiling again and he still played billiards once or twice a week. However, as two perceptive members of the family observed, His Grace of Glasgow was showing ill grace. He did not take kindly to the new arrangement and would have preferred the maintenance of the 'ancien régime'. Yet despite his displeasure, the new arrangement prevailed for some time

It could have continued, but...

One day a daughter of the house, who was a teacher in a Catholic Primary off the Garscube Road, suddenly found the Archbishop standing in her class-room. 'Your Grace,' she said as she curtsied. 'How nice to see you!' she added as she rose. That was a lie but it was a lie compelled by good manners. 'Good morning,' observed the prelate. 'I happened to be passing,' he said and that was his lie, for he had called on purpose. 'So I thought I would look in and ask you to convey a message to your Papa,' he continued. 'Please be so kind as to tell him that I am of a mind to call this evening with a view to playing billiards and, if perchance, that is not suitable, he could send a man-servant to me and suggest some other dates'.

Slightly flustered, the young lady observed that she was not 'au fait' with her father's arrangements and commitments for the week but that she would gladly convey the message, adding that she was sure that were he to be free, she was confident that her father would be delighted to see His Grace.

After the slightest of pauses, she then suggested that the Archbishop might care to address the boys.

At this he demurred. 'I am not very good with children,' he commented, thereby giving voice to the under-statement of the year.

But, emboldened, the girl tried again.

This time the Archbishop succumbed and turning towards the forty-plus boys asked which boy could tell him about the Blessed and Holy Trinity and in response to the query a dozen or so hands were raised. To his misfortune the Archbishop gesticulated towards a boy with a fine head of red hair and with a helpful, kindly smile. 'Please, Father,' he said, 'Ah don't know awfy much aboot ra Trinity, but dae you know ye hiv shite on yer boots?' Some horse manure had attached itself to the boots of the ordained, who gave voice to an embarrassed shriek and fled .... and was not seen by the family for the better part of a year.

And that was almost the end of our story. I say almost because I believe it should be reported that for a year to eighteen months after that incident, indeed until the boy of the red hair, the smile and the innocent guileless compassion left the school, 'wee week-end parcels' as they came to be called worked their way each Friday from the father's shop near St George's Cross to the school and then by the boy to his parents' house further up the Garscube Road. These were little gestures of gratitude from the family in Pollokshields to the family of the boy, who, like an exorcist, had sent someone or something fleeing.

As well, the manager of the shop exercised good judgement in selecting the gifts from week to week. Thus, it started with a chicken to be followed by two dozen eggs then two pounds of butter followed by the same weight of sausages. Bacon and ham appeared and at one Christmas it was a duck.

In the fullness of time His Grace of Glasgow returned for occasional games of billiards but the man who returned after his Sabbatical was more accommodating and less haughty than the man who had fled from the class-room in the school.

Once upon a time I was severely rebuked by two Presbyterian ministers, one Catholic priest, an Episcopalian Bishop and a Salvationist Major for having said that the Holy Spirit worked in weird and wonderful ways. Wonderful, yes, but in no way weird, never weird.

My friends had the better of it but I like to think that on one occasion in late nineteenth century Glasgow His chosen instrument was a wee boy with red hair and a lovely smile.

Moriarty

'If you ever go across the sea to Ireland ....', take the advice of the wise American who said: 'Go West, young man, go west!'

Ireland is a soup-plate. Its magnificent mountains run round the edge of the country. The middle is substantially a flat bog, interspersed with rivers and loughs and a million and one small fields. I suppose the Central Plain has its own charm and like the rest of the country gives rise to the forty shades of green. Furthermore, the pubs, the music and the craic are as good in the middle as they are on the periphery.

But for beauty, for colour and for breathtaking seascapes and skies one has to make for the hills and the shores beyond them. In particular you should go to the South-west and the West. My wife and I reckon that West Cork and Kerry – not least Killarney and the Ring of Kerry - are absolute musts. The Burren, Connemara, the mountains of Donegal painted again and again by Maurice Wilkes should all be seen and the hills of the Antrim Coast road and the Mournes warrant the same attention.

Yet, for all that, our favourite place and the one we find the most captivating and the most magical is the Dingle Peninsula in County Kerry.

The main thrust of this story is about a very fine couple, Robin and Christine, who went to the Dingle for their honeymoon.

The story, however, has two beginnings. The one involving me occurred on a day in the late sixties in the staff coffee lounge of the Scottish College building of our University. I was sitting on my own – a gey rare phenomenon – when Dr. Bill Aitken came over and being of polite disposition asked whether he could join me. Bill was Reader in Librarianship and was an exceptionally competent and experienced librarian. Before coming into the University he had been County Librarian in the counties of Clackmannan, Perth and Ayr. 'Tom,' he asked, 'what do you know about students' grants?' and with the modesty for which I am renowned I told him I knew everything about students'grants. 'Great,' he observed. 'My daughter is going up to St. Andrews in October. Could you help me complete this form?' and that we did.

Such was my introduction to the life of Christine Aitken who was in time to marry Robin.

That was the late sixties. Move the clock forward by ten years or so and naturally changes had taken place in our lives. In the case of Bill's daughter, Christine, she had gone to St. Andrew's where she graduated with distinction and then gone to Moray House in Edinburgh for her teacher training and then proven herself as a very good and competent teacher doing most of her teaching in Cumbernauld.

More importantly, she had met Robin Davis, fallen in love, got engaged and married him.

For their honeymoon they went to the Dingle Peninsula and stayed in a modest hotel in Dingle town.

In my case I became Head of a small Department in the University and was sitting on three or four Government bodies but so far as this story is concerned a more pertinent matter was that I had become an external examiner in the Republic of Ireland.

The circumstances leading to this appointment were somewhat bizarre.

One day in 1976 I received a telephone call from a Professor of Mathematics at University College, Cork.

Some years earlier the Irish Government had created two new educational establishments which in broad terms were to do in Ireland what the Polytechnics were doing in the U.K. They were to be Institutes of Higher Education but they were not to duplicate the work of the existing Irish Universities. They were to be less theoretical and be more practical. It had worked, but not for long. Now they too wanted to be Universities.

The Government had invited the National University with its four constituent Colleges to assess the new institutions. The University had argued it could not assess them as they, the new lot, had been created to be different from the Universities. Somewhat peeved at this spirited reply, the Government told the University to find people who could and would assess the aspirants.

So it was that my senior lecturer, Mary Ferguson, and I found ourselves with a motley crew of academics from Europe and North America in Cork being briefed for what was to prove to be a fascinating and occasionally controversial exercise.

I digress to report that Mary Ferguson was a remarkably able and brave lady. During the Clydeside Blitz a land-mine had landed on the close adjacent to the Ferguson home in Dumbarton. In time Mary had 56 minor and major operations. She lost an eye and they were taking glass out of her body as late as 1962.

We were assigned to evaluate some of the work being done at Limerick N.I.H.E. and I remember that late one evening before we left Cork we were at a party in the back-room of a pub. I admit to having been in a very pleasant alcoholic haze and suddenly becoming aware of both my condition and my surroundings. I was sitting in an ingle-nook with Tighe Carey who later became Principal at Cork. We were discussing Irish literature and at Tighe's instigation I was endeavouring to assess the merits of two kinds of snuff.

What had brought me to my senses had been a loud roar from the rest of the party and it had been provoked by the fact that the Professor of Classics was kissing Miss Ferguson.

It transpired they had been singing and after innocent Irish songs had started to drift into nationalist and republican anthems. It had been argued that this was discourteous to some of the guests, whereupon Mary had been persuaded to sing. She had sung *Auld Lang Syne* and *Loch Lomond* but done so in impeccable Latin. The Classics man pronounced he had never heard anything better in all his life... and had rounded it off with his kiss!

The next morning a caravan of cars set out for Limerick N.I.H.E. This was a magnificent campus off the Dublin road, a few miles to the east of the city centre. The main building was a wonderfully preserved eighteenth- century mansion which had once belonged to Clive of India. The architects and landscape people had built the teaching and admin. blocks with a consistent stone in much the same way as at the University of Stirling. In this campus, however, they had gone one better and had laid out the buildings so that they weaved around the centuries-old trees.

The initial visit and the deliberations which both preceded and succeeded it led to our being appointed assessors for the review and that in turn resulted in our visiting the site three times a year for an initial run. Our interim report was very much in line with that of the assessors in other disciplines: there was little doubt that it would eventually qualify for University status, but such standing would have been inappropriate at that stage in their development. When, with much celebration, University status was conferred we were invited to stay on as external examiners. In addition the Irish equivalent of the C.N.A.A. in Britain appointed me as an external to three of their Regional Colleges, those in Waterford, Tralee and Athlone.

So it was that my wife and I and Fergie's successor, Mary O'Connor, together with a friend, Joe Foley, would have expeditions which took in all these academic ports of call, to which trips we would add on a few days' holiday which almost always took us to Killarney, the Ring of Kerry and the Dingle Peninsula.

There are two main roads into the Dingle. One runs from Tralee and the north-east corner of the peninsula. It runs across the back of the peninsula in a westerly direction and brings the traveller to Dingle town. The other starts as a long, flat, straight road running along the south side of the hill. It has a well-nigh continuous run of houses with occasional shops, churches and wee garages until it starts to climb to go over the hill to the town. As it starts to climb, the sand-dunes on the left give way to a truly magnificent beach which runs due south for well over a mile. Not infrequently, when we visited it, it would be deserted while enormous rollers came pounding on to the beach, having come all the way from Long Island or Cape Cod. This is the beach they used for the shore scenes in 'Ryan's Daughter' while the temporary village had been built on the dunes behind the beach. That beach on its own makes a trip to the Dingle worthwhile.

Dingle town is not much better than your average Irish town, most of which are rather drab. It was a wise man who said: 'The Celts are not an urban race.' When one finds an attractive Irish town, such as Adare, it has almost always been laid-out by an English factor for an Anglo-Irish peer.

Notwithstanding that reservation, our party found three places in Dingle to be of some fascination. One was a Gents' Outfitters, McKenna's, in which my wife was always struck with a streak of generosity and bought me something for my wardrobe. The second was a very fine bookshop - albeit half the books were in Irish – with a first-class coffee shop in the attic. The third was Moriarty's, which was a small cave-like shop on a bend of the road as it swept through the town. Moriarty's was the epitome of clutter. The window display was a delight for those playing 'I spy with my little eye something beginning with...' It was totally devoid of order. It had, for example, a statue of the Sacred Heart standing on a toilet roll!

Every visit to Dingle involved a visit to Moriarty's which always seemed to be the same. It was a thousand light miles away from Harrods though both were in Retail Distribution.

When on their honeymoon Robin and Christine arrived in Dingle after a long journey by train and bus from Dublin they booked into their hotel, unpacked and had an evening meal. After the meal they went out to discover the town.

That was when they found Moriarty's. The happy couple saw something that our party had missed: we had been oblivious to it!

What they saw, what we had missed, was a sign in block capital letters. It read BICYCLES FOR HIRE.

Over breakfast the next morning, they discussed the hire of bikes. They soon decided they wanted them... but for how long? Discussion eventually resolved the matter. Were the hire to be inexpensive they would take the bikes for ten or twelve days. On the other hand, were the charge to be rather expensive, they would settle for a week.

Within an hour they were stepping out of the sunshine into the darkened world of Moriarty's cave.

Moriarty himself, a veritable leprechaun of a man, stepped forward to greet them and enquire what he could do for them.

Hire bikes? Why, of course! He would be delighted to meet their request. But there was a difficulty, a major difficulty. He had no bikes to let.

Resilience and hope, though, seemed to be part of his nature. 'But look in tomorrow,' he said. 'You never know, you might be lucky then!' So they looked in the next morning and the next and the next again and it was always the same again. Moriarty would explain with an apologetic smile that he had no bikes but that they should try again.

Robin and Christine are Quakers and so are slow to anger and they strive to see the best in others. Yet Robin was inclined to be a bit peeved and even sceptical. He voiced his disquiet to Christine. Could it be that Moriarty had bicycles but did not want to do business with people from Britain? Were they the innocent victims of misplaced Irish nationalism?

It was against that background they resolved to see it out. They would go in every day after breakfast but the situation did not change.

Did not change - that is - until their last full day in Dingle. They went in as usual fully expecting the usual apologetic explanation. But that day was different. Beaming and smiling and almost laughing Moriarty pronounced the unforeseen words. 'Bikes today!' he proclaimed and thereupon escorted them through the back of the shop and out into the yard where there was a large metal shed like a mini aircraft hangar. Undoing the lock, Moriarty threw open the doors, revealing a shed full of bicycles. Standing in the very front of this array was one bike devoid of a cross-bar. Stepping into the shed Moriarty lifted that bike and while handing it over to Christine said: 'For you, my dear. You have been very patient!'

With the ready rapport that couples have, both the young people realised what had happened and realised that the other shared this reading of the situation.... Moriarty could not bring himself to offer a bike with a cross-bar to a young lady who always wore a skirt or a dress. Such was the innocence of 'once-upon-a-time' Ireland, in particular in the far west. The environment of the Tiger economy and the increasing secularism have seen a marked erosion of that quieter, softer, innocent existence.

Ireland is markedly more prosperous now than it was in the world and days of Moriarty and his bicycles but it is good to have known it as it was.

Women In Labour

Mrs. Dobson was always well dressed. She was never 'over' dressed and certainly never 'sair' dressed. She was invariably neat and tidy in her appearance and always with more than a touch of style. Not for her the old coat from the hook behind the door which served for almost every occasion except going to the kirk on Sunday.

Boys of tender years below the teens are notoriously oblivious to what adults are wearing and I was no exception to the rule, but even I was vaguely aware that this lady was out of the ordinary.

I was ten when Mrs. Dobson first entered my life. It was the spring following our first winter in our 'new' Corporation house. It was about half past four of the afternoon and I was at the last stage of my walk back from the school. Mrs. Dobson was a lady from the close next to ours but it was a close which meant very little to me and my pals as it had no boys of an age to be interested in playing football in the street. This rather fine lady stepped in front of me and addressed me by name. 'Tom,' she said, 'I have a job for you to do. I would like you to distribute leaflets for the Labour Party and to do so after tea-time in Bennan Square and Hickman Street. Could you ask your father and mother if that is all right? I think they will say that it is ... and if it is come up to my house when you have finished your tea and I shall let you have leaflets. Will you do that?'

Somewhat embarrassed, I said that I would, at which she nodded and said 'Thank you, Tom,' and she left to go towards her own close. I felt something which I had never before experienced. I felt 'grown up'. That night in early May saw the beginning of my involvement in the affairs of the Party and beyond it in the wider Labour Movement.

As the years rolled by I did not see all that much of the lady. Until we left for the Forces, she would organise me and some of my friends to distribute leaflets, chalk streets and do other minor tasks associated with electioneering.

In the wake of my demobilisation I joined the Party but although we were in the same Constituency Party I did not see all that much of her. Occasionally we would meet in the street and would chat about Party and other matters. From such conversations and from chatting to others, I gleaned that she was as active as ever in the Women's Section and in the Co-operative Guild but that she did not aspire to sit on the Constituency Executive.

In her own way, this lady epitomised all that is - or maybe that should be 'was' - good in the Labour Party. She was innately good and decent, she was considerate and compassionate. She had standards of personal and social dignity and responsibility and steadfastly adhered to them.

She was religious and was a life-long member of the Church of Scotland. I doubt whether she had ever heard about Dale, the nineteenth century Congregationalist who, in and around Birmingham, preached his social gospel, but his standards were her standards as they were for virtually all who constituted the great Nonconformist Tradition which set the tone and early criteria for the Labour Party and Movement and which ran in harness with those from the Catholic Social Guild and Jewish intellectualism.

Mrs Dobson and those like her worked for the Party motivated by a deep-set conscience and a deep-rooted sense of social responsibility. They served the Party extremely well and the tragedy is that there are very few of them left.

The last time I saw her was at a rather important meeting in the centre of town. I was running a large estate car at the time and had given a lift to five ladies from Castlemilk, one of whom was responsible for some embarrassment when she loudly asked: 'Tom, whit dae we dae again? Dae we pit oor hauns up when you pit yours up?'

I spotted Mrs Dobson sitting on her own and slipped in beside her. We talked of yesteryear and she mentioned that she had seen that my mother had died. She was wearing a matching outfit in pale blue and was one of the four ladies in the hall who were wearing hats.

Ten minutes late, the Chair as he chose to be addressed, came on to the stage and started the meeting. Mrs Dobson winced audibly and murmured that she had never thought she would see a Labour Party meeting of some importance chaired by anyone dressed like him. Doubtless the young man regarded himself as being fully at one with fashion. For my money and clearly for Mrs Dobson's money he was a mobile disaster area.

Sadly, I never saw Mrs Dobson again.

For eight years in the sixties we lived in King's Lynn Drive in Kings Park which together with Croftfoot was a large private housing estate which had been built in the inter-war years by the Glasgow firm of Mactaggart and Mickel.

We loved that house and were very happy in it. The back door and the living-room window looked out over our garden, a lane and the tops of the houses in Kings Park Avenue and Menock Road to the trees in the park which had been donated to the city by the builders. That was a southern exposure and on a good day the sun would shine on it from early dawn till well-nigh sunset. On going into that house we were very fortunate. We collected the keys on the Friday of a September Weekend and that day was the first of a protracted Indian Summer which lasted to the end of the first week in November. It was with great reluctance that we left that house, doing so only because we needed extra bedrooms.

It was my mother who became friendly with Mrs Thomson, sometimes referred to as old Mrs Thomson. By that time my mother was in her early seventies and Mrs Thomson was reckoned to be ten to twelve, maybe fifteen, years older.

We lived in the middle of the Drive and Mrs Thomson at the bend where our Drive dropped down to the main artery of Kings Park Avenue where we caught the bus.

As she progressed towards the bus-stop, my mother would on occasion encounter Mrs Thomson pottering in her front garden. To begin with, they merely acknowledged each other but in due course that progressed to comments on the weather and speculation on the weather to come. It soon transpired that Mrs Thomson had, in her day, been a very keen and competent gardener though she was no longer as able as she had been. Exchanges about bulbs and bushes extended to recipes for tablet and chocolate cake and then to such delights as rhubarb and ginger jam and other jams of both obvious and obscure fruits. As the days shortened, it was revealed that both ladies were avid readers. Here it turned out that they had similar tastes. They liked the Glasgow novelists such as Guy McCrone and Quigley with his novels on the whisky trade and read such authors as Howard Spring, Mary Stewart and Charles Morgan. Being book-lovers they knew not to lend books to each other, that borrowing and lending books tended to ruin friendships rather than fortify them.

So it was that the acquaintanceship developed into a mild yet warming friendship. As this occurred, it transpired that each had a son employed by the University of Strathclyde. Mrs Thomson's son, George, was the Registrar whereas I was a mere Senior Lecturer though as a result of my being on both Court and Senate I saw more of the Registrar than did most non-professorial academics.

For my part I held George Thomson in high regard. He was fair and considerate and in no way was condescending - attributes sadly all too frequently lacking in those in high command. Moreover, this favourable view of the Registrar was formed early in the University's existence and long before I came to realise he was related to the Mrs Thomson to whom my mother chatted over the privet hedge.

Remarkably, he seemed to like or at least approve of me. For years I could neither understand nor explain this approach, then I came to realise that he approved of all the academic staff who taught competently, cleared their desks timeously of their administrative duties and conducted their research with acceptable competence. Yet, with that as a bench-mark, he went further in giving, as it were, a further seal of approval to those who went the extra mile and contributed to the corporate life of the institution. During this time I was active in the Staff Association, on the Committee of the Staff Club and was an elected member of Senate as well as sitting on Court, all of which won smiles of approval from this exceptionally fine administrator. When he retired he was succeeded by a man to whom I never warmed.

In 1964 Labour won a General Election and returned to power after thirteen years in the wilderness. One day in the run-up to the election the ladies revealed that not only were they intending to vote Labour but that both had always voted Labour, indeed in the case of Mrs Thomson it went further in that it transpired that for many years she had been a Party member. It appeared she had not been in any way zealous in attending meetings but had worked in all sorts of different ways for the Party.

Towards the end of the sixties we moved to Cathcart to a late nineteenth-century house set over three floors. One unfortunate consequence of this move was that my mother no longer enjoyed her chance encounters with Mrs Thomson though they sent each other a Christmas card.

Many, many years later Labour won all ten constituencies in Glasgow. This brought conversation round to the events in the early Twenties when ten of the then fifteen Glasgow constituencies went to Labour or to the I.L.P., a situation which led to the 'Red Clydeside' tag.

In the wake of that election in the early twenties the ten men who had been elected left on a night train from St. Enoch's station to travel to London to take their seats. A crowd came to see them off and to cheer them on their way. Some reports put the crowd at 200 and others at 2,000. Flasks with tea and coffee and parcels of sandwiches, cake and buns were handed in to fortify the travellers on their journey. In the course of the chat about these events, I learned that the lady responsible for the provisions was our Mrs Thomson, this being yet another manifestation of her dedication to the Labour Movement.

But there is another important aspect to the story of that night.

As the guard waved and blew his whistle and the train started to pull out of the station the crowd spontaneously burst into song.

The question at issue is: what did they sing?

Was it *The Red Flag*? No.

Was it *The International*? Wrong again.

Was it *Jerusalem*? No, not in Glasgow.

Was it *Auld Lang Syne*? No, it was not.

Was it *Ye're no' awa' tae bide awa'*? Still wrong.

Was it *Scots wha hae*? No, not that.

Was it *I belong to Glasgow*? No, it was not that either.

So what was it? What did the crowd sing?

They sang *Now Israel shall see*, the Psalm 77 of the Covenanters.

And here we encounter a dreadful and woefully sad irony.

These events occurred some 85 or so years ago but back then the Nonconformist tradition shone through the entire Labour Movement, not least because the vast majority of the activists believed they had souls.

As I write, the Labour Party is led at national level by a son of the manse and at Scottish level by a daughter of the manse, yet most of the members are totally devoid of religious commitment while the fortunes of the Party plummet.

Now Israel shall see... Not one member in a thousand in this first decade of the twenty-first century would recognise it and its significance.

The Fife Holiday Maker

It was my friend, Jim Craigen, then a senior administrator with the S.T.U.C. and, later in his career, the Labour and Co-operative M.P. for the Maryhill constituency of Glasgow, who was responsible for my being invited to be a lecturer/tutor at their Summer School in St. Andrews. This was a commitment which was to prevail for the following twenty-plus years.

At the time I was delighted to accept. We were not having the best of summers and, God forgive me, I was only too keen to be a refugee from the nappies round the fireplace.

My teaching was to be on the Monday, Tuesday and the Wednesday; I travelled through by bus, though our English friends would say 'coach'. This was well over forty years ago but I can still recall with devastating clarity my delight at the journey on the Sunday afternoon. It was a rather fine summer's day, warm with lots of blue sky and some glorious white clouds. The Scottish countryside was at its best. Travelling through the Hillfoot towns was fascinating and the Fife towns, villages, fields and hills even more compelling. The whole experience was a delight.

On the Monday I was not due to teach until after the morning coffee break, so after breakfast I returned to my room on the ground floor. About quarter-past nine I was standing by the window looking out at the pleasant view when the door was flung open with a resounding bang and a cleaner in a brown overall came striding into the room. She was neither up nor down at my presence but I was rather taken aback at the nature of her entrance; after all I could have been in a state of undress... Worse: I could have been 'à la scud' as they say in Govan.

Gathering myself together as best I could, I felt compelled to address the lady. 'As you can see,' I said, 'I have made up the bed. I hope you do not mind.' The lady beamed: 'Naw, naw,' she replied and raced on: 'In fact, that's a graun help. Ye see, Ah'm no awfy faur furrit wae ma work this moarnin.' And thereupon she lifted the Sunday newspaper from the waste-paper basket, waved her duster as a sort of farewell gesture and left ... with another bang of the door.

The Tuesday morning was a virtual repeat of the Monday. Again I had made the bed. Again she barged in without knocking. Again she observed that she was not awfy faur furrit with her work. Yet again she deigned to remove the paper from the bin, waved the duster and withdrew.

The Wednesday was different. Being due to give one morning lecture and leave after lunch I had stripped the bed and packed my grip. As the corridor clock chimed the quarter, the door was flung open and in she came. When she saw the stripped bed a scowl appeared on her normally cheery face.

I felt compelled to explain the difference in my behaviour. 'I stripped the bed as I am going home today,' I explained. The lady was for none of it! 'Naw, naw,' she said. 'You've no' tae gang hame until ra-morrow. Ah've goat a chitty here.' She rustled in a pocket and extracted a crumbled piece of paper. She looked at it and then looked at me as though I was an errant child. 'Aye,' she pronounced, 'you ur Mr. Cadbury.... like the chocolate folk, ur ye no? Well, it says here you've tae stay till Thursday.' To her credit she exercised considerable authority. Yet I had to correct her so I explained that later in the morning I would have finished my teaching commitment and then be travelling home to a family which expected me, but I finished with an offer of help.

'If you like, I shall help you make up the bed.'

The lady beamed. 'That wid be a graun help,' she observed, adding: 'Ye see, Ah'm no awfy faur furrit wae ma work this moarnin.' So it was she left and returned with fresh sheets and pillow-cases.

To my surprise I found that helping the lady change the bed was an embarrassing experience. As our hands almost touched as they raced along the sheets, it was not sensual but it was strangely uncomfortable - so much so that I felt compelled to say something however fatuous.

'Remarkably good weather we are having,' I said in a remarkably squeaky voice.

'Aye,' she said, 'Ah fair hope it hauds,' and then added: 'Ah'm gaun ma hoalidays oan Setterday.'

'That's nice,' I commented. 'Are you going somewhere interesting?'

'Ah'm gaun hame tae see ma family,' she replied.

I felt my eyebrows rising. Home, I thought, and felt tempted to say 'All the way to Pittenweem!' but I pulled myself back from such a sarcastic gibe. Instead, I looked at her and asked where that was.

'Ye widnae ken much aboot it,' she replied. 'It's a wee place outside Rotterdam. Ah'm Dutch, ye ken!' Dutch! Dutch! It was impossible. I was overwhelmed with incredulity. The lady must be mistaken: she must be teasing me.

'Dutch!' I almost roared. 'You must be kidding me; you must be having me on.'

She stopped working. 'Naw, naw,' she said. 'Ah widnae hae ye oan, no' wae you being sae decent an' helpful, like. Naw, it's true. Ah met an merrit a Scotch sodjer at the end o' the waur, like, an when he goat demobbed in '46 he came tae oor place an broat me ower here an here Ah um!'

For my part, I muttered comprehension but now it was her turn to experience perplexity. She looked at me with a compassionate sympathy.

'Right enough, Ah kin understaun yer being confused. Efter a', they tell me Ah speak like a Fifer!'

For many an ensuing year I taught at Summer Schools in that same Hall of Residence and many was the bottle of whisky I won by betting that other folk could not identify the country of origin of my wee lady from outside Rotterdam.

A Case Of Christian Principles

Gregory Gilhooley was known in his neighbourhood as 'a decent wee man', not that he was all that small. He and his wife and their two children lived in a pleasant house in a rather fine Council Housing Estate in the east end of Glasgow. In the inter-war years Glasgow Corporation, inspired by the Wheatley legislation, built four magnificent estates – Knightswood on the north-west side of town, Mosspark in the south-west and Carntyne and Riddrie in the east and north-east of the city. They were good when they were built and they are still good and they were good when the Gilhooleys were in residence.

Mr. Gilhooley was a middle-ranked executive in one of the Departments of the Corporation. His Department was not as prestigious as the Town Clerk's Office or that of the City Chamberlain, nor was it given the quasi-reverential regard bestowed on the Education Department but it was seen by most as a 'jolly good Department.' Gilhooley was not disliked by his colleagues and the junior staff but then again he was not popular. He tended to be a bit of a loner. Thus he did not drink and consequently did not join those who sloped off to pubs at five o'clock. He did not gamble and so was not involved with the passing-on or the receiving of tips. On top of all this, he neither listened to nor re-told blue, risqué stories.

The youngsters in the Department had two nicknames for him. The less offensive was when they called him 'horse' or 'stallion' which were thought to be appropriate because his initials were G.G. The rather more offensive name came from those who referred to him as 'Mick the Mix'. The somewhat tortuous reasoning behind this came in two parts. The use of 'Mick' was a reference to his Catholicism, 'Micks' being a derisory local term for all Catholics but particularly for those of Irish extraction. 'The Mix' was an allusion to Gregory's Mixture, a popular medicine of the day.

One fine evening in early summer the family went up to Hogganfield Loch to walk round the loch three times. As the children raced ahead the father and mother discussed the future of the two children. They had come to realise that they had two very bright kids on their hands and that the boy, Bernard, was exceptionally clever. The question at issue was what they were going to do about it.

By the time the third loop of the loch had been completed and they were making for the tram-car to take them home, the matter had been resolved. It had been decided that they would send the children to the best Catholic schools in the city – the girl to Notre Dame which was under the auspices of the nuns of that order and Bernard to St. Aloysius College, the Jesuit school in Garnethill in the centre of town. It would not be easy. As well as fees, there would be uniforms and sports equipment to be bought; there would be books to be purchased; and on top of all that there would be fares into and out of town and no doubt summer excursions to God knows where ... but with the Grace of God they would do it. And they did.

To ease the financial burden of the two schools' commitment, Gregory, who was a very good pianist and a passable clarinettist, started playing in a small part-time dance band mainly on Fridays and Saturdays in Church and Scout Halls and those of Tennis and Bowling clubs. The money was very welcome but the smokey atmosphere did nothing for his health. He enjoyed the playing but on occasion was known to voice his disquiet about the venues and in particular about the smoke.

When Bernard arrived at 'the College' it did not take the staff – both ordained and lay – long to realise that they now had in their ranks an exceptionally talented and bright boy. He sailed through the school and when, not long after his seventeenth birthday, he sat the Scottish Higher Leaving Certificate examinations, he was awarded six Highers, all with grade A.

The headmaster invited Gregory and his wife to come and see him. When they met he recommended that Bernard should stay for a sixth year in the Upper School and take his 'A' levels. The parents agreed and come the day the school directed him towards what was seen as the most prestigious 'A' level board in England.

He took four subjects and when the results came out, not only did he have another four A grades but more spectacularly he had won the Gold Medal in Latin and the Silver Medal in Greek. On the occasion of the presentations some weeks later, a Professor of Classics who was a member of the national exam Board was heard remarking that they could not possibly have given two Gold Medals to a Glaswegian who lived in a Council house and who attended a school which was not then a member of the Headmasters' Conference, though it is now! The inference was plain. Had justice prevailed, Bernard would have had two Gold Medals.

When it came to choosing a University the young man elected to go to one of Scotland's four ancient, pre-Reformation Universities. When there, he resolved first to take an Honours M.A and of course did so in the Classics.

As students moved into the final Honours year they were confronted with a challenging 'class' examination in Latin which resulted in their being divided into potential tutorial groups of five. The leading Professor was a very well qualified man called Samuel Isaac Fletcher who was regarded as a man of exceptional Christian righteousness, not least as a well-known lay preacher. There were, however, two other factors of import. Fletcher took the top group of five for their tutorials (and it was said that this was his total teaching for the entire academic year). This was the first factor. The second was that in all the years of this arrangement no known Roman Catholic had ever been in the top five.

So as the exam loomed three questions kept being asked.
They were:
Would Gilhooley be in the top five?
If so, would Fletcher take the top five?
And if so, what would happen?
The answers to these questions were:
Yes! Not only was Gilhooley in the top five, he was top of the five.
Yes, Fletcher took the top group and only the top group.
As to what happened, Fletcher did not speak to Bernard for the entire year. Instead, he would address another student, nod towards Bernard and say to the other student: 'Ask him if he has any thoughts on why Cicero used the pluperfect in that situation.'

And so they progressed.

All that happened long, long ago. Bernard is now Lord Gilhooley and virtually at the top of his profession. Professor Fletcher has gone to enjoy the heavenly reward which he confidently knew awaited him.

A Grandfather's Reward

The last time I saw David Goldsmith was about a year ago: I could do with seeing more of him. On that occasion he was, as he generally always is, in grand form. He was as charming and witty as ever and had, as he always has, a salacious piece of gossip. David will now be in his early to middle seventies and is living in happy, contented and relatively healthy retirement on the south-side of Glasgow.

David's high-level career lasted about forty years running from about the time of his thirtieth birthday until he eventually retired when he was knocking seventy. David had been a journalist who transformed himself into an extremely successful and effective Public Relations and Press Officer. During his long years of such activity he was a kenspeckle character in the city, particularly in the better bars and restaurants. He knew thousands and tens of thousands claimed to know him. As I understood it, he worked for four different organisations over his critical forty years, doing about a decade with each of them. Of the four, two were in the Private Sector and the other two in the Public Sector. As he left, all four were sad to see him go and never again received the same publicity and column-inches.

Despite all that success and the countless stories and anecdotes to which his career gave rise, my story about David Goldsmith is confined to matters before and matters after his forty glorious years.

David left school shortly before his seventeenth birthday, doing so with a healthy and commendable Scottish Higher Leaving Certificate. He wanted to be a journalist so he applied to all three of the evening newspapers sold in Glasgow at that time. For years the newspaper vendors in their afternoon and early evening activity had given voice to the cry of '*Times, News* and *Citizen*' and somewhat miraculously all three survived the war years. One of them took him on but shortly after he turned eighteen he disappeared for two years to exotic places and returned to the town as a supposed sophisticate of twenty and resumed working for his paper.

A few months after his return he attended a Jewish wedding in Giffnock and there he met and was bowled over by a delightful and beautiful Jewish "princess" of seventeen. He dated the girl and on their first night out took her to the Paramount Cinema. As they walked down Renfield Street the gallant David enquired whether the young lady would like a coffee. She said she would, whereupon David realised that he did not know where one could get a coffee at that late hour of the night except - that is - for the tea and coffee van that stood in St. Vincent Place, so foolishly he took her there. The diverse customers who thronged around the van included some "ladies of the night" who were having a last coffee before proceeding to Blythswood Square and its environs.

These ladies engaged in some affable albeit ribald exchange with David, all of which his princess found to be highly amusing, so much so that when she was back home she blurted out the whole story to her father.

The father was not amused. He sent for David and proceeded to rebuke him soundly, telling him he was a disgrace to the Jewish community. He concluded by pronouncing that David must never see the girl again. To his credit David observed that as a journalist it was part of his duties to cover the courts for stories concerning football players, boxers and other supposed celebrities on drunk driving or wife-beating charges. When he was in court, he encountered the ladies of the night when they were pleading guilty and paying their fines. This innocent encounter was his only linkage to the ladies and their professional activities. For his part the father conceded this had a plausibility and so he withdrew his veto on David seeing his daughter. It was in the wake of that event that David made two critical mistakes.

The first was that he related the story to the police officers who frequented the courts and they in turn told the tale to other police officers. By the end of the week the Chief Constable was the only member of the force who did not know the story.

The second mistake was that he took the young lady once more to the Paramount. This time as they walked down Renfield Street, a police car pulled up beside them and three officers, with much mischief in mind, jumped out. One pinned the girl against the wall while the other two grabbed David and bundled him into the back of the car and shouted to their colleague to join them. He in turn mumbled an apology and released the girl.

The whole episode was over in not much more than ten seconds. The car proceeded to St Vincent Street and went along to West Nile Street and up that street to the dull, featureless bit at the rear of the Paramount. There they dumped David on the pavement. As they did so, one of them shouted at David: 'Right, David! Now explain that tae the lassie's faither!' But he was never afforded an opportunity for comment or explanation. And that was the end of that!

It is at this juncture in our story that we must leap forward by more than fifty years. It is a fine late spring evening and David is not out for a quiet stroll, neither is he in an up-market bar sharing a couple of bottles of wine with some friends. Instead, he is sitting with some distaste in a hall in Clarkston where there is to be a Dancing Display. Here I would contend that if Purgatory exists it involves having to sit through a Dancing Display. David is a widower, his wife having died of cancer some four or five years earlier. A daughter had persuaded him to attend the dreaded event and David is hoping he will be so bored that he will fall asleep.

David was taking no interest in the people in the hall; he was not even looking for his daughter when a very well-dressed and impressive lady sitting some five or six seats away smiled over at him and said: 'Good evening, David. Do you not recognise me?' It was the princess of yesteryear, now a widow. When David related the tale to me he confessed that they retreated to the back row of the hall where they conversed throughout the entire performance of prancing which purported to be dancing. And he concluded his narrative by observing with a wry, yet shy, smile '...and we have been inseparable ever since!!' I regarded the story as delightful and still hold it in high regard.

That said, there are some reservations. Thus: they are reported as being inseparable but being the shrewd, astute people they kept each their own house and their own bank account. But for all that, they do see a great deal of each other and frequently go on holiday together.

When one day I related this story to Charlie Niven I ended by saying: 'Ah well, good luck to them and God bless the two of them.'

'Amen to that,' said Charlie and then he added: 'He may well bless them. Come to think of it, He might be related to David and knowing David, He probably is!'

A Pathetic Mourning

It was sad, and initially at least it seemed a simple and straightforward situation. Charlie Mulgrew - or rather Mr. Charles Joseph Mulgrew, Member of the Order of the British Empire, Knight Commander of the Order of St. Gregory the Great (a Papal Knighthood), Fellow of the Royal Society of Edinburgh, Fellow of the Educational Institute of Scotland, Fellow of the Royal Society of Arts, First Class Honours M.A. in Geography and M.Ed both of the University of Glasgow and for fun a B.A. in History of the Open University and a half-written PhD. thesis on the life of John Henry Newman, and former Head-teacher of the biggest and most successful R.C. comprehensive school in the Glasgow conurbation - was dying. He was in his bedroom, the master bedroom with en suite facility, in his substantial, ten-apartment villa in Newlands on the south-side of the city.

When he had been in the hospice by the river in the middle of town, the staff there had looked after him magnificently but knowing he was dying Charlie had intimated that he wanted to return to his home and to die in his own bed. There had been two considerations behind his pronouncement. First, he wanted to be in his own home environment at the time of his death. His family might be around the bedside but even were they not to be in attendance, he would have the familiar sounds and smells reaching him by the staircase. The second reason was that he wanted to make his last and general confession and to receive his last communion and the last rites of the Church in the privacy of his bedroom rather than in the hospice with a curtain round the bed. The hospice authorities assured him more private arrangements could be made but Charlie thanked them and said he would go home. So far as the administering of the sacraments was concerned, he told his family that he wanted them to ask his long-standing friend Canon Gerry O'Driscoll to attend to all three.

The family had decided that rather than having a string of visitors and friends coming over a string of days and giving rise to a lot of work for their mother it would be better to steer folk towards a Sunday when they and possibly their spouses could be there to help. It was further agreed that the Canon should be asked to come over on a quiet day.

But there had been confusion as to the dates. What and why things went wrong and who was responsible were questions that were never resolved. On one and the same day the house was louping with friends, neighbours and relatives all looking for tea, coffee, cakes, biscuits and sandwiches and maybe a stronger drink or two. Moreover, and this was the serious mistake, the Canon was expected that same afternoon.

Charlie Mulgrew and his wife Maureen had six children who had arrived with remarkable symmetry i.e. a boy, a girl and a boy, followed by a boy, a girl and a boy. On the day in question, the day on which it all went wrong, Margaret Mary, the older of the two girls, was rushed off her feet. She was frazzled. So far as she was concerned three things had gone wrong and there was no likelihood of relief.

The first problem was that there were over forty folk in the house. There were over ten in each of the three public rooms. There were four in the kitchen but they were not working, on the contrary they were engaging in what they clearly regarded as witty yet erudite conversation. Others were sitting on the stairs while three men and a woman she did not recognise were in the garden smoking. Her difficulty was that she had been left on her own to cater for this minor invasion. She was having to deal with requests for tea, coffee, sandwiches, biscuits, scones and cakes, soft drinks and wee drams of whisky and other alcoholic drinks. She had to scurry round the rooms collecting crockery and glasses, wash them, dry them and deploy them to serve those who awaited their diverse requests to be fulfilled.

The second difficulty was that viewed from her end of the telescope some of the guests were being rather unreasonable. Mrs Nicholson, their next door neighbour, was insistent that she must have brown sugar with her coffee. Mr. McTeague from the church wanted black coffee but with cold milk, while his wife wanted cream. Mr Sneddon, who had been a teaching colleague of Charlie, put his head round the kitchen door observing: 'I just wanted to remind you I cannot take butter in my sandwiches,' while a man she did not know told her in no uncertain terms that he really must have soda water for his whisky. And so it went on. Worse, no-one seemed to be going home.

The third difficulty was that the plan whereby the family would all rally round and help with the work had never really been feasible and the wee bit that had possibilities of implementation had dissolved. Her young sister, Philomena, who had promised she would be there, had phoned to say that one of her children was poorly and she felt obliged to stay and look after her. Margaret Mary had seen Phil as her one likely help-mate. Her younger brother, known within the family as Father Tim, was in a mission station in a rain forest in Latin America, whilst the three sisters-in-law were individually and collectively useless. The wife of the eldest son was a fashion-plate and a ridiculously high percentage of the annual family income went on her wardrobe. As soon as a garment had spent two years in her possession it was taken to a charity shop. She assumed there would be boutiques in Heaven. The wife of the second son was a Reader in an obscure branch of medicine in the University of Glasgow and she did not try to hide her disdain of the two other Mulgrew wives.

As for the wife of the third son, her favourite resting place was a bed in a Maternity Ward. She loved children and revelled in being pregnant and even more delighted in cradling and breast-feeding a new-born child. No help was forthcoming from that unlikely trio and it was significant that they had distributed themselves over the three public rooms, one in each.

Each of the wives in her own way had let it be known that she expected her husband to stay in attendance upon her lest she required his services. Margaret Mary was very much on her own!

It was after the Canon arrived that everything went so dreadfully wrong, not that he was responsible though he was to be deeply involved. When his car was seen sweeping into the drive Maureen and half-a-dozen others went out to greet him. He was not rude or even discourteous but by a firm yet tense smile and more particularly by body language he resolutely conveyed that this was not the time for tittle-tattle. He, at least, was immensely conscious that he was bearing the Host. As for those who cooed around him, they should have realised this and behaved accordingly. There was most serious work to be undertaken. It could be there would be time for casual pleasantries later in the afternoon but the exercise of three Sacraments held precedence.

As Maureen escorted him up the stairs she was - as usual - inclined to prattle but this was Maureen. Cutting through her commentary the Canon confirmed that Charlie was in the master bedroom where he had visited him when he was ill with severe bronchitis.

When they went into the bedroom and acknowledged Charlie, the Canon swept his eyes around the room and ascertained that all was in order: the room had been prepared for his visit and for what had to be done. Thereupon he took Maureen by the forearm and while thanking her for the thorough preparation ushered her to the door, put her out onto the landing and firmly closed the door.

For the next five to ten minutes the Canon engaged in conversation with Charlie. This was in part to put Charlie at ease but more importantly it was to confirm that Charlie was in command of his faculties. When the Canon had ascertained that Charlie was composed and was fully alert and capable of the Sacraments, he went to the door and out onto the landing and called for a member of the family. Significantly it was Margaret Mary who responded to his summons. She had just delivered a tray with tea, coffee and drinks to a group of four sitting half-way up the staircase.

The Canon explained that he was about to start administering the three Sacraments to her father. He asked her to tell everyone in the house that they were not to be disturbed. When they were finished he would come downstairs and, if time permitted, have some tea, whereupon others could go up and see her Dad. To her credit, Margaret Mary went about her new task most thoroughly. She spoke to the tea-party on the stairs and caught a lady coming out of the first floor bathroom. She went into the three public rooms, in each case taking command of the situation and in a loud clear voice conveyed the priest's message. She spoke to those who were in the kitchen and went out to the smokers in the garden. Notwithstanding her thorough approach, she did not catch her mother who had obliged old Mrs Nicholson by slipping next door to her house to collect the lady's reading spectacles.

It was some five or ten minutes later that disaster struck!

Maureen returned and in her usual proprietorial manner went upstairs and without knocking swept into the bedroom.

'Well now, Canon,' she pronounced and was about to add: 'You will be ready for a really good, strong cup of decent tea and not that watery stuff the nuns give you when you visit that convent of theirs up the road and you will ...'

The priest did not merely interrupt her or speak to her. He roared at her. 'Get out, get out, get out of this room, woman, get out this very minute! How dare you interrupt a man making his peace with his Maker! How dare you come in here prattling about tea! Get out with you! Get out now!'

Maureen did not just leave, she fled doing so in confusion and indignation. As she crossed the landing and started her descent she was angry not at herself for her intrusion but at the fact that she had been spoken to in such a manner and this in her own house. It really was quite intolerable.

But it was when she was about half-way down and negotiating her way round the tea-party who were shuffling to let her pass that Maureen realised something dreadful, absolutely dreadful. To her horror Maureen realised that as she had crossed the room she had heard her husband confess to having committed on frequent occasions when he was a young man sins which she regarded as vile and abominable. He had already confessed them when he had returned to the Church in his early to middle twenties but had felt he should confess them again as death confronted him.

Maureen felt debased and cheated. She was married to a beast. She had given herself to this creature, she had borne his children. She felt dirty and defiled. She wished she were dead. Maureen never smiled again. From that moment on she was the epitome of misery.

So busy was Margaret Mary that it took her an hour to discern that something was seriously amiss.

The first she knew of it was when a moderately helpful member of the mid-staircase party came down to the kitchen with a tray bearing the used cups and glasses and reported that she and the others had heard the Canon shouting at her mother which had been followed by Maureen descending the stairway in some visible distress. She went on to observe that they had been shocked at the Canon's behaviour, not least as he was the guest and it was Maureen's house.

On receiving this intelligence Margaret Mary resolved to find her mother, reassure her and see what she could do to alleviate or retrieve the situation. It took her some time to find her mother who had taken herself off to a spare bedroom. Through her tears Maureen confirmed that the Canon had raised his voice to her, that she had not meant any harm in inadvertently going into the bedroom. She told Margaret Mary that it was not important and would soon be all over and forgotten. The ladies hugged and Margaret Mary returned to the kitchen not at all convinced by her mother's placatory account.

Later Margaret Mary was inclined to think that she was responsible for the unfortunate incident in that she had failed to locate her mother and inform her of the Canon's injunction. Later still she was inclined to exonerate herself, taking the view that her mother, an experienced Catholic matron, could have been expected to know not to intrude on the Sacramental proceedings in the bedroom.

Maureen, of course, had said nothing about over-hearing part of Charlie's confession.

Before the month was out Charlie was dead. Over five hundred relatives and friends attended the Requiem; the small church was swamped and the congregation had spilled over the steps and out onto the pavement. The Mass was concelebrated but it was the Canon who delivered the panegyric in the course of which he quoted John Wesley. Wesley had said: 'Our people die well'. So too had Charles, observed the Canon.

Maureen did not go to Communion; instead she muttered to her daughters about 'not being up to it'. When the Mass was over she walked up the aisle supported by her two daughters. They followed the coffin carried by the three sons and various cousins or uncles.

Some three or four months later Maureen went to confession in St. Mungo's church in Townhead. She told the priest about her anger and resentment. She said she was sorry but the priest had his reservations about both the depth and direction of her sorrow. He reminded her of the injunction to forgiveness in the Lord's Prayer. He pointed out that he had gathered that whatever Charles had done he had not committed any of the four sins described in the simple catechism as those 'crying to Heaven for vengeance.' He asked her to reflect on people who had done dreadful things but who, by the Grace of God, had come to be honoured by the Church. Saint Peter had denied Christ three times before the cock crowed and Saint Thomas à Becket, before martyrdom, had led a life of debauchery in the company of his friend, the King. He sent her away to reflect further and to come back to confession a week or so later.

On a bright, sunny, warm day in June Maureen found herself in the shopping area at the top of Buchanan Street. She was in town to buy birthday presents for two of her grandchildren. She was almost glad to have these puny commitments. They took her mind, however fleetingly, off her well-nigh constant misery.

As she was going into the John Lewis store she ran into her cousin, Barbara Conroy. They were not only related, they had been friends since the time they had been resident students in their Teacher Training College in Dowanside. Barbara thought Maureen looked ghastly - which was understandable as she did look ghastly.

The ladies took themselves off to the nearby Costa Coffee bar. Over the coffee Barbara asked whether Maureen had a wish. 'Yes,' she replied and went on to say that she wished both the Church and the State took a more compassionate stance on suicide.

Barbara was shocked. 'Dear God,' she thought, 'she must have loved him so very much and cannot wait until she is with him in Heaven.'

Barbara could not have been more wrong.

Murdo Ewen MacDonald

It so happened that I knew quite a lot about Murdo Ewen MacDonald for some time before I met him and first shook his hand.

My knowledge of him dates from the early fifties. At that time I was the Statistics Clerk in an Employment Exchange in the East End of Glasgow. The manager was a Miss Isabella Lamb who travelled daily from Edinburgh where she lived with her elderly mother in a terraced house on the main road near Haymarket Station. Every Monday afternoon I had to report to the manager between quarter past and half-past four to her office. I would bring with me each week the appropriate statistical reports due to be signed by the manager before they were entrusted to the postal authorities for delivery to our Scottish Headquarters in Drumsheugh Gardens in Edinburgh, about half a mile from the house in which the manager resided.

Miss Lamb's predecessor had been a gentleman called G.D.T. Wilson who, according to the bulk of the female staff, looked like Gregory Peck. When I reported with my 'returns' to him he had asked a few questions: almost always his queries were predictable and did not 'throw' me or give rise to problems. Miss Lamb was much more inquisitive and frequently her questions revealed that she was very well informed on what was happening in the office and this, in turn, obliged me to be no less well informed.

The number of documents for signature – and consequently giving rise to possible questioning – varied a great deal from week to week. At one extreme there were Mondays when all we had were a few sheets on weekly reports. At the other extreme there were two horrendous Mondays each year. On these two days I found I had to forego my lunch break; I did not even have time for a cup of tea. On these two days we had weekly, monthly, quarterly and six-monthly reports to send to Edinburgh.

On some of the quiet Mondays – some, but by no means all of them – Miss Lamb would engage me in conversation. On such occasions the work always took precedence. But occasionally, when the sheets had been signed and the questions asked and answered to her satisfaction, Miss Lamb would visibly relax a notch or two, go into a different control mode and as often as not open with a question with no connection whatsoever to do with the work of the office or of the Department. She knew that I was 'doing' a part-time course at Glasgow University and not infrequently her opening gambit would be a query about the course or about my progress – or the lack thereof. She seemed to be intrigued by the fact that someone on a part-time course could have the same status within the University as a full-time undergraduate and, for example, be registered as a 'civis' of the University.

As time went by she started talking to me of matters of interest or of concern to her and her mother. So it was I learned that the two ladies were members of St. George's Church at the West End and that they were very pleased with and immensely proud of their minister, a certain Murdo Ewen MacDonald. Quite often she would tell me about his sermon on the Sunday and we would discuss the central theme or issue of the sermon. The more she told me, the more we discussed the thrust of his argument, the more it came over to me that her minister was a man broadly in accord with Dale, the great Congregationalist of Birmingham and his Social Gospel. It seemed to me, albeit not to Miss Lamb, that he was two snorts and a hiccup from the line which would be forthcoming from a Christian Socialist.

It would be a gross exaggeration to say that Miss Lamb was delighted when I was in a position to report that I had met Murdo Ewen MacDonald, but she was visibly pleased and almost excited. She let me know that she wanted to know all about it. How had it happened? Where had it happened? What had I made of him?

I explained that I attended quite a lot of weekend schools and had spent the preceding Saturday and Sunday on the east coast at a school organised by the Workers' Educational Association, which was not at all as left-wing as the name suggested. The weekend school had been on the impact of religion and morals on the National Health Service. When we had booked in at the hotel where the school was to take place, we were informed that the main speaker had gone down with shingles but that Dr. MacDonald would take two sessions on the Saturday and that two other gentlemen would be with us on the Sunday.

I was able to report that he had been most impressive: each address had clearly been well prepared and this notwithstanding the short notice he had been given. Both speeches had been well-argued and he had dealt magnificently with the questions, not least those which had been designed more to trip him than seek elucidation.

In an informal chat before dinner he had been gracious, well-informed and witty. He had in no way been condescending. Best of all, he had agreed to take another school later in the year and I had already booked for it. As the ensuing years rolled by, I was to meet him occasionally. We were never close friends but I was very pleased to be in a position wherein I could say that I knew him and admired him. There were two particular occasions when I had been in his company. They had been moments of import which I was destined never to forget. And these I am about to relate.

In one sense it is regrettable that I do not have full and precise recollection of the first of these two incidents. In another sense it does not matter in that I do recall with reasonable clarity the story he told me and it is that which is important. The bit on which I am uncertain is where we were when he told the tale to me and when it all took place. That said, I am fairly certain it was in a hotel in Edinburgh and I have a half notion that it was in the very early sixties. I think the hotel was the Roxburgh at the far end of George Street, diagonally across from the great 121 George Street of the Kirk, and looking out across Charlotte Square of the money men and nowadays of the money ladies.

His tale was simple but highly significant. At the time it occurred he was a post-graduate student and on his own admission was seen as the 'lad o' pairts' who was destined to go far in the ranks of the national church. He was home in the family house in their village in Harris. One day his mother came in and reported that she had met their former minister, a Mr. McQueen, who some years earlier had taken quasi-retirement by moving to and accepting the charge in the smaller village round the headland. She said he was anxious to see Murdo Ewen and would be grateful if the lad could see his way to walking over the hill one day as he was sure they had lots to talk about. The lad had placated his mother by observing that he would but admitted to me that he had been gey dilatory about doing it. It had taken three reminders from his mother to move him to the day, rather late in the vacation, when he put on his walking boots and set out for the next village and its manse.

On the day of the visit, the lad had cleared the breakfast table and washed and dried the dishes and stacked them away. He was not the most domesticated of men but then few are. True, he did this most mornings when he was home but it seemed even more appropriate that morning: after all, his mother would be deprived of his company for a lot of the day. Neither foresaw how long it would be.

As he made his farewell and set out at a moderately brisk but sensible pace, he reckoned he would be with Mr. McQueen by quarter or twenty minutes after eleven o'clock, but as he approached the door of the manse he heard the half hour strike. The old man greeted him warmly and as it was a fine warm day they sat initially on the bench that faced the sun. The conversation flowed fast and furiously. Sometimes it was learned and profound while at others it was if not quite trivial then certainly of lesser import, yet whatever the level it was always interesting and stimulating.

When he had arrived Murdo had hoped to be offered a cup of coffee but no such offer was forthcoming. From twelve to two there was wit and wisdom but no suggestion of food. After three had struck the young man had asked for a drink of water and that was exactly what was provided. So it was the day progressed. When five o'clock had gone the lad made overtures towards leaving but his first four attempts were ignored politely by his host.

It was that time of year between late summer and early autumn and the dark was coming earlier every evening. When there was just enough time for an agile youth to go over the hill before it was really dark, the minister acknowledged that their day was over. 'But hold you there, Murdo,' he said and then went on: 'You will be having something to eat!'

And with that declaration behind him he led the way into the kitchen. There he opened a cupboard and took out a battered, dented tin box commemorating the Coronation of George V. From the tin he extracted three oatcakes and then taking a dish of rancid butter from a grilled space in the wall he dipped two fingers badly stained with nicotine into the butter and proceeded to spread it on the oatcakes which he then put on a plate. 'There you are, lad,' he said, 'you can get that into you to fortify you for your journey' and with that he handed over the plate. He stood watching as Murdo ate all three oatcakes, thanked him for a most interesting day and took his leave.

Sitting in the hotel – I think - in Edinburgh Murdo smiled at me and said thoughtfully and wisely: 'I knew it was an exercise in humility. What he was telling me in a quite indirect way was that no doubt I would have a fine career and probably achieve much which many of the ordained never attained but at the end of the day I was no better than the others. I was and am dust. The rest is what God allows me to be – for a while!'

So far as the second of these two incidents is concerned, I am much clearer in my recollections. It occurred in the middle sixties not long after the emergence of the University of Strathclyde. It was at a seminar, held at Turnbull Hall, the well-appointed Catholic Chaplaincy of the University of Glasgow named after Bishop Turnbull of Glasgow who in 1451 obtained from Rome the Papal Bull creating a University in the city. The original location of the University was about two hundred yards north of Glasgow Cross on the road up to the Cathedral. It stayed there for about 400 years until it was transplanted to its existing site on Gilmorehill.

The seminar was a good, successful event. We spent the day examining the problems being encountered by Christian Chaplaincies in the Scottish Universities.

The final session was taken by Murdo Ewen. He gave a quite brilliant summary of the day's findings and then went on to some 'obiter dicta' of his own in which his most startling and dramatic pronouncement was his own belief and prediction that by the year 2020 the Christian community in these islands would be a beleaguered minority of some ten to fifteen per cent of the population and no longer capable of maintaining the luxury of their doctrinal differences.

I write as the first decade of the new century comes near to its close and the nearer we race towards 2020 the more it seems possible to me that Murdo Ewen could be found to have been right.

One last point about this wonderful, delightful man. When he was at University he was friendly and shared digs with another Divinity student, a man called John Ebenezer Brown, who in later life was to be the father of a man who became a British Prime Minister. Talent befriends talent.

The Fundamental Objective

This is not just a short story, it is a very short story yet it concerns the most important relationship in the whole world.

There are only two characters although their exchange is about a third who never appears.

The first of our two characters is a lady who was one of four daughters in a minor aristocratic family and who had married into a middle-rank aristocratic family. Both families were recusants, that is to say they had clung to their Catholicism like shell-fish to the rocks through the very difficult years of the sixteenth, seventeenth and eighteenth centuries. This formidable and somewhat demanding lady had called, without an appointment, at Ampleforth, one of the leading Catholic public schools, to see the Headmaster who was the late Basil Hume, who was in time to become the Cardinal Archbishop of Westminster and who in the view of many is destined, in due course, to be canonised and become a saint.

The lady explained that her mission was simplicity itself: she wanted the Headmaster to accept her son Nicholas. It was true that he had a colourful history of having been invited to withdraw from a plurality of other schools but much of this had been due to unfortunate misunderstandings and/or to the young man's spirited approach to life. To all of this the Headmaster was inclined to be unsympathetic but to each of his protestations the lady's response was to embark on yet another repetition of her case.

In due course the Headmaster weakened. Truth to tell, he had wearied of the situation. He sighed deeply. 'Very well, Madam,' he said. 'Send the boy up in September. I shall take him then!'

Madam was delighted and said so again and again. In due course she collected her small bag, her large bag, her umbrella and her gloves. She thanked him again in even more effusive terms. She rose and made for the door. Normally, when a visitor, particularly a lady visitor, intimated by spoken or body language that the business was completed, Father Basil would have risen from his chair to escort his guest to the door of the room. He would have opened the door for the visitor and ascertained that the visitor knew how to find the main door. He would have shaken hands and wished his guest 'God speed' and a safe journey.

This time he did not do so and this left him ill-at-ease with himself. Later, still smarting from his minor discourtesy, he examined his conscience. Why had he not risen and escorted the lady to the door? He found that the explanation came in three parts. Firstly, he was not himself: he felt a cold was imminent. Secondly, he was peeved at himself for having given in so readily to the lady's overtures. He was already sure he had given voice to the wrong answer. As for the third factor, his leg was playing up and he did not want to walk on it unnecessarily.

So the lady had been left to see herself to the door. As she reached it and put her hand on the door-knob she looked back. 'By the way, Headmaster, can I just ask? For what do you prepare your boys?'

Basil looked up from his desk. 'Death,' he said. 'Death and Judgement'.

The Agnes Stewart Story

This is not really my story: it is Agnes Stewart's story. It is a football story which I regard as one of the finest football stories I have ever heard and this despite the fact it has nothing to do with the playing of the game – nothing to do with goals, injuries, penalties and incompetent referees.

Mrs Stewart is a former tax inspector who for some years has been a member of an N.H.S. Trust. I met her when we were both involved in dealing with complaints against the Health Service. One day I had gone to her house in Cathcart to discuss a particularly 'tricky' case which was proving difficult to resolve. When we had completed our business Agnes generously produced piping hot coffee and delicious home-made scones.

As I munched my way through a third scone, Agnes asked whether I knew John McCabe. 'John McCabe – one time headmaster of the primary department at St. Aloysius College in town?' I replied. 'Yes, I know him. Why do you ask?'

Agnes went on to say that her late husband, George, John McCabe and another gentleman had been friends and avid Celtic supporters. They went to virtually all the home games and nearly all the away games. On one famous Saturday they were due to go to Dunfermline where there was to be a Scottish Cup game. As usual they met at a pub just off Argyle Street in the middle of town. From Agnes's account I took it to be the Mitre Bar, sadly now closed.

Having met, the trio had a round of drinks and then a second round and in due course a third round. All this, of course, pre-dated the now-current provisions on drink-driving.

As they rose to make towards the car, John asked whether they could go through the Milton on the North side of the city. 'Why would we do that?' enquired the car owner. 'Because it is my mother-in-law's house,' explained John and went on. 'I said I would look in for a while.'

'For goodness sake, John, could you not have mentioned this earlier? We did not need the third drink. Come to think of it, we did not need the second one either. As it is, we shall be pushed to make it for the kick-off.'

When they arrived at the appropriate close, John hastened from the car and proceeded to run up the staircase. The other two sat and engaged in meandering conversation about former games and heroic players of yesteryear. After ten to fifteen minutes had slipped by, one of the two turned to the other. 'This is ridiculous,' he said. 'Toot the horn.' So the driver played the horn vigorously – but to no avail. After a further ten minutes the impatient one blew his top. 'As I said, this is really ridiculous. Now we shall be lucky to be there by half-time. Toot that horn again and keep tooting loudly till he comes.'

This time the recourse to the horn produced a result - a dramatic result. John came bouncing down the stairs. He was being pursued by

Frances, his wife, who was trying to hit him with a dish towel. This was not exactly a weapon of mass destruction though her fury suggested she wished it was. As she ran she was shouting derogatory remarks.

'You are dreadful,' she proclaimed. 'You are the worst husband in Scotland. I wish I had never married you. You are terrible ....' But it was all to no avail.

John called to his friends to open the door of the car. When he reached it he jumped in and called on the driver to move it – which he did with great alacrity.

As the car screamed round the first two corners while en route to the main road, the driver asked what that had been all about.

'Well,' muttered the contrite John. 'My father-in law died last night. Frances and her mother took the view that having regard to the circumstances I should have been prepared to spend more than twenty minutes with him and them.'

'They were right,' said the driver – and they drove on in silence.

I had found the story mind-blowing. I thanked Agnes for telling it and went on to report that by a remarkable coincidence I was due to see John for lunch the following day in the Glasgow Art Club.

Within 24 hours I found myself sitting opposite John McCabe at a table for two by the window of the Art Club in Bath Street. When we had enjoyed our meal and the coffee had been served, I looked over at him.

'John,' I said. 'I want to tell you a story. More, I shall be grateful if you do not interrupt, do not intervene. I would have you hear me out. When I finish I shall ask you one question and, in light of the answer, might go on to ask a second question. Is that acceptable?'

John intimated that it was.

So I told him the story as I have told it here – and many a time between the two events. As I unfolded the tale John sat quiet and silent. His face was devoid of animation. He sat there with a face akin to those on Easter Island. When I finished I caught his eye. 'Now, John, is that story correct in all regards or is there an error or two?' I asked.

John enlivened and smiled. 'There is one error, one mistake,' he said.

I smiled to myself. I believed he would confirm what I had long suspected, namely that his father-in-law had not been dead. He had probably been ill with bronchitis or a very severe winter cold.

'Right, John,' I exclaimed. 'What was wrong?'

'It was not Dunfermline,' said John. 'It was Raith Rovers – it was Kirkcaldy!'

The Day I Nearly Killed the Principal

The Royal Charter creating the University of Strathclyde came into force in late May of 1964.

It was the first Scottish University since the Reformation, the other four – Aberdeen, St. Andrews, Edinburgh and Glasgow – having all come into being in the pre-Reformation period.

Earlier in the same month of May two degree-granting Colleges had merged so that the prize of University status could be conferred on the having-been-combined unit. The bigger and better known of the two was the great Royal College of Science and Technology, known affectionately throughout the conurbanation and beyond as 'the Tech'. It went back to the seventeen-hundreds and its distinguished alumni include Doctor Livingstone of missionary fame.

The other and smaller College was the Scottish College of Commerce which produced almost all the teachers of Business Studies in the secondary schools in Scotland. It had also proven to be very successful in entering candidates for degrees from the University of London.

There are various versions as to how this merger came about.

My own view was that it was substantially the work of three men. They were Dr Samuel Crowe Curran F.R.S., the last Principal of the Royal College and the first Principal of the new University, and Professor Donald Pack, a distinguished mathematician and later Vice-Principal of the University. As the fifties rolled over to the sixties, Donald Pack had written to the Principal setting out the case for the College aspiring to University Status. It was a very well-written and most impressive paper.

The third of the three was a Senior Lecturer in the Maths department called John Eaton. John Eaton, however, went further in his vision in that he wanted the new University, as and when it was achieved, to be markedly more democratic and participatory than the four ancient institutions. In the older Universities power was exercised by and confined to the Professoriate. Eaton wanted all the teaching staff to have an involvement by having an element of non-Professorial staff elected by their colleagues to sit on both the Senate and the Court. And so it came to pass.

The liberal, progressive provisions for the implementation of our 'democratic' charter proved to be very acceptable – if not in the short run, at least in the fullness of time. The arrangement was that, so far as the Senate was concerned, there would be one 'elected' member – elected from and by the non-professorial academic staff – for every three ex officio members and they in turn consisted of all the professors, certain office-holders, for example the Librarian, and the non-professorial folk who were in charge of small departments. Initially that last group consisted of the director of the hotel school and Bill Tyler who headed the department of librarianship (and who later became a professor and Vice-Principal).

In the summer of 1964 the total ex officio content was 24 which meant that eight staff members were to be elected.

As I recall it, the first meeting of the Senate was to be held in September which meant the election was to be in late August. The election was to be held on one day and was to be conducted in the Assembly Hall of the Royal College Building in George Street. Voters had to attend in person, there being no provision for postal voting. Voters did not have to avail themselves of all eight votes.

While all this was happening I was a Senior Lecturer in the Scottish College and was secretary of its Staff Association.

One brilliant day in the middle of Glasgow Fair Fortnight I was working in an otherwise empty lecture room in the Scottish College Pitt Street Building. I was in casual clothing and sorting out my lecture notes and reviewing the hand-out material which I distributed to my students.

In the early afternoon two gentlemen called to see me. They were Bill McHutcheson who taught in the Department of Thermal Dynamics and Walter Martin, a mathematician. They explained that they represented the Executive Committee of the Royal College branch of the Association of University Teachers, which had admitted them and their colleagues to that body.

They reported they had both a problem and a proposed solution. The problem was that they had eight members on their Executive Committee and since it would be invidious to have to choose likely candidates for the Senate Election, they wanted, indeed they proposed to run all eight as a preferred list thereby confidently expecting to have all eight elected.

We – my colleagues and I in the smaller College – constituted the problem. What they proposed was that we would 'stand-down' and not contest the forthcoming election. More, we should discourage our members from competing.

As a sort of reward, or quid pro quo for our cooperation, they would refrain from contesting the further election which would be virtually certain to take place in 1965 following the expected flow of further professorial appointments. I readily admit that my response was cautious.

I said I would have to consult my committee. Our President Alex Smith was on holiday in Kilchattan Bay on Bute but would be back with us in early August. In the meantime, could I ask some questions? I observed that I took it that all eight did not receive the same vote. Presumably John Eaton had been first: could not the bottom two or three be dropped? They were appalled at this suggestion.

I pointed out that the Royal College had some 320/330 members or non-professorial academics while we in the Scottish College had about 110. This suggested to me that a joint preferred list of six Royal College members and two Scottish College folk would be fair. Had they considered such a situation, and if so with what result? The two visitors reported it had been considered but had been rejected because, of course, it involved the selection of six from eight – which invidious arrangement was totally unacceptable.

We concluded our business by my thanking them for their visit and their candour. Clearly I could not commit my committee. I would strive to obtain our reply and convey it to them at the earliest possible date. Thereupon they left.

In the run-up to the election the Royal College A.U.T. Committee nominated themselves but unfortunately for them some maverick departments put up other candidates. We in turn nominated Alex Smith and myself, and only the two of us. We recommended that our members voted for the two of us and only the two of us. Come the day, the Royal College achieved a turn-out of just over 30% whereas we had a turn-out of 92%, the committee members working all day persuading our colleagues to attend the Royal College Assembly Hall and vote.

When the results were announced John Eaton was top of the poll, Alex Smith was second and I was fourth. Bill McHutcheson tied with John Paul for the final and eighth place. They went off with the Registrar and a pack of playing cards was found. Bill won. Interestingly, John Paul was elected a year later.

So it was a 6:2 distribution which we had regarded as equitable and the Royal College folk saw as a tragedy. John Eaton and I met and readily agreed that all eight of us had to work as a team. We formed an elected members' group which met prior to Senate meetings and which strove to achieve a unified policy on the agenda items. John Eaton became Chairman of the group and I emerged as the Political Commissar. We had occasional spells of tension but by and large it worked extremely well.

All that saw us through the academic year of 1964-65.

Our story moves forward, to a day in the late sixties.

As the sixties were falling away like autumnal leaves and the seventies loomed towards us, I found myself not only as an elected member of Senate but as one of the three elected members who were appointed to sit on the University Court. It was appropriate that there were three of us, for the court had three major committees – finance, property and staff. The court in turn could assign us to one each. I was on the staff committee.

One day we were having a meeting of that committee. The chairman was Sir Pat Thomas, a West of Scotland industrialist who was a lay member of Court. At the top table with the chairman were Sir Samuel Curran, our Principal, and Louis McGougan, the Bursar. Over the piece we liked the Principal but he could be short-tempered and irritable. To make matters worse, he both disliked being at University meetings when he was not chairman and secondly, he tended to become easily annoyed by Sir Pat, who lived a different lifestyle from the Principal's origins in Wishaw.

The agenda and the business were not exactly a thrill a minute. Boredom was creeping up through the floorboards and the carpeting. Then we came to a report on recommended academic promotions. It came from a sub-committee which had reviewed the nominations. The report was straight-forward. Two Readers were to be given Personal Professorships. Two Senior Lecturers were to be promoted to Reader and it advised the appointment of eight new Senior Lecturers.

Sir Pat made it clear he expected this to go through without demur. 'Is the report acceptable? May I take it we endorse it? Yes? Thank you ...Oh, Carbery, did you want to say something?'

'Only a small point, Chairman, but I believe it to be important. May I continue?'

'If you must! But I trust you are not going to be troublesome and question or oppose the report,' said the Chairman.

'No opposition at all, Chairman. I readily endorse all of the recommendations. All those to be promoted are worthy of it. I would remind you and our colleagues, Chairman, that one of the reasons we have elected members from the non-Professorial staff on both Senate and Court is that we tend to have a knowledge of staff across the whole spectrum of the University, whereas the Professoriate tend to confine themselves to their own and related disciplines. I would argue, Chairman, that I am the only one here today who could recognise and make commentary on everyone mentioned in the report.'

Pat Thomas scowled. 'And that is all you wanted to say?' he growled.

'No, not quite, Chairman,' I observed. 'Whereas all the promotions are laudable, I can tell you that almost certainly the promotions are all attributable to worthy research achievement.'

'And what is wrong with that?' growled the Principal.

'In one sense, nothing,' I observed. 'But, Chairman, I would remind the Principal, you Chairman, and the Committee that there are three criteria for promotion – research, teaching and administration. We are told that there are Faith, Hope and Charity and that the greatest is Charity. By the same token we and sister Universities have research, teaching and administration. It would be nice, indeed it would be prudent, if we could have an occasional promotion based on teaching ability and exceptional administration performance.'

'This is old hat,' said the Principal. 'Everyone thinks he is a good teacher. We can identify and evaluate the research. We would like to recognise exceptional teaching but we just cannot identify the good teachers. The same is true of exceptional administration.'

Sir Patrick smiled broadly. His body language clearly indicated that he regarded me and my unnecessary intervention as duly spiked. He endeavoured to retrieve control of the meeting but at that juncture a young secretary entered the room quietly, nodded at Sir Pat, and gave a note to the Principal and leaning forward whispered in his ear.

A formidable scowl crossed the Principal's face. He nodded at the young lady, rose, barely acknowledged the Chairman and turned and followed the secretary out the room. The ensuing silence was broken by a Professor of Engineering. There was always a Professor of Engineering, (and we had eight of them by 1970) who raised a point of order. Then a lay member got in on the act and so my colleagues meandered all over the place, most of them making points which were irrelevant.

Then the door opened and closed with a bang and a clearly very annoyed and angry Principal returned. He threw himself into his chair. He was known to be trying to give up smoking but without a 'by-your-leave' he stretched across and lifted Louis McGougan's cigarettes and matches, stuck a cigarette in his mouth, lit it, drew on it, inhaled deeply three times, crumpled the cigarette in an ash-tray and then cutting across a city accountant lay member half-turned to Sir Patrick.

'Right then, where are we now?' he queried.

Sir Pat was irked but he was not prepared to take on the Principal. 'I am afraid Carbery still has us bogged down on this promotions report.'

On receiving this intelligence Sir Samuel was nearly apoplectic. I realised I had to defend myself. 'Chairman,' I said in what I hoped was a fairly loud but firm tone. 'I really must protest. It is true we are still on that item in our agenda. But that is not my responsibility. I would point out that I have not spoken while the Principal had to be away. That we are still on this item is entirely due to you and your Chairmanship.'

Now it was the turn of Sir Patrick to be apoplectic. As the Chairman scowled the Principal, somewhat appeased, said 'What is Carbery's point?'

I did not wait for the Chairman to reply. I jumped in and reiterated my concern that whereas all the proposed promotions were fine, we were concentrating on research to the detriment of teaching and administration.

'Oh, is that what it is all about?' voiced the Principal. 'Well, I can tell him that last year before he came on this committee we promoted two men because of their teaching!' He beamed with a smile which read 'check-mate'.

'Well now, Carbery, do you accept that?' asked Sir Patrick.

'Certainly, Chairman,' I said. 'It is most gratifying to have the Principal's assurance – though I confess to perplexity in how we managed to promote staff members whom – according to the Principal himself - we could not identify.'

Some members of the Committee laughed and the Principal was once again apoplectic. I genuinely thought he was going to take a heart-attack and die.

Normally the Principal and I had a good relationship – not great, but good. For some four or five months following that meeting he cut me dead.

Then one day we met as one was going into and the other leaving the gents' toilet across the corridor from his room. As I held the door for him, he looked me straight in the eye.

'You know your trouble?' he muttered. 'You are too cheeky for your own good!'

And with that he patted me on the shoulder – and normal relations were resumed.

A Fortunate Promotion And The Lost Ten-Shilling Note

Almighty God was wonderfully kind to me on the matter of my civil service promotion in 1954.

When at school, I found to my embarrassment that I had no great ability with languages, ancient or modern. At the time, equipped with the limited knowledge of a very early teenager, I thought this deficiency ruled out aspiring to a university course, so I looked at other possibilities and concluded that the Civil Service entrance exam was the thing for me. Memory plays tricks with age, but as I recall it success in the pre-war clerical entrance examination to the Home Civil Service called for an ability higher than the Scottish Highers and virtually the height and weight and cubic capacity of 'A' levels. Success also brought good material rewards in the Britain of the day. Thus a seventeen-eighteen-year old school-leaver could enter the service with a starting salary of £150 per annum. This may not sound much to-day, but it was more than many a time-served tradesman made in a year. The advantages did not end there. I could be wrong but as I recall it the top of the clerical scale was about £400 a year and one promotion put one on a scale running to £650 a year, and this at a time when a bungalow in, say, Clarkston could be bought for £600. Nor did the benefits end there: a handsome pension awaited those who reached the retiral age, and this without having to contribute the 6% or thereabouts of salary which others were contributing in both the private and public sectors.

True, there was a down side: one was liable to be sent anywhere in Britain.

And then disaster struck. The Home Civil Service decided there would be no examinations during the war years. However, as the war drifted to its close, it was announced there would be a reconstruction examination when all those denied their chance during the war and certain other groups could have their opportunity to retrieve the situation. So it came about that in 1946 while stationed outside Swindon I spent the better part of a week travelling to Reading to sit the examination. In due course the Civil Service Commissioners advised I had been found acceptable. I opted for the Ministry of Labour and National Service as it was then called and following my demobilisation in the summer of 1947, I took up my first posting in Kinning Park Employment Exchange in early September of that year. Four months in that office, eight months in Troon interrupted by an attack of rheumatic fever, and then from autumn 1948 in the delights of the Bridgeton office saw me through to the dramatic events of 1954.

Here, I would digress to say that duri[...]years of Churchill's coalition government, the Minister of Labour with a seat in the Cabinet was Ernest Bevin, a prominent trade union leader. He and his department did extremely well. A number of post-war surveys indicated that of all the major countries involved in the war, it was the United Kingdom that was by far the best in making use of its manpower. We did better than the capitalist U.S., better than Nazi Germany, better than Fascist Italy, the Communist U.S.S.R. and better than dynastic Japan.

From a national point of view this had been highly commendable but it had been achieved by a rapid extension of the Ministry of Labour which in the immediate post-war period had an inflated number of staff at the executive grades. The result was that for well nigh the whole of the first post-war decade there had been no promotions from the Clerical Officer grade to that of Executive Officer or in the parlance of the Ministry of Labour, from grade 6 to grade 5.

By early 1954 it became apparent that the situation was changing. Death, ill health and attainment of retiral age had thinned the hitherto well-stacked executive grades; and it was announced there were to be promotions. So many officers were recommended for promotion that there were to be not one but two hurdles for the contestants; thus in the case of Bridgeton Miss Lamb our manager made twelve recommendations. Of these seven of us were invited to appear before a promotions panel. That body could at best nominate some to appear before a second more formidable panel. Three of us won through to appear before that body. By the grace of God I was one of the three – a situation seen by some as remarkable as I was still in my twenties and the youngest of the original twelve.

In those years I had not been idle. Reporting to Bridgeton in September 1948, I had used that winter to take a Certificate in Unemployment Benefit, doing so by attending classes at the then Glasgow and West of Scotland Commercial College, a fore-runner of the Scottish College of Commerce. As I registered for that course it never occurred to me that some years later I would be the teacher on that same course.

From 1949 to 1952 I had taken a Diploma in Public Administration from the University of Glasgow and by 1954 and the early summer panel interviews I was half-way through an Honours B.Sc. Econ. (External) from the University of London.

Of the three of us to appear before the second panel, my friend Bob McCrae was seen by the staff as the No.1 seed. Bob was bright and popular and a natural leader of men. He had been a Sergeant in the Signals Corps. He was very good at his work and was known to be in the Masonic Order. He too had studied and had an A.C.I.S qualification. Before he retired Bob was to be a Senior Executive Officer or Grade 3 and to be manager of our Motherwell Office. But to his great disappointment he was not promoted in 1954.

Those successful in these promotion exercises were listed in what became known as waiting lists. I can still recall Bob's utter delight when, later, in 1961 he appeared on such a list for promotion to Higher Executive Officer or Grade 4.

But as indicated he did not make the 1954 waiting list for promotion to Grade 5: he made that in 1955.

I was lucky. I was very fortunate. I did make the 1954 list and was the only one from Bridgeton to make it. More, almost immediately following the publication of the list, 10 promotions in Scotland were announced. Of the 10, nine were pre-war entrants to the service whereas I had been 14 when hostilities began.

So on the 1st August 1954 I became a Junior Executive Officer in the Ministry of Labour and my salary rose from £440 a year to £500.

I said that God had been kind to me. He was kind to me in that I was given promotion in a very competitive situation.

Further: while I was almost sent to the Shetlands, I landed a Glasgow posting in an 'out-house' of our Scottish Headquarters. That Glasgow posting allowed me to continue my studies for the B.Sc. Econ.

The good fortune continued in that I revelled in my new duties. I was made an Insurance Officer and charged by the Lord Advocate to decide on questionable or doubtful claims for Unemployment Benefit. There were seven of us working in the Glasgow office and dealing with all such matters for the Glasgow conurbation. I not only liked the work – I loved it – and it brought out the lawyer *manqué* in me.

And as for my final bit of good fortune re promotion at that time, my boss was Alex Lambie. Alex was a good boss in that he was pleasant and congenial, and by and large did not intervene with our exercise of our duties where we had a very substantial degree of independence, as have Magistrates in their courts and High Court judges in theirs. He also gave advice and this on a range of topics which ran far beyond our duties. For example, he knew my wife and I were in the market to buy a house.

'Don't buy a bungalow,' was Mr. Lambie's succinct advice, though when asked why such a purchase should be avoided he replied at great length. His argument was that bungalows are always cold, not least as they have four external walls exposed to the elements. Such houses may be fine in high summer but in winter they are the cause of either misery or very high fuel bills. His supplementary advice was to buy a mid-terrace house with only two narrow walls exposed to the world – which is what we did.

Alex, though I never called him by such familiarity, was a Grade 4 officer. He had been very seriously wounded in the First World War. It was believed that his survival was a sort of miracle. He was very friendly with Jack Brennan who was younger than but senior to Alex, a situation which arose from Brennan being a graduate who had entered the service as a cadet at Grade 5 level but virtually guaranteed promotion to H.E.O./ Grade 4 before attaining one's thirtieth birthday. In the middle fifties Jack Brennan was a Grade 3 officer and Manager of Glasgow's South Side exchange. The friends had a lot in common. Both were Catholics, but not ostentatiously so. They were more concerned with the sacraments than with the sacramentals. They were bookish and read a lot of 'catholic' material - Chesterton, Belloc, Newman and Hans Kung. Both were married while neither couple had children. Both wives had converted to Catholicism, one with modest enthusiasm and the other with maximum enthusiasm.

The two couples went on holiday together. Every summer they took themselves off for two weeks in a popular holiday resort. The resorts chosen tended, of course, towards the douce rather than the brazen. Scarborough, Southport, Bournemouth and Eastbourne were visited. The Brennans were very fond of Llandudno where they had spent their honeymoon.

One year they had gone to Torquay and one morning coming out of a coffee-shop, Alex found a ten-shilling note lying on the pavement. They took it to a police station but when they reported their business the desk sergeant was neither enthused nor pleased.

He looked at Alex.

'Do me a favour, sir, find a church and put it in the poor box. Let me explain …' And he did just that. His case was that if he took it he had to enter it up in a log-book, yet even if someone reported the loss of such a note and could even give an indication of the appropriate location, the police could not hand over the note unless the deprived could quote the number of the note. 'And no-one ever knows the number of such a note, sir,' he observed. But he was not finished. He went on to point out that if they, the police, still had it at the end of a year they had then to send the money to the finder – but not the full amount. On the contrary they had to calculate and deduct the cost of both the postal order and the postage. 'Look, sir,' he concluded, 'it's just not worth it. It is a lot of work to little purpose. As I said, sir, do me a favour – find a church with a poor box.'

But they compromised. They found a church – a Church of England church – with a poor box. Each couple put in half-a-crown and they sailed forth to spend the residual five shillings which they did over and over again. Thus the ladies bought coloured berets from C&A on the strength of the five shillings. They had afternoon tea in a five-star hotel on the strength of the same five shillings. Nor did it end there. They had a sail around the bay on the same money and to cap it all they spent a day at Buckfast Abbey on the strength of the five shillings.

It was all this that led to the best of all Alex Lambie's wonderful pieces of advice. 'Never find a ten-shilling note, Tom,' said Alex, and then he added ruefully: 'It's not worth it: it is too expensive!'

It was, as were all his commentaries, excellent advice.

But of course all that was long ago. Inflation has done its work. For ten shillings read five pounds. The up-date on the Lambie advice is: 'Never find a £5 note.'

This tale of the lost ten-shilling note could do with an addendum. In essence I believe I should reveal that when I had my second interview in the run-up to the promotion, Jack Brennan was on the interviewing panel and that he and I had an exchange.

In the days prior to the interviews I encountered a man I knew who was a veteran of interviews, having considerable experience of both sides of the table. 'Be ready for them,' he advised. 'It is not unusual for one of the panel members to 'rough you up' a bit – to give you a hard time, not too hard – but hard. It is done to see how you react. Do you fold like a tent when the ropes are slackened or, at the other extreme, do you fight back and nearly or fully lose your temper? Or again are you capable of defending your stance, fairly and firmly, and with luck, with dignity or as much as you can muster?'

The second interview took place on a Saturday morning. My interview was destined to be the last of the day, indeed the last of the week. The panel could have been excused for being a shade weary, depressed and experiencing the *déjà vu* element in virtually every candidate's responses.

The chairman was a Miss Robertson, a Deputy Controller. At the interview, she was supported by two men – Jack Brennan and the Manager of our Dundee office. Miss Robertson welcomed me graciously and introduced her colleagues.

The early exchanges went well. The issues they raised were predictable. I felt fairly comfortable: I was not scoring sixes but I was winning the odd single or double, and even the odd four.

Then Mr. Brennan took up the running.

'I see you took a Diploma from Glasgow University. What was that all about?'

I told him. Though not overly impressed, he did look interested.

'And now you are studying for a London degree. Is it markedly more demanding than your diploma?'

So again, I told him.

This time he smiled like a chess player about to say 'check-mate'.

'May I take it, may we take it, that you would readily concede that all this study stuff interferes with your work?'

I recognised the ploy. Did I crumble and concede? How should I play it? I decided to tell it as I saw it.

'I would acknowledge that there is an intrusion – a well-nigh minimal intrusion. Thus on a few occasions – very few but some - my thoughts at work stray to some aspect of one of the subjects I am studying. Then again, when the results come out, there is a little flurry of private phone calls from fellow students. I do not make such calls, but I do receive them. There is one point, however, I would make by way of mitigation,' I said.

'And that is?' asked Brennan.

'It is my experience that virtually every active member of staff allows something to intrude on the working day. In my case it is study. In another it could be table tennis tournaments or bowling outings requiring considerable planning and organisation.'

Jack Brennan scowled. It was well known that he organised table tennis tournaments and arranged at least two bowling outings each year.

Miss Robertson laughed a gentle laugh.

'I think our young colleague has the better of that exchange, Mr. Brennan. I think we should move on,' and turning to the Dundee man invited him to raise a new topic – which he did.

Remarkably they promoted me.

To his great credit Jack Brennan never held this exchange against me.

A Dicksonism

There was a time in the late fifties when I endeavoured to have a new term introduced to the English language. This became a one-man campaign based on a surname.

English has many examples of this phenomenon, my own favourite being Boycott, that of the sad and pathetic Captain Boycott, the English gentleman who in the nineteenth century had an estate in the West of Ireland. Boycott by inept man-management alienated his workers to such an extent that the workforce withdrew its services. More, the local community in support of the employees was not prepared to replace them.

The overall result was that Boycott could not harvest his crops and could not attend to his animals. For him it was a disaster. From that incident we acquired a new noun – a boycott, and a new verb - to boycott.

Other examples abound. Dr. Spooner who mauled his deployment of some phraseology gave rise to a spoonerism and the medical man, Parkinson, found his name applied to the dreadful disease which he identified and from which my friend Robert Crampsey tragically died in late 2008.

Another widespread example was the application of the name Hoover to all electrical carpet sweepers, the name not being confined to those sweepers manufactured by the company of that name. Not many young people use this terminology, but on the other hand many of the elderly do.

Thus in a recent court case in England, a witness in her eighties observed: 'When I called to see her she was hoovering her carpets and apparently did not hear me ringing her door bell.'

My new term would have been a Dicksonism. This would have been based on my boss in the Civil Service, a Miss Agnes Dickson, who appropriately was seen by many in the department as an example of the Peter Principle (itself an example of the surname phenomenon) which argued that many executives are promoted to a grade beyond their competence.

Miss Dickson's forte – and consequently the basis of my new noun – was the deployment en passant of a phrase which managed to convey that the speaker was of a somewhat higher social status than one might have thought.

An example of this very situation came through on the radio in an early episode in 'Hancock's Half-Hour.' Hancock was giving an account of his time in the army, and in particular of the retreat to Dunkirk. He described how, devoid of motor transport, they were marching along a minor road when someone shouted 'Stukas!' and sure enough, in came the dreaded German fighter-bombers, firing machine guns and dropping bombs before peeling away. Virtually everyone dived into the ditches by the roadside. Hancock went on to report that as luck had it he found himself lying beside the Brigadier. Never one to avoid confrontation, he reported he had looked the Brigadier in the eye and observed rather grandly: 'This is a bonny pickle in which we have landed.' The Brigadier had stared back and said: 'Sir?'

Within my own coterie of friends we had one man of similar disposition. We all told war stories but most of his reminiscing involved his batman – which was his way of reminding the rest of us that he had held a rank which entitled him to a batman.

So far as Miss Dickson was concerned, her first notable instance was in the late autumn of the year when female Civil Servants began their seven-year march to equal pay. Hitherto, women were paid less than their male counterparts. As I recall it, the Treasury was 'unco cautious' in that march to parity: it was to take seven years with an increment each year. Before we could say that parity prevailed, the ladies had to be patient.

Nevertheless, many of them celebrated by venturing abroad for their holidays. Folk who in the past had gone to Scarborough, Southport, Llandudno, even Torquay and daringly Newquay, started going to the Dutch tulip fields, the Belgian coast, to a Rhine cruise and one brave soul went to Paris.

Her troops having had their holidays, Miss Dickson went in September. In due course her postcard arrived. It had a flourish. It had a Dicksonism: 'Florence is as wonderful as ever.' In other words, think not that I am one of the nouveaux travellers like you lot.

As the years progressed, I became a sort of Lieutenant to her. We started work at 9 a.m. but she lived in Uplawmoor, travelled by train to Glasgow Central and took a tram to our Sauchiehall Street location near Charing Cross. She would arrive at about ten minutes past nine. As often as not, before she went into her own room, she would put her head round the door of the large room where the rest of us worked. 'Tom,' she would call: it was never a bellow but it was a firm, peremptory summons. I would rise and follow her into her room. As she hung up her coat, peeled off her gloves – always there were gloves – and laid her briefcase, handbag and umbrella on a side table, she would talk. It was not that she always had a Dicksonism but very often she did.

'That brother of mine is a gem, Tom, a positive gem. Last night after our overtime, I missed the train to our high station and had to settle for a later train to the down station. I telephoned to report what had happened and without demur he took the Bentley out of the garage and came down to collect me. He is a treasure!'

On another occasion she said:

'Dear God, Tom. That train this morning was dreadfully busy. The number of people at Thornliebank who came into our first class compartment was just scandalous, and not an apology from a single one of them.' With Dicksonism after Dicksonism, she sailed onwards and onwards.

All of that was more than 50 years ago. I failed in my campaign to see 'Dicksonism' becoming an acceptable and used term.

But maybe this is the start of a new campaign and just maybe ...

Pew Rents

As I recall it, my friend Robert Crampsey could have continued in his post as Rector of St Ambrose's Secondary in Coatbridge until 1995 but he chose to take premature retirement about 1990. Having left early, he decided to supplement his pension by writing the histories of golf clubs. I believe that by the time he stopped he had written eight in all, the most distinguished being the Glasgow Club at Killermont.

One of the other clubs was Cathkin Braes. While he was in the early stages of his research, some Committee members made the eminently sensible suggestion that he should interview the last remaining member of the Stuart family, the one-time owners of the great Castlemilk Estate on part of which the club played its golf. Originally the club had rented the land.

It was pointed out that the club had offered Honorary Membership to the members of the family – which consisted of the owner, his wife and their solitary child – a daughter. The parents, it was said, seldom played though very infrequently they had made a gesture, but one which showed neither skill nor aptitude. The daughter on the other hand had played a bit more often and played to her very high handicap.

By the time Robert was working on the club material, the daughter was an elderly lady and a resident in an up-market Nursing/Retirement Home near Dundonald in Ayrshire. It was agreed that Robert and two Committee Members should go and see her.

The visit took place on a Sunday afternoon. The Committee Members observed that, when they met, the lady would offer Robert a glass of sherry. They urged Robert to accept. That way she too would have one but the arrangement would have the advantage that when she offered a second drink he could decline whereupon she too would desist. It was argued that if Robert declined the first drink the lady would smile and say, 'You will not mind if I have one myself,' and thereupon have a second and possibly a third and then probably fall asleep, thereby negating the purpose of the visit.

As the interview got under way Robert asked about her childhood.

It transpired the family had a regular pattern from year to year. July was always spent in Arran and August with cousins and their parents in Eaton Square in London. It took eight wagons to take their staff and the luggage from Castlemilk to St. Enoch Station.

Fishing for background information, Robert asked about both vacations. 'When in London,' he enquired, 'what did you do on Sundays? Did you go to St. Columba's Pont Street or to St. George's Eaton Square?'

The lady was not at all put out by the question, nor did she express surprise at the question.

'We went to the Church of Scotland in Pont St. for three of the four Sundays. On the fourth we went with my cousin's family to St. George's. It was a sort of gesture of good-will.'

And then apropos of nothing, the lady added: 'Father paid four Pew Rents to St. Columba's.'

'Four?' queried Robert. He was perplexed as he knew there were only three members of the family.

'Yes, FOUR!' confirmed the lady and then sensing the perplexity of her guest she offered the explanation.

'One for Papa, one for Mama, one for me – and one for Papa's Top Hat!'

My only regret about this story is that I did not learn of it earlier than I did.

Throughout the seventies I was a member of the Independent Broadcasting Authority. Our impressive 8-storey office block was in Knightsbridge diagonally across from Harrods. We met twice every month and this for all-day meetings. Generally we had guests joining us for lunch. About once a quarter the guest list included Dr. Fraser McCluskey, the Minister at St. Columba's. We became quite friendly and I was sad that some of his congregation were sniffy about his marriage. I was very happy for them both when he was made Moderator of the General Assembly of the Church of Scotland.

I did not see much of Dr. McCluskey thereafter. This was sad. I would have liked to have seen his face when I asked him how well he was doing in Pew Rents for Top Hats!

Bernard Stuart's Legacy

There is one matter arising from this story of which we can be entirely confident. Our hero is not going to sue me on grounds of defamation. This not just because I am confident that in telling the story I shall not malign him, but because he is long dead.

Bernard Stuart was a Scot. More, he was a Benedictine priest. In the sixteenth and seventeenth centuries, Europe was in the turmoil of the Reformation, with many regions involved in religious wars. This did not impinge on the Reverend Stuart. On the contrary, he was settled in the confident, Catholic atmosphere of Salzburg where he was Chaplain (and sweeper) to the Cardinal Archbishop of Salzburg, a man called Firmian.

One day the Cardinal turned to Bernard Stuart and in a manner both haughty and friendly said: 'By the way, Father, I want you to build me a Schloss. As you know I have purchased a site on the southern side of Hohen-Salzburg which will give rise to magnificent unfettered views of the Alps, and as you know, we are enjoined in Holy Scripture 'to lift up our eyes to the hills.'

Father Stuart was both competent and obedient. He had absolutely no knowledge of architecture or of building science. So he wrote to the Librarian of the Vatican Library, asking him to forward books on both subjects. Some two to three months later three donkeys arrived with pannier bags well-packed with books. Most of them were in Latin, some in emerging Italian and some in French.

Initially, Father Stuart worked on his own. Once he had his plans completed, he engaged a master of building who in turn recruited a labour force, and in due course construction commenced.

Some eighteen months later a magnificent building had been erected and was ready for occupancy.

Cardinal Firmian and his entourage moved into their new home and work-place.

And almost immediately Bernard Stuart was given affirmation of the dictum that the reward for a job well-done is to be entrusted with another task, at least as demanding as the first.

The Cardinal congratulated and thanked his Chaplain and added: 'And now, Father, I want you to make me a lake, an artificial lake which looks like a natural lake, so that I can see the sunlight dancing on the water and we can occasionally play games on the ice in the depths of winter.'

Still compliant and obedient Father Stuart produced the lake.

All that was some four to five centuries ago. Remarkably both the Schloss and the lake are still there.

The house has had an interesting history.

When one of Firmian's successors decided to move back into less pretentious accommodation in town, the Schloss was sold. It became a hotel for a while and then a private residence and again a hotel. Then in the early 1930s it was purchased by Max Reinhardt, the Austrian-Jewish theatrical director and entrepreneur who proceeded to spend a small fortune renovating it. For example: he bought a library, both shelving and books, from a monastery in Italy and had it installed in the East Wing of the building. His mistress was Heidi Lamarr and Reinhardt had a secret staircase built which led from an alcove on the balcony of the library to the room of the film star.

With the Anschluss in 1938 and the German take-over of the whole of Austria, Reinhardt found it prudent to escape to America. The Germans appropriated the building and during the war it was the Gestapo HQ for the entire Salzburg Region. As the war was ending, Hitler's private pilot committed suicide in the beer-cellar.

When the war was over and the American forces were in command of the South and South-West Sector of the four occupied zones, some young, liberal, idealistic American officers got in tow with a young Frenchman called Clément Heller. Their common concern was that a lot of young Europeans of diverse nationality had been deprived of university or indeed any form of tertiary education. They – the Americans allied with Heller – resolved to lay on demanding courses to which they would recruit some bright Europeans. They saw their arrangements as having three probable advantages. Firstly, the Europeans would have a taste of higher education. Secondly, former Axis nationals would meet, mix with, study alongside, argue with and possibly become friends of Americans, Britons, French citizens as well as those from countries from Norway to Luxemburg, from Poland to Greece which had been occupied. Thirdly, with luck, those who availed themselves of such courses would go home looking on the United States more favourably than hitherto, although in fairness one should note that the third aim had slight statistical weighting vis-à-vis the other two.

With all this in mind they scrounged some old Nissen-type huts from the US Army, and they recruited tutors, mainly but not exclusively American academics, administrators and captains of industry and commerce.

It was a wonderful success. Somehow the young Americans won the resources and persuaded a wide variety of folk to help them for small or no monetary reward, while those who were the temporary students revelled in the experience and never failed to express their appreciation. The arrangement came to be known as the Salzburg Seminar in American Studies.

It is here that the two strands of our story come together.

One night at a private dinner in a very up-market penthouse flat in fashionable Manhattan, the hostess, herself a generous donor to the Seminar, waited until the coffee stage where she invited a young army officer – one of the original set – to tell her other guests about what he and his friends had achieved.

The hope of both of them had been that cheque books would have been extracted from pockets and hand-bags and cheques, generous cheques, would be written.

One lady guest went further: 'You mentioned your problems with accommodation,' she observed, 'but I have recently acquired a mighty fine schloss just outside Salzburg. You can have that if you want it.'

She was the American widow of Reinhardt and the new Austrian Government had recognised her entitlement to the building.

I have heard two versions of the terms on which the Seminar acquired the use of the building. One was that they were given the building 'for free'. The other was that they were charged a peppercorn rent.

The Seminar continues, albeit in a modified form but still doing exciting, valuable work though students tend to be in their forties rather than their twenties.

The Schloss and the lake are still there and both were used for a scene in 'The Sound of Music' movie and so are part of 'The Sound of Music Tour' which takes place more than twice on every working day in that delightful city of Mozart and spires.

In the redevelopment of Gorbals-Hutchesonton, we in Glasgow paid for a run of houses to be designed and built in Crown St. When constructed, they looked the part. I still recall seeing an elderly lady attending to her roses by her door and radiating pride as she worked upon them.

As I remember, we gave gold medals to the architect and commendation to the builders. It did not take long for it to become apparent that the houses might have done well in the South of France or Morocco in North Africa: they were not well suited for Glasgow and its climate.

Condensation was experienced. The tenants were urged to open their windows even in days of inclement weather.

Heating bills soared, and after a decade or more of quarrels and bickering and reports and protestations the houses were demolished. My recollection is that they survived for ten or twelve, maybe fifteen controversial years. They came, but they did not conquer. They went.

Meanwhile, Bernard Stuart's Schloss and lake remain and they are photographed day after day by blue-rinse matrons from the States, beer-bellied Germans and diminutive, myopic Japanese tourists, and the photographs are shown with pride to friends in Little Rock, Colorado Springs, Hamburg and Tokyo.

Informing The Masses

He came from an Irish-German American family and his name was Michael Hans-Jurgen Tiedemann. His mother came from an Irish family called O'Keefe and she, his grandmother and his great-grandmother who was 92 and resident in the St. Francis Nursing Home, run appropriately by Franciscan nuns, were all daily communicants. The German side of the family originated in Bavaria but in the nineteenth century three brothers, although land-locked, became obsessed with boats and shipping in general. They had studied Nautical Engineering and on graduation moved to Hamburg.

I became friendly with Michael through the Salzburg Seminar in American Studies, where, being bi-lingual in English and German, he had been invaluable.

By profession, academic attainment and experience he straddled Economics and Accountancy and had specialised in Public Finance. He was in his early thirties and was a middle-rank executive, with great promise and probable prospects in the Bureau of the Budget in the Private Office of the President.

Life was good. He was held in high regard by his peer group and his superiors. He was happy in his work and was engaged to be married to a beautiful, clever and shrewd daughter of a Boston-Irish whisky merchant who was an effective political operator in the Democratic Party. And then the President made his life difficult.

Schlesinger, Sorenson, Goldberg, brother Robert et al had all been arguing to John F. K. that their administration, like others before it, was too Washington and New York based. They argued that the Administration needed to talk to, go out and meet the American people.

So the President told the Cabinet (to their delight) that they should tell the Administrators that every unit had to provide two speakers, each with an appropriate topic, to go out and speak all over the country at a wide variety of public meetings.

Michael was flattered but not enthused to find that he was to be one of the Bureau's nominees. He was given three days to come up with what was hoped would prove to be an acceptable subject and title. He was to report to Bill Carey, the Senior Executive Officer of the Bureau.

Michael, however, tried to be clever. He was pleased to be asked but he did not want to have to go to New Orleans, San Diego or Santa Barbara County to give his speech. He did not want to be apart from his recently acquired fiancée. So he decided to choose a topic which, with luck, no-one would want.

When he reported to Carey, Bill asked him whether he had chosen his subject and title.

Yes, he had.

What was it?

'New Monetary and Fiscal Goals for the American People,' said Michael.

'Fine,' said Bill.

Two weeks later, Michael was told by Bill Carey that he and another young man from the Department of the Interior had been assigned to Chicago. They were to give their talks in one of the city's finest theatres on a Sunday evening. The other man would be speaking on 'The Future of our National Parks.' Michael would be the second speaker. They had been booked into a five-star hotel quite near the theatre. They were to fly to Chicago on the Friday evening and back to D.C. on the Monday morning. The flights had been booked and their tickets, a copy of the hotel booking and their guidance for the Sunday night were already with their secretaries.

Bill turned to go. 'By the way,' he added, 'the dress code is black tie - a bit formal, but you know Mayor Daley' and with that he turned and was gone.

In Chicago on the Saturday evening before their joint performance the two young men gave themselves a rather fine dinner and a generous nightcap. On the Sunday morning the Department of the Interior man attended the Presbyterian Church in the middle of the town. Michael had thought of attending the twelve o'clock concelebrated High Mass in the Cathedral but settled instead for an early morning 8 o'clock mass in a small local Church.

They had a late lunch and agreed to forego dinner but, instead, to have a sort of afternoon tea about 4.30 p.m. and have a late-night supper - probably a steak and French fries – about 10.30 p.m when they returned from the theatre and the post-lecture reception.

Over late afternoon sandwiches and coffee the two potential speakers speculated on the size of the likely audience. The other young man suggested something between 500 and a thousand but probably around 650. Michael thought this was ridiculously optimistic but was too polite to say so. What he did say was that he reckoned they would be lucky to have some 300 to 400 – scattered over the theatre which would be substantially empty.

When they and the Chairman, the Deputy Mayor of the city, went out from the wings onto the stage, to be received by tumultuous applause, both of them were shattered to find the theatre full. There was not an empty seat in the house. It was rather difficult to see but in a quick exchange they agreed the place was full – front stalls, back stalls, dress circle, upper circle and gallery absolutely full – and full with men. There was not a female to be seen other than the usherettes. More, every man, dress circle to gallery, was wearing a tuxedo.

The other man spoke first. The audience was solemn but there was occasional laughter. After a generous comfort break it was Michael's turn.

Early on, having failed to receive any reaction to his quirks and his controversial points, Michael decided that in his preparation of his material he had not been sufficiently serious and detailed. He concluded he had been 'talking down' to his audience. He decided to abandon his prepared script and to plunge into very detailed, complicated material. When giving them that material he knew no-one, except the Director of the Bureau and Bill Carey, could have done better or could have been more detailed.

Yet the audience remained unmoved. They did not scoff but equally they did not applaud. They sat with faces akin to those on the statues of Easter Island.

At last his ordeal was over.

Yet when he finished there was a roar of approval. Was it relief? No, for it was followed by protracted and thunderous applause. It was a standing ovation.

Back in the wings the Chairman turned to them both but particularly to Michael.

'Great,' he pronounced, 'absolutely great. JFK will love it. Tremendous!'

'But the response and lack of response of the audience was confusing,' suggested Michael.

'Those bums,' exploded the Chairman. 'Forget them. There was not an accountant in the lot of them. That, my son, was the entire wage-related staff of the Chicago Sewage Department. Boss Daley told them to attend and, of course, they did what they were told!'

The Challenged Advertisement

There is an apocryphal tale that goes the rounds in Aberdeen, though I am sure it is to be heard in many another Scottish town. The version I heard dates from the late fifties or early sixties. It concerns a tram driver who went home for his lunch. As he went into the kitchen his wife, Jessie, was fussing about the table. 'Oh, Alex,' she said. 'Ah went doon tae Union Street tae get an engagement present for yon lassie Bremner an' Ah saw the ugliest man Ah've ever seen in a' ma puff!'

'That's strange,' said her man. 'Ah didnae ken George Middleton was tae be in Aberdeen to-day.'

At the time, George Middleton was the General Secretary of the S.T.U.C. and was regarded as clever, crafty, hard-working, hard-drinking and of unbecoming appearance if not positively ugly. There were those who said that was a harsh assessment: he was not always hard-drinking, only sometimes.

George had a sweeper, a sort of alter ego, a man called Robert Muir. He was very clever: indeed, some of us think he was brilliant. He had risen through the newspaper industry and had a great facility with words and never used a small word when a big one was available. He was, we believed, a member of the Communist Party. His family background was that of minor aristocrats. He was a descendant of the Muirs of Uplawmoor, who in the fourteenth and fifteenth centuries had lived in the keep or tower near Caldwell Golf Course. Whoever else had prospered, Robert's branch of the family had fallen on what, for them, was hard times. It was our understanding that when Robert was a boy they had been well nigh obliged to move from a substantial villa in the village of Uplawmoor to a tenement flat in Glasgow.

Yet everything is relative. In Nesbitt's book *The Railway Children*, when the father is sent to prison, the mother and the three children move to an eight-apartment 'cottage' in the country: mark you, it was near a railway line. By the same standards of deprivation the Muirs' flat was a six-apartment in a rather fine red sandstone building in Shawlands: it was a thousand light miles from the one- or two-apartment flats in the Gorbals where one family shared an outside toilet with two or three other families.

When Robert was about seventeen or so he decided to join the Y.C.L. – the Young Communists' League. He cut the appropriate coupon from the *Daily Worker*, completed it and sent it to the League's H.Q. in London. They wrote back assigning him to the Gorbals Branch as his nearest and advising him when and where the branch met.

When Robert 'reported' he found he was expected. He was given a warm reception by the chairman and secretary.

When the meeting started, the chairman introduced Robert who was acclaimed by a mild round of douce applause. Once the meeting was well underway, there was a fierce and occasionally acrimonious debate which surrounded a motion which had been moved by a lad called Connell.

Everyone was alluded to as a 'Comrade' so the debate was peppered with contributions supporting and disagreeing with Comrade Connell. As the debate progressed and became even more heated, the chairman perceived that Robert had something to say. He interrupted a young girl in full flow. 'Sorry to interrupt you, Comrade, but it is your third contribution to the discussion. I believe our new Comrade wants in. The floor is yours, Comrade Muir.'

Robert beamed and rose. 'Thank you, Comrade Chairman. I shall not be tedious. I just wanted to say that as I see it, Comrade Candle has the better of it.'

There was a mixture of perplexed grunts and laughter, but Robert had thought in referring to Comrade Connell the others had been using the common, frequently used Glasgow mispronunciation of 'Candle' – and had thought that had he done so, it would be seen as affectation.

To those of us who worked constantly or occasionally with them, it seemed George Middleton and Robert Muir went everywhere together.

One fine day they had set out from the S.T.U.C. offices in the Park Circus airt by Kelvingrove to walk to the offices of a white collar union in Cathedral Street, on the opposite side of the city centre. They could, of course, have gone by taxi or even public transport. The uncharitable would say they were walking but intended to claim the taxi fares in order to supplement their drinking money.

It was Robert who gave me his account of what transpired. 'There we were, Thomas, progressing quite satisfactorily on a fine summer day, when we were approaching Buchanan Street, and those heavens, in which you purport to believe, opened up on us and extremely heavy precipitation descended on us. Not only were we and our clothing subject to being soaked, but as you know, George dyes his hair. Without the dye his hair is grey. With it, the hair is black. I took command of the situation: 'Look you, George, we shall have to take refuge! Behold there at no great distance is the spacious foyer of the Skerry's building.' (This was an educational establishment, purporting to be an Institution of Higher Education). 'And there we waited, but time was speeding on the wing and we were already late for our appointment. Then George gave voice to a conclusion: 'There is nothing for it, Robert,' stated George, 'I'll have to buy a hat!''

Robert continued the story. 'I said, look again, George, I shall take myself to the intersection. When the traffic flow diminishes I shall gesticulate and you can withdraw from this protection and scurry to me, and together we shall traverse the thoroughfare. There on the other side is Gerrard's, a moderately-priced gents' outfitters.'

Robert went on. 'This we did, Thomas, and when we entered the darkened, cavernous ill-lit establishment I perceived a youth with pimples pretending to be a salesman. He was standing beside an advertisement which proudly proclaimed: 'Attaboy hats – the hat for every face.'

'I clicked my fingers. My man, my man,' I declared, 'I have here a challenge to your advertisement!'

A Study In Political Ethics

Les enfants terribles of Gorbals Constituency Labour Party in the late forties and early fifties were Pat Lally, who was destined to be the city's Lord Provost, Walter Fyfe who was a Church of Scotland minister and social community worker – and myself. We were all in our early to middle twenties and were the only folk under 45 in the C.L.P.

The power-house of the C.L.P. was John Mains, a hard-working, hard-driving man, of political skulduggery and guile. In the parliamentary elections of 1950 and 1951 he was the agent for our M.P., Mrs. Alice Cullen. As I recall it after one of these elections, I was landed with the task of cross-checking his completion of a return of a form under the Representation of the People Acts of 1948 and 1949.

John solemnly certified that the total expenditure incurred in pursuit of Mrs. Cullen's candidature had come to precisely £53:13:4. This had been mainly spent on chalk and the rent of a hall for a pre-election meeting. The chalk was liberally used at key intersections where our labourers in the vineyard printed exhortations to 'Vote Cullen, Vote Labour.' The intensity of such messages reached its zenith in the environs of St. Francis' Church in Cumberland Street and Sandyfaulds Street. It was a large church with seven masses on a Sunday from 6 a.m. to 12 noon. The Western Catholic calendar gave the estimated Catholic population of the parish at 26,000.

There was substantial correlation between this Catholic community and Labour voters.

Although the bulk of our voting support was Catholic and the same was true of our paid-up party membership, the Catholic element did not constitute a majority of the membership of the executive committee. This was a body of some sixty or so men and women. The biggest block was almost exclusively male. It consisted of trades union representatives, mainly from 'craft' unions. Many of them wore pin-size Masonic badges in the lapels of their jackets. There were also men and some women from the two big unskilled and semi-skilled unions - the rather left-wing Transport and General Workers and the more cautious and loyal to the leadership General and Municipal Workers. There were also representatives of the white collar unions, particularly the National Association of Local Government Officers and U.S.D.A.W. - the shop-workers' union.

The next largest block was made up by those representing the rank and file members in the branches. Representatives from the Women's Section, from the Co-operative Party (mainly members of the Co-operative Women's Guild), the Socialist Societies (such as The Fabian Society and the Socialist Medical Association). Most of the intellectual and philosophical content of our deliberations came from four Jewish members – two lawyers, one accountant in a Jewish firm and a doctor in a local hospital.

John Mains 'ran' our C.L.P. but chose at that time not to be Chairman. That task he entrusted to an agreeable and pliable engineer in the A.E.U. John was using the time to have himself elected to Glasgow Corporation.

For our normal monthly meetings we met in a former shop in Rutherglen Road. After these meetings we three young bloods took ourselves to Lombardi's Café near the intersection of Rutherglen Road and Crown Street, where we conducted our own post-mortem on the meeting. When we held our A.G.M. or other important meetings we rented a large room in the St. Mungo Halls in McNeil Street, which halls were owned by the U.C.B.S. – the United Coop Baking (or was it Bakery?) Society.

One year we had an eventful A.G.M. As usual we were running late and the wee Chairman was anxious to bring matters to a close. 'We come now to 'Any other competent business' and we never have any so ....'

'Just a moment, Chairman,' I said. 'I have a matter which I want to raise.'

'Oh, dear,' said the Chairman. 'I do hope you are not going to be difficult.'

'I would hope not, Chairman,' I replied. 'But if I have to be, so be it. My point is this, Chairman. There is a rumour circulating in the constituency that if anyone works for us, for the party, at three successive elections, then he will have his Corporation house soon after it and this irrespective of how many points he has in the Housing Department's lists. Now I am not asking whether this is true or untrue. What I shall say is this. If it is true we had better desist now before the press gets wind of it; and if it is untrue then we nail it, and nail it now and expose it as fallacious.'

Silence prevailed. One could hear the proverbial pin drop. Then the whispering and shuffling of feet broke out only to be interrupted by the Chairman.

'This is a dreadful allegation,' he observed. 'You must be wrong!'

'I am not wrong, Chairman. It is literally the talk of the steamie. We are very, very lucky the papers have not got onto it by now.'

At this point John Mains took over. 'Comrade Chairman,' he opened. 'Those of us who have been around for years know our young friend has raised a matter of great complexity. As you indicated earlier, we are running late and we do not want to have to pay a surcharge on the rent of the hall. As we saw in the financial report, our finances are very tight. If our young comrade is agreeable, I shall enlighten him later. In the meantime, if there is no other A.O.C.B., you can declare the meeting closed.'

The Chairman grasped it. 'Yes. Thank you. I sense we have no more business. I declare the meeting closed.'

There was a round of applause, a scraping of chairs, a lot of coughing and a lot of noisy converse. I knew I had been out-manoeuvred.

As we made for the door John came up to me and grasped me firmly by the arm. 'You are at it, Tom,' he declared with an air of controlled anger. 'You are clever. You understand these things. It is all a case of X's and Y's, isn't it?'

I was bewildered. I gazed at him. 'John,' I said. 'I do not know what you are on about. What are you saying?'

'Alright,' said Mains. 'We'll make it easy. We'll forget the Y's. We'll keep it to the X's – right?'

'John,' I declared, 'I am still not with you.'

By this time John was visibly angry.

'Look,' he said. 'If the Tories are in power, they will build 3X houses. Right?'

'John,' I said. 'I am still not with you. Yes, the Tories will build houses, but where do you get your 3X figure?'

'You are fussing,' said John. 'As I say, if the Tories are in power, they will build houses, fewer than us, but some. Let's say 3X. Whereas, if we are in power, we'll build 5X. In other words, when we are in power there are 2X additional houses every year. Tell me this! Who deserves some of these extra houses more than the guys who got us into power to build them? These guys deserve these houses. That's fair, isn't it?'

And without waiting for an answer he nodded towards the door where Pat and Walter were waiting for me. 'Good night,' said John with the confident and satisfied air of a man who had won.

Acquiring Property

In the preceding story John Mains was a principal character.

It was based in the early fifties. If we move forward to the middle seventies we find that John had made considerable progress in the ranks of the Labour Party and the Labour-controlled Corporation of the City. In this story he has been a councillor for some time and is now a Bailie. He has been Convener of the Health Committee, during which time he conducted a campaign on the detection and cure of tuberculosis. For this commendable and successful campaign John had been awarded an OBE of which he was immensely proud. He had been Education Convener, a post in which he was very active and incurred some controversy. By the time of the events of this story, he was Leader of the Labour Group and the most powerful member of the Corporation.

I too had moved on. I had left the Civil Service and was a Senior Lecturer in a University.

When John became Group Leader he sent for me. Direct as ever, he lost no time in telling me he wanted his own personal 'Brains Trust' and I had to form it. He would draw on it – or some of it – as and when it suited him.

About twice a month he would phone and say he wanted to see me. He invariably finished with the same injunction: 'And bring Alex Smith. He is very good. He is much better than you are.'

As a reward for our advice he would have us join him for lunch in the Members' Dining Room in the City Chambers.

I knew of his ambitions, although later I was to know why they had been stilled.

Some years earlier on a visit to the City Chambers I had been in the gents' toilet nearest to the Members' corridor. As I washed my hands, a councillor I knew sidled up to the adjoining wash-basin.

In a throaty whisper he said: 'Don't look now, Tom, but the future MP for Gorbals has just come in.'

When I did turn to look and dry my hands I expected to see John – but it was not John, it was Jerry O'Sullivan. Somewhat surprised, I turned to my acquaintance. 'Excuse me,' I said. 'But my understanding was that the broad plan was for John, John Mains, to be the member after Alice.'

'Oh, he is,' said the other. 'But Jerry is to get it after John.'

I looked at him steadily.

'I have heard of Apostolic Succession, but this is ridiculous,' I declared.

As it came to pass such succession did not occur. Some of us managed to persuade John that he was better being a big fish in the relatively wee pond of Glasgow Corporation than being a miserable, thwarted wee fish in the very big pond – or sea – of the Commons and the Palace of Westminster.

Moreover, Jerry O'Sullivan did not succeed Alice. She was followed by the ebullient and delightful Frank McElhone. John was miffed but seemed to take it well. Or did he?

One day when I was seeing him, I was alone, Alex was teaching. He, John, was in excellent sparkling form, entertaining all the rest of us at the lunch table. When he was in full stride, however, a Corporation officer in the official green and gold uniform came up, jangling a brown package which clearly had metallic contents. He knew better than to interrupt John the raconteur. Nevertheless, his presence and thoughtless, nervous jangling was beginning to annoy John. The storyteller struggled to the end of his story. He won the appreciative laughter he sought but it was less noisy, less fulsome than he would have wished. Turning to the staff member he looked up at him.

'Ay, whit is it?' he asked.

'Sorry, Bailie,' said the uniformed man. 'But Charlie sent this for you.'

'Charlie?' growled the Bailie.

'Aye, Charlie,' replied the man, risking a thin, unconvincing smile.

'Charlie?' said John, demonstrably still perplexed.

'Aye, Charlie – the joiner fella,' said the man, oozing embarrassment.

This time John caught up with what was happening.

'Och, aye! That Charlie!' and with that he accepted the package. 'Thanks,' he said.

'Tha's a' right, Bailie,' said the man and with relief radiating from him turned and departed.

John put the heavy package on the table. He turned towards me – all the others had drifted away – but his features were devoid of amiability. Indeed he was poised to growl.

'Did you work for McElhone at the election?' he asked me. It was almost a snarl, an accusation.

'Yes, of course I did,' I replied.

'Why?' he asked.

'Why??' I replied. 'Why? For two reasons. Firstly, because like you he is a personal friend, and secondly, because he was the official Labour Party candidate. Either would have been a good reason: together they constituted a very good reason.'

John softened visibly.

'Aye,' he said. 'You were right. You are right.'

There was a pause. Then in softer, friendlier tones, he almost smiled at me. 'You would see our rooms at Gorbals Cross?' It was more a statement than a question, but the query was there as well.

'Yes,' I said. 'I was in them fairly often.'

'What did you make of them?' he asked.

'They were good – very good,' I said and went on: 'Very, very good for temporary accommodation.'

'Aye,' said John who gave voice to a deep, deep sigh.

Again there was a pause.

'And what did you make of the SNP rooms?' he asked.

'Well, I wasn't in them,' I said.

Again he was quite angry.

'Oh, I know that,' he half-roared.

'They certainly looked the part,' I said. 'They were big. They were bright. They shone out over open ground. They shone like the Cloch lighthouse. Then again, there were lots of cars parked opposite. They gave the impression of great activity though I reckoned some of the cars never moved. But you have to give it to them. It all looked the part.'

'Aye, they did,' said John. 'You know the SNP crowd in here was bumming about how much they had spent on them. The building is due for demolition in about five to ten years' time. They think they have the tenancy until the building comes down. They don't. They did not double-check. Their occupancy finished at midnight last night. I've got the tenancy for us since then. That was a joiner from the Direct Labour Department out changing the locks. They are ours now. Come the general election they will be ours.'

There was another pause. Then John changed the subject. He was due to be interviewed on television later that evening. The topic was to be school closures. With diminishing school rolls the city had a surplus of schools. The city leaders felt obliged to close some schools, not least in the centre of town. He would be asked what was to become of the buildings.

I suggested he should talk about clinics, community centres and the like but that he should try to turn the subject to city centre schools. The school on the island at Woodlands Road across from the 'Dough School' could go to Glasgow University while Allan Glen's, opposite Strathclyde University, could go to that establishment. Indeed, that latter solution would be a very appropriate transfer in view of the mathematical and scientific tradition of both the institutions involved. I argued he should readily acknowledge that the universities were experiencing liquidity problems – in other words, they were 'skint' – but that he could say he was certain they could negotiate a peppercorn rent, not necessarily as dramatic and romantic as a snowball on Midsummer's Day, but something not inordinately expensive.

John on live television was an unpredictable performer but that night I was proud of him. He batted very well and at the end he was talking as though he had been 'au fait' with peppercorn rents all his life.

When I arrived in my office the next morning at 8.45, my secretary, who had been in since 8.30, told me in an authoritative tone not to undo my coat: the Registrar wanted to see me ASAP.

George Thomson had retired and a man called Richardson had succeeded him. I did not warm to him and frankly we did not like each other. When I was shown into his room he turned on me immediately.

'Did you prime that clown Mains for his television interview last night?'

'Yes, I did. Why?' I replied.

'Why??' he almost shouted. 'Why?? You know that it is our declared policy and certainly that of the Principal that we shall never go north of Cathedral Street,' he replied.

'Yes, but it smacks of a policy fated to be abandoned. Property and sites to the south of our campus are twice and thrice the price of those to the north. Moreover, Allan Glen's people and former pupils would be delighted to see their school and its nomenclature become part of this University,' I explained.

'No, they wouldn't,' said the Registrar. 'They would hate us for destroying their school.'

'We would be doing no such thing. The Corporation and demographic change are doing that.'

'Well, I'm not asking you, I'm telling you. Do not interfere with matters of University policy on buildings. Sir Samuel (Curran) does not want to cross Cathedral Street or go east of High Street. Court agrees and that is that. Now go back up the hill and get on with that for which we pay you.'

'And which I do rather well,' I ventured. 'Good morning, Registrar.' And with that I left.

Some time later – not all that long afterwards – we learned that the Collins Company, the book publishers and famous printers of the Bible, was intent on abandoning its huge building on Cathedral Street, on the north side of the street, let it be noted, and moving their activities to a new custom-built facility in Bishopbriggs. We were interested in acquiring the about-to-be-abandoned building – despite its northern location. So we bought it at a bargain price.

Part of the deal was that we would do the bulk of the cleaning: the Collins folk would concentrate on their new location.

In the course of our cleaning we came across one of those large metal signs which used to decorate the nation's railway stations and carriageways such as that which swept up to St. Enoch's station and hotel of the same name. I can see them still:

'THEY COME AS A BOON AND A BLESSING TO MEN,
THE PICKWICK, THE OWL AND THE WAVERLEY PEN.'

Virol for growing girls.
(Nothing for growing boys.)

'Guinness is good for you.'

'Bovril prevents that sinking feeling.'

The metal sign we found was magnificent:

'Holy Scripture, writ divine,
Bound in leather – one and nine.
Satan trembles when he sees
Bibles sold as cheap as these.'

[One and nine was or had been one shilling and nine pence – less than ten new pence.]

I thought then and I think now that the advertisement was magnificent, despite using an adjective where I would have used an adverb. But - quibbles apart - it is wonderful.

And one last point. Having purchased and obtained the Collins Building we re-named it after the Principal. It was and still is the Curran Building – even though it is on the north side of Cathedral Street.

Nelson Gray

Nelson Gray came from the Edinburgh area.

On leaving school during the war he volunteered for the Fleet Air Arm, which took its young men at 17 - unlike the RAF which, while accepting and recruiting men of 17, did not call on their services until they were 18. For the intervening months they were assigned to the Air Corps and remained civilians. They had a small silver badge to wear: I know, I wore one.

But Nelson went to the Fleet Air Arm. He was instructed to report to Portsmouth. He knew better than to report in short trousers and his two full-length pairs did not look the part – so he reported in a kilt and a tweed jacket. When he approached the main gate a fat, heavily-built C.P.O. who was directing the traffic through the entrance, first gave voice to blasphemy and then added: 'We're in trouble now. Bonnie Prince Charlie has come to join the Navy.'

Later that night Nelson sat with his fellow recruits marking their newly-issued uniforms and gear with their names and numbers. Introductions, self-introductions were in vogue.

'I'm Trevor and I come from Cheltenham,' said one youth.

'And I am Jonathan Woodcott and I live in Tonbridge Wells,' said another as the process continued.

They had Ralph from Scarborough and Glyn from Swansea and Jack from a village in rural Leicestershire.

Nelson could see his turn was coming. Was he going to say he was Nelson and give rise to hoots of laughter, maybe scepticism and maybe derision? 'What about you?' asked Trevor turning towards Nelson.

'I am Hamish and I come from Edinburgh,' was the report and the invisible baton passed again.

'My name is Raymond. Our home is in Somerset but we have a town house in Kensington and I have been living there.' And so the introductions ceased.

It says something about the myopia of youth that as the weeks passed no-one commented on the fact that 'Hamish' had put N. Gray on his equipment. Later, when asked, a friend said he assumed Hamish was a second name.

Nelson became a pilot and, thank God, avoided injury and survived the war. On release he enrolled to study for the ministry of the Congregational Church. He did well and on ordination was appointed an assistant minister in one of the largest Congregational Churches in Edinburgh. Within a year or two he obtained a charge in his own right. It was in the Parkhead District of Glasgow.

Such were the modest beginnings of his Ministerial career.

Yet he was destined to spend the last 20 or so years of that career as Head of Religious Broadcasting at Scottish Television, a job which he did extremely well. He had another Minister as his assistant: Eric Hudson was a Church of Scotland minister and still is, though he no longer works for Scottish Television where, as with all British broadcasting, religious programming is in decline. Nelson's department was one of the best in the company. In addition to the two ordained there was a delightful layman called Paterson and a young director of programmes called McDonald. Their output exceeded in both quantity and quality that of any other ITV company of comparable size and frequently outshone that of some of the large network companies such as ATV and Granada.

When Nelson had taken over at his Parkhead charge it soon became apparent that it was well within his competence. Yet the acceptance of the Parkhead ministry presented Nelson with a quandary. The difficulty was this. Nelson had long complained about bus-loads of football supporters travelling across Scotland to support teams located miles away. For his part, Nelson had long argued that every man should support his local team. Nelson's church and modest manse were in Parkhead and, of course, the local senior football club was Glasgow Celtic – with its predominantly Irish-Catholic support. Nelson saw – saw only too clearly – that it was time to 'put up or shut up!' But which?

Nelson pondered long and hard. He resolved to go to Celtic Park and, although he could ill afford it, to go to the stand. At the end of his third or fourth visit he was making his way slowly towards the exit. He was walking along the long, broad concreted area at the back of the old seating area when he was accosted by a wee man in an ill-fitting navy blue suit.

'Excuse me,' said the man, 'but did you pay to come in here?'

Although normally of a benign and slow-to-anger temperament Nelson was inclined to bridle. 'Of course I paid! What are you suggesting – that I sneaked in or something like that?'

'No, no! You misunderstand me. You are a minister, aren't you? You don't wear a dog collar – well, no' when you come here. But you are a minister. You have the church in Westmuir Street. Well, that's it, isn't it? The clergy, the cloth get in for nothing. So you don't need to pay!'

'I knew Roman Catholic priests were given free admission. But I never heard of it applying to others. Are you sure you are right?'

'Oh, aye,' replied the wee man. He hesitated. 'You have to be ordained. Are you ordained?' And having acknowledged Nelson's half-mumbled assent, he raced on: 'Well, you might as well accept it. No' many of your folk come. But you are no' very well paid, are you? The stipend – that's what you call it, isn't it? – is no' very big so the money might as well stay in your pocket.' He paused: 'Mind you, you have to come in a special gate, but my pal Liam is in charge of it.'

163

With that he turned and acclaimed a tall thin man who in reporting to the call shuffled over.

'Liam, this is – whit's your name again? Oh, aye, it's on the board across from the Wayside Pulpit board. It's Gray, isn't it? Liam, you'll let Mr Gray in through your gate, won't you?'

'Oh, aye,' said Liam. 'Mind you, Mr Gray, you've no idea the tricks some folk play in trying to get in – second hand Salvation Army uniforms, collars turned back to front and a second scarf but I know you noo an' Ah'll be glad tae see you, Sir.'

And so it was for what I believe was the better part of eighteen years Nelson and Liam played their parts in a fortnightly litany.

The queue shuffled forward while Liam stood by the gate and pronounced:

'Afternoon, Father.'
'Afternoon, Father.'
'Afternoon, Father.'
'Afternoon, Father.'
'Afternoon, Canon.'
'Afternoon, Father.'
'Afternoon, Father.'
'Afternoon, Father.'
'Afternoon, Father.'
'Afternoon, Monsignor.'
'Afternoon, My Lord.'
'Afternoon, Father.'
'Afternoon, Father.'
'Hello there, Mr Gray ......'

It was Nelson who told me all this. I used to tell Nelson that when he wrote his autobiography the title had to be 'Hello there, Mr Gray.' Sadly he did not live to write his autobiography.

I did the obituary for the *Glasgow Herald*, as it then was. I reported the Celtic Park story, but two ladies telephoned me to rebuke me. Nelson, I was told, had been very active in CND. Why, I was asked, had I not reported that? That was much more important than silly stories about men going to football matches.

No doubt the ladies were correct, but I could not report something I did not know. In any event, I preferred the football story and I reckon that most Glaswegians would.

A Formidable Lady

Her name was Lindsay Tomlinson and was destined to become Lindsay Tomlinson-Massie. And this is how we know her. That said, it is not quite true – for there are three good reasons why we cannot use her real name.

She was and is delightful company. She is an unusual lady – a one-off. She is tall, at least an inch or two over six feet. She is large-boned and consequently is well built. Yet she is not unduly heavy and on a dance floor conveys not the slightest suggestion of being over-weight.

But it is her personality that is her strongest feature. She is lively and entertaining. She makes friends easily and having made them keeps them. She always has an anecdote or a joke. She is a gifted conversationalist and is capable of slipping into company of any social status. She is slow to take offence and never offends.

When some friends and I first encountered this formidable lady she was married to a Baptist minister and living in a city on the east coast of Scotland. For much of the year she spent three days and two nights away from home as she was teaching at a young offenders' institution in the central belt. It was rumoured that when the pupils became obstreperous, her tactic was simple: she took a skull in each hand and banged them together. As a result she was said to be the institution's only teacher who had no disciplinary problems.

Some time before we met her, Lindsay and her husband had bought the manse in which they were living. The church community had been experiencing a liquidity problem. The young couple suggested they could alleviate the problem by purchasing the house. The church authorities accepted the offer so the legal work was done and the money transferred.

This piece of business could have been expected to lead to a phase of marital bliss. And by all accounts it did – but not for as long as expected. The situation deteriorated even further and separation and then divorce ensued.

The settlement was that Lindsay took the house, having, as it were, bought out her now former husband. So we found Lindsay living like a pea in a whistle, on her own in her 8-apartment stone-built villa.

Some twelve to eighteen months after the settlement Lindsay threw a party. It was a great success – like most things organised by this most efficient and capable lady. In the course of the evening one guest asked whether she had considered selling:

'This house would make a very fine manse,' said the guest.

Lindsay patiently asserted that it had been a manse – once upon a time! She added that she had no wish to sell. In light of what followed, we must conclude that either the guest misunderstood – or chose to misunderstand.

Two or three weeks after the party the door-bell rang and when Lindsay opened the front door, she was confronted by a cheery-looking wee man in clerical garb. He introduced himself, explained that he was acting for the local Episcopalian Bishop and that his Lordship understood the house was likely to come on the market and was inclined to think it could prove to be a suitable manse.

Lindsay tried to disabuse him but observed that if he wished to 'see over' the house he was very welcome. So she invited him to enter.

We never learned whether he took a shine to the house but it appeared he took a shine to Lindsay. A situation which seemed to be substantiated when he moved in and became resident.

As one of our crowd observed, it was wrong to jump to conclusions as he might have been a lodger, a celibate lodger. Nevertheless, our majority understanding was the gentleman who was not old but was of moderately mature years had been a fairly recent late entrant to the Anglican priesthood. Again, our majority understanding was that Lindsay and the gentleman made lovely music together...

Such we believed was the scenario for some months and then one afternoon there was another ring on the door-bell. This time the visitor was the Bishop. He expressed his dismay at the domestic arrangement, he did not mince his words in demanding that either the couple should marry or the curate should move out of that house and sever all association with Lindsay.

It seemed only weeks, but maybe it was months, after receiving that intelligence that we learned that Lindsay was to be married. Naturally we took it that the groom was our curate/priest/minister/vicar.

But NO!

The groom we learned was a consultant at a local hospital. He and Lindsay had met at a dinner-party and it had been an instance of 'one enchanted evening' stuff: they were madly in love. It was as simple as that.

And so they married. Two of our crowd were at the reception which followed the ceremony in a Registrar's Office. Within a year Lindsay was pregnant and had a boy who was a hefty twelve pounds at birth.

Perhaps I should have explained earlier that Lindsay and the folk I knew who knew her were all members of a Government Advisory Committee which met six times a year, generally in Glasgow but on occasions in other towns such as Inverness and Stranraer. The Secretary of the committee was a man called Smillie: he was pleasant, friendly and efficient. He was, however, a worrier. One day some months after the birth of Lindsay's boy, Smillie telephoned me. He was in a state of great agitation.

'Mrs Tomlinson-Massie is coming to the next meeting,' he declared, clearly shocked.

'Good,' I replied.

'But she is intending to bring her baby.'

'So be it,' I said. 'Either the child is quiet or it is noisy: if it is quiet there is no problem whereas if it is noisy she and the baby withdraw. It is simple as that!'

166

'No, Chairman,' said the Secretary, 'I am sorry to disagree but it is not as simple as that. She is nursing the baby; she is breast-feeding it.'

I acknowledged that this was a shade more difficult.

'Nevertheless,' I continued, 'neither you nor I shall comment. Let her bring the child. If the situation becomes, shall we say, 'difficult', I shall deal with it. Is there anything else?'

Somewhat miffed Mr Smillie said 'No' and wished me good-day.

Come the day of the meeting the committee assembled in a Glasgow hotel. Like the Count of Monte Cristo Lindsay arrived to the striking of the clock. She had the baby in a sort of carrier-bag, placed it on two chairs at the back of the room and took her place at the table, helping herself to a cup of coffee and two chocolate biscuits as she did so.

The meeting got under way and we made good progress through the Agenda. Then as noon approached the young Tomlinson-Massie started to gurgle. To begin, it was a soft gurgle. Undismayed, Lindsay rose, lifted the child from his cot-like bag and brought him to the table and started to undo her blouse.

Immediately there was an uproar of protestation. Nearly every female member was talking and two male members chipped in as well.

'Lindsay, my dear,' I pronounced, hoping I sounded authoritative. 'As you see, some of your colleagues are distressed at the idea of what you intend to do. My view is that the men should not determine the propriety and acceptability of what you propose. I believe that ladies and only the ladies should decide.'

So I declared a comfort break.

'I suggest you and your female colleagues discuss the matter while all the men withdraw. On our return you can advise us of the findings though it may be apparent which side prevailed.'

When the men were returning, with some diffidence, we met Lindsay coming out with the baby tucked under her arm like a rugby ball. 'I lose,' she declared, 'lost 4 votes to 2 with two abstentions. Instead of the privacy of our committee room, I am going to have to feed him in a public corridor' – though it should be noted that it was a very quiet corridor.

It was clear that Lindsay regarded her female colleagues as reactionary – whereas she was very much her own girl. She contributed wonderfully to our committee and to others on which she served. She deserved high recognition in the Honours lists but such recognition was not forthcoming. Perhaps the Establishment found her too independent and too spirited.

Lindsay went on to write a brilliant novel which was to have been the basis of a British-made movie but the entrepreneur who was to be the main source of funding withdrew and the scheme foundered.

Lindsay now lives contentedly in the Hebrides. She was a formidable and wonderful lady – and still is.

The Would-Be Traveller

This all happened rather a long time ago – back in the days when the Glasgow Tourist Office was not in its present well-appointed premises on the south side of George Square, but in a wooden construction on the east side of the square. As I recall it, it was a summer's day in the early to middle sixties.

At that time queues forming in banks, railway booking offices and enquiry offices did not form one queue with clients called forward in an orderly manner but instead individual queues formed up in front of the various positions as they still do in some airports. As most folk arrived seeking attention they had to choose which queue to join and then and now, in the few instances where the 'old' arrangement prevails, most members of the public understandably elect for the shortest line. Some, however, hold back and try to figure whether some queues are moving more quickly than others and whether, if this is so, which is the fastest.

On going into the Tourist Office I too held back and tried to assess the merits and demerits and for better or worse chose not the shortest line but one which seemed to be moving more quickly than the others. As I was reaching the point where I was third in line, I could see that I was destined to be dealt with by a young man who was probably still a teenager. He looked nervous but he appeared to be dealing quickly and efficiently with his clients.

Eventually I was second when the man ahead of me stepped up to the counter. He was a tall American with a build and carriage which suggested he could play alongside James Stewart or Gary Cooper in a movie about the development of the West in the eighteen-eighties.

The boy addressed him.

'Aye,' he said. 'Whit kin Ah dae fur ye?'

The American hitched his trousers and ran his other hand through his hair.

'Well, now,' he started. 'I'm sortofa, kindofa interested in this trip where one goes by train to Ball-lock (he meant Balloch) and proceeds on a boat called 'Maid of the Lock' which sails on Lock Lomond to Inversnaid where you join a coach which goes to Stronacklackar where you take a second boat, a smaller boat 'Sir Walter Scott' on Lock Katrine which takes you the length of that loch to …'

He did not manage to complete his sentence. The young man cut across him.

''Sno' gaun',' he interjected. 'Rra biler's burst!'

There was a pause. The American was confused and clearly had not made much of the young man's comments. His body-language suggested that at best he regarded it as a Gaelic greeting.

'Yeah, yeah,' said the American. 'As I was telling you, I'm kind of keen on this trip by Lock Lomond and Lock Katrine ... '

Again the young man interjected, on this occasion with a visible irritation.

'Ah telt ye afore, 'sno' gaun'. It's rra biler. It's burst!'

The American was confused. He stood annoyed and dumb-founded. Trying to be helpful I tapped him on the shoulder.

'Excuse me,' I opened. 'But I believe the young man is endeavouring to tell you that one of the vessels is out of commission. It appears the boiler is in need of repair.'

The American's face was a combination of enlightenment and annoyance.

'Well, why the hell did he not say so?' he exploded.

I tried to sound sympathetic and to suggest I understood his annoyance.

'I believe he was doing his best to do just that.'

Nowadays the staff in the Tourist Office speak conventional English – and some other languages to boot!

Language Matters

It is one of the regrets in my life that I have no affinity with other languages. It appears I have neither the feeling for them nor the ear. At school I did badly at French. There was no rapport whatsoever with the French master. Rather, there was a mild mutual antagonism.

During my five years at that school I was given corporal punishment – 'scuds' – twice. Once I was given four of the best for throwing snowballs. Why does Almighty God send us snow if not to enable boys to throw snowballs? Then in my final year the French teacher gave me twelve for swearing at him in French. Surely he should have known that I was quite incapable of such competence.

I am equally bereft of any ability to play a musical instrument. And I am barely competent as a swimmer.

But I have no regrets about my lack of affinity with and competence in gardening. The day God gave out the green fingers I must have been at the Rangers end waving a large Union Jack.

During Holy Week of 2009 one of the books read on BBC Radio 4 was the fine work *Sisters in Sinai*. This work relates the experiences of Agnes and Margaret, the twins from Kilbarchan in Renfrewshire. Following the early death of their mother their father resolved not to re-marry but, instead, to take care of the girls himself with the assistance of his domestic staff. Finding the girls had a facility for languages, the father persuaded them to study modern languages and as an inducement promised that on mastering a language to a level of modest competence the girls could have a holiday in the appropriate country. As a result their application led to vacations in France, Germany, Spain and Italy and all before as late teenagers they attended a finishing school in Kensington where they stubbornly declined to cultivate an Oxbridge accent and, instead, continued to speak their English with a fine Scottish accent.

These ladies went on to work in Egypt, the Holy Land and Syria on early Christian documents, not least in the language spoken by Jesus, and became two of the most distinguished Biblical scholars of their day, a status which resulted in a spate of honorary degrees from home and abroad.

My envy of their skills in languages reminds me of another story about languages. This comes from a BBC Radio 4 programme of some twenty-plus years ago. This told the story of a German aristocrat and his Russian aristocratic wife and the story of their schloss and their vineyard in the Rhine.

We learned that in the closing months of the War a British bomber returning from a raid deeper in the Reich had been obliged to jettison its incendiary bombs. These had fallen on the schloss and the resulting fire destroyed the building.

The BBC interviewer asked the owner whether he had been and, perhaps still was, angry and resentful. He, in turn, made it clear he was not resentful. There were, it transpired, two reasons for the apparently relaxed response. First, he saw the incident as part of the vagaries of war. 'These things happened,' he observed. The second reason was that he was relieved that it was the house that had been destroyed and not the vineyards: the schloss had been re-built in one generation whereas it would have taken several generations to restore the vineyards.

Towards the end of the programme the interviewer turned to the question of languages.

First to be interviewed on this topic was the wife. We learned that as a girl and as a young woman she had spoken Russian, Polish, Hungarian, English and French. Later she acquired German. How had that all come about, she was asked.

She explained that her family had estates in Russia, Poland and Hungary which explained the presence of the first three. The English had come from an English governess and the French from having French maids.

When it was the husband's turn it emerged that he had German, of course, and Russian, acquired on the Russian Front, English and French, not least as he too had been subject to an English governess and his family had employed French maids. The interviewer was clearly most impressed, so much so that she ventured further.

'Are you prepared to tell me what language you use – how shall I phrase it? - in the bedroom?'

'Yes,' he replied.

'And what is it?' asked the interviewer.

'Spanish,' said the estate owner.

The microphone picked up the audible gasp of the interviewer.

A Weekend In Dublin

Lewis Brodie was one of a group of exceptionally clever and talented students who attended the Scottish College of Commerce in the early sixties. They were working for an Associateship of that College and for the B.Sc. in Economics of the University of London. Many of them were destined to have quite illustrious careers.

On graduating, Brodie joined the Administrative Staff of London University where, having established himself as a competent and hard-working administrator, he was entrusted with the formidable task of gathering-in some eight, ten, twelve disparate Teacher Training Colleges and Colleges of Education into the one Faculty of Education of the University. Not only did he succeed in this venture, he did it within budget and within the time prescribed.

Shortly after this achievement he was appointed Registrar of the Glasgow College of Technology which at the time was a Local Authority College but which was destined to become a Central Institution and, later still, the third University in the city.

Here it should be revealed that he and I had an agreement or understanding. The intention was that he would become Registrar of this institution while I would become Principal. He succeeded in achieving his part of the plan but I failed. I did succeed in being one of the final four candidates for the Principalship but in their lack of wisdom and courage the committee appointed one of two internal candidates and I do not regard it as churlish to observe that his administration was undistinguished. It was all rather sad. I genuinely believed that Lewis and I, working in tandem, could have brought a kind of synergy to the scene and this to the benefit of the staff and more importantly to the students and to the city.

Having accepted the College appointment Lewis persuaded his wife that they should live in Aberfeldy in Perthshire and then, sometime later, in a village on the south side of Loch Tay. He drove each day from there to the city and back in the evening. It was a long and dangerous journey as reference to a map will confirm. In addition, he smoked eighty strong cigarettes each day and these two factors regrettably explain why this brilliant and most congenial of men is no longer with us.

It is here that our story takes a turn. One evening Lewis and his wife were in a pub in Aberfeldy when it transpired that a young policeman was anxious to sell his tickets for the Ireland v Scotland rugby international. The young man had been looking forward to the trip, but a middle-rank member of the royal family was coming to Strathtay to visit friends over that same week-end and as a result all police leave had been cancelled. Lewis took a notion to go and see the game and a fellow former student and consequently bought the lad's tickets.

The package deal involved flying out of Edinburgh on the Friday evening and returning by an early morning flight on the Monday. On reporting to the airport on the Friday Lewis reckoned that he and two others, a minister of the Kirk and his Divinity-student nephew, were the only sober men embarking the plane and later it emerged that the same trio were the only travellers not charging the trip to expenses.

On the Saturday he slept late, lunched early, enjoyed the game though Scotland lost and then, in the evening, visited Denis Mitchell who after a short successful spell in broadcasting had taken a law degree and was working for the Irish Government. They had a fine meal and then over more than one bottle of brandy talked about cabbages and kings and of their days as students in Glasgow.

Eventually, between one and two in the morning a taxi was summoned. As the taxi pulled away Lewis asked the driver whether his hotel would still be open or whether he would have to call on the services of the night porter. The driver's response was to bellow with laughter and he nearly drove his cab up a lamp-post. Three blocks from the hotel they could hear the noise. On arrival at the hotel Lewis could see that a temporary bar had been erected in the foyer but that the rest of the foyer had been taken over by one enormous rugby scrum. Some eighty to a hundred Scots were pushing one way while an Irish force of customers of about the same size was pushing with equal if not greater force in the opposite direction.

Sitting on a high stool at the end of the bar was a shabbily dressed Dubliner with a badly stained raincoat and a battered soft hat set at a rakish angle. Every now and again he would take out his wallet, extract another bank note and nod at a young barman who was clearly serving him and him alone. The barman was pulling pints of stout and carefully ensuring that each was of full measure and had the expected layer of frothy cream. As each pint was drawn it was placed conveniently beside the customer.

The particular matter which intrigued Lewis was what the man did with his recurring purchases. Was he drinking them? No, definitely not!

Nor was he distributing them to deserving warriors in the two armies, doing so with commendable objectivity rather than partisanship.

No, what he was doing was to take a pint carefully, slip from his high-stool and then with great aplomb, drop-kick the glass tumbler over and into the scrum. The liquid poured over many while the glass hit one unfortunate and then fell or slithered to the floor where it was pulverised into the carpet.

As Lewis reported, this was remarkable, and what was even more remarkable was that no-one remonstrated, absolutely no-one objected.

Our overall conclusion was that the rugby world is a world apart. One such weekend was enough for Lewis. He continued to see his friend Denis but not over rugby weekends in Dublin.

Workers' Unity

This story concerns and was told by the late Robert Crampsey. Within the Crampsey family and to a small, close coterie of friends he was known as Bert. When he became a national figure he was known to the wider world as Bob.

In the Thirties of the twentieth century a very select and influential political group was known as F.R.B.C. which stood for 'For Roosevelt Before Chicago', that city being the location of the 1932 Democratic Party Convention which saw F.D.R. emerge as the Democratic Candidate for the Presidency of the USA. Some of us were privileged to be members of K.B.B.B. – Knew Bert Before Bob.

This story concerns one of the summers of the late forties or early fifties when Robert was an undergraduate at the University of Glasgow. In those days almost all the students from working-class and lower middle-class families found it prudent - no, necessary - to take a summer job. One year Bert spent the summer as a porter and general 'humpher' in a hotel in the Kyles of Bute. In the summer of our story he was a conductor on the tram-cars of the wonderful Transport Department of Glasgow Corporation.

On his first day Bert reported early to the depot, not far from his home in Shawlands. He was wearing an already used green uniform, which had been cleaned and pressed for its new recipient along with the matching hat. While he was one of many sitting around waiting for allocation, a wizened wee man with a gnarled face walked up to him.

'You a student?' he asked. Robert acknowledged that he was.

'Right,' said the man, who was known throughout the depot as Wily Willie Whylie. 'That will be one and ninepence.'

'What?' remarked Robert.

'Aw, naw,' said W.W.W. 'Don't say you are gaun' tae be difficult!! Ah telt ye afore – wan an' ninepence!'

As the wee man was speaking Bert quietly debated the matter deeply within his own mind. His initial reaction to the demand was to hold out for a lucid – and acceptable – explanation. But he thought better of it. He reckoned it was prudent to go along with it.

'All right,' he said, and proceeded to count out and hand over a shilling, a sixpenny piece and a three-penny bit.

'Fine,' said the wee man and continued: 'And congratulations. You are now a fully paid-up member of the Depot's Branch of the Transport and General Workers Union and as such you are entitled, comrade, to all the benefits thereof!'

And after the slightest of breaks raced on: 'Right, see us yer hat,' whereupon he took the hat off Robert's head, glanced at the label and cried out: 'Who is six and seven-eighths?'

'Me!' called a right towsy untidy man with oily hair.

'Right,' cried Whylie, and he marched over to the untidy man. The shop steward, for such he was, took the oily hat off Sanny, the oily man, and plonked it on Bert's head, and tossed Bert's hat over to his new comrade, the hat's new owner - Sanny.

'Now,' he said to Robert. 'You pay attention. You speak posh, like, so they'll put you on a posh route – like Clarkston or Giffnock or Rouken Glen. It's posh folk and big hooses oot there. Auld women pour oot the big houses and come on yer tram. Don't you take their insults. They think they're haughty but they are just rude. They'll react and tell you they're gaun' tae report you. 'I'll take your number,' they say, and open up a big haun-bag and bring oot a wee notebook or diary with a wee pincil up its bum an' they start tae write doon the number oan rra cap. But it's no' your number, is it? It is Sanny's number, for it's Sanny's hat, is it no'?'

W.W.W. continued: 'When a complaint comes in the clerk who deals with it marks it up. 'Complaint arose from Giffnock Route but conductor of the number quoted was on the Springburn/Garngad run. Apparently number misquoted. No action possible'. The clerk then files it away! You unnerstaun'?'

At that point Robert and Whylie nodded to each other in agreement. Whylie concluded the induction: 'Welcome aboard, comrade!'

The Cruise Round The Northern Islands With The Great Jimmie Currie

This started as another short, short story, but it grew of its own volition.

So far as my involvement was concerned it happened as the century turned from the twentieth to the twenty-first. At the time one of my part-time activities was trying to help a very fine body based in the Dixon Halls in Crosshill in Glasgow. The organisation strove to help and care for carers, those wonderful folk who find themselves working long, hard and unpaid hours looking after others, mainly relatives, who are severely incapacitated. On one occasion I produced a business plan, but it was not very good. I was assured by kind colleagues that there were other occasions when I was a bit more useful.

Each year, as a side activity, the Committee organised a concert and buffet meal for Senior Citizens in the district. One year – and I fear it was only one year – I was asked to be the M.C. and interlocutor at the concert.

Life has taught me not to envisage what form a 'new' event was likely to take, so I approached the concert with an open mind. I was then somewhat surprised to find about 200 folk at the event and even more surprising was that nearly half of them, and almost all of them ladies, were of Indian sub-continent origin. Perhaps rather uncharitably I assumed that most of this group were primarily, if not exclusively, interested in the food and that they almost certainly were not looking forward to Archie singing 'The Road to Mandalay' or the Boys' Brigade piper doing his bit or Sadie singing 'The Rose of Tralee' or Willie McShane on his mouth-organ and least of all my trying to be funny.

In opening the entertainment I explained that my contributions linking the events would consist of ten or twelve supposed jokes. All of them were jokes I had acquired from men and women who were ordained (or near-ordained). I hoped that no-one would be offended at material emanating from such a source. If, however, offence was taken I would privately reveal the branch of the Churches from which the particular joke had arisen and the offended could raise it with the raconteur's superiors – if, that is, that branch of the church had superiors.

For all my reservations and apprehension the concert went reasonably well and apparently my jokes were acceptable and some gave rise to moderate laughter. The buffet was a greater success.

By the time the tea and coffee were being served a very well-dressed lady with an air of great respectability came up to me and asked to speak to me.

'I just wanted to say that my sister and I – that's Elma in the blue dress and the polka-dot silk scarf – enjoyed your jokes, very much indeed.

Actually, we recognised three of the jokes as stories told by the Reverend Mr James Currie. Last year we, that is Elma and I, went on a cruise – 'Northern Islands' it was called. We sailed from Leith and went to Orkney, Fair Isle, Shetland, the Faroes, Iceland, an island off Greenland, St Kilda, two islands in Ireland – Achill and one of the Aran Isles - the Isle of Man, Rathlin, our Arran and we disembarked in Greenock. We had an after-dinner speaker on each of our twelve nights and on three of them the speaker was Mr Currie. This is how we recognised his jokes. They had the stamp and style of Mr Currie, didn't they? Elma and I discussed all this over the buffet and we agreed I should tell you all this and tell you as well what we regarded as the funniest, the best of his jokes, so I would like to tell it to you so that you can add it to your repertoire.'

So she did just that – and here it is.

There was a Church of Scotland Parish Minister in Skye who was seen as having, almost epitomising, all the attributes of an exceptionally good minister: knowledge of the Bible; intriguing, interesting preaching; compassionate and genuine pastoral activities; piety; and modesty. He had been born and raised on one of the smaller islands but all his ministry had been conducted in Skye. It had started with his being an Assistant Minister in a large church in Portree, then a charge in a small community near the west coast of the island. Now he had charge in a parish very near to Portree.

It was then a matter of some delight when he was awarded an M.B.E in the Birthday Honours list. His kirk session discussed the situation and the unanimously supported outcome was that they would approach Presbytery with the suggestion that the two bodies share the cost of enabling him to fly to London for the investiture and providing him with sufficient funding to enable him to spend four or five nights in a good four-star hotel. Presbytery agreed, and the whole venture was given a generous write up in *Life and Work*. The writer gave the piece a personal touch and the members of the wider Kirk learned he was a widower and had not taken a holiday since his wife had died some five years earlier.

So off he went to London. On the evening of the day of the investiture he gave himself a good dinner.

On leaving the dining-room he went through to the spacious foyer and bar area and sat at the end of a long couch. In due course a very smart well-dressed young lady came into the hotel and sat down at the other end of the settee. They nodded to each another.

After a while one of them remarked that the foyer was very well lit; indeed, some of the lighting arrangements were very clever and tasteful. After another pause the other said that the curtains were most colourful and well designed. Yet another silence ensued and then the first to speak commended the quality of the carpeting. The other agreed.

There then ensued a fairly long silence, but in due course it was broken and it was the Minister who broke it. 'That's a very fine outfit you are wearing,' he observed. The young lady agreed and went on to say she was very fond of it.

'You must have a very good job, to afford a magnificent outfit like that,' he suggested.

The young lady gave a knowing smile and re-crossed her legs. 'Yes,' she said. 'You see,' she went on, 'I'm a call-girl!'

'Oh, how very interesting,' enthused the Minister. 'I am from Tiree myself!'

The Case of The Wet Cloot

Most folk who encountered Mrs. Annie Kelly for the first time saw her as a big, heavy, hefty, clumsy woman who was almost certainly obese and over-weight. More, they suspected she had lost any agility and fleetness of foot which she had ever enjoyed.

They were wrong.

Annie Kelly was large-boned and well-built. As a girl she had been more than competent at the Irish dancing - shades of 'River Dance' and all that hectic footwork. Even in her late fifties she retained an ease of movement which her bulk belied. Furthermore, she was strong and could lift and re-position many a load which most men could not raise from the floor.

At the time of 'the incident' as it came to be known, she was employed as a cleaner by Ritchie's, one of the many small to middle-sized engineering firms in the Bridgeton area of Glasgow. This undistinguished firm, which was fated to collapse and disappear some ten years later, employed three cleaners. The senior of the three was a Miss Stewart who worked on the top floor of the office block where she looked after the rooms occupied by the Chairman, the Managing Director and the Senior Executives such as the Chief Engineer and his Finance and Accounting counterpart. This remit extended to the smaller offices occupied by the secretaries to these gentlemen, to the Boardroom and to the Executives' toilets and the small kitchen from which appeared the tea, coffee and snacks which fortified the company's captains of industry.

The second cleaner, a Mrs Alice Gilmour, looked after all the offices on the first and second floors and the toilets on these floors. Annie Kelly was responsible for everything at ground level, which included the fairly impressive entrance area, the areas used by the Reception staff, the Telephonists' room, the Postal and Stores rooms and all the toilets and washrooms at the level, not least those in the large and noisy workrooms which constituted the factory. She worked from 6 a.m. until 9.30 and again from 5.30 until 9 in the evening. From 9 am to 9.30 she was expected to scrub, not mop, the extensive floor of the Reception area. It was there that 'the incident' took place one morning in the early fifties. There was a high degree of agreement in the ranks of those primarily concerned as to what had happened on the morning of the incident.

It was about 9.25 as Annie Kelly, who had scrubbed the entire floor, was proceeding to wipe it over prior to her departure that three staff members arrived late. They were not unduly put out at their late arrival. The three consisted of two senior draughtsmen and a senior engineer called Sammy Dobbie. As they crossed the floor they were in good humour which was described by another witness as 'laughing and jostling'. Dobbie proceeded to slip on the wet surface and grabbed out at one of his friends

179

in order to prevent himself falling. As he slithered to the floor he shouted at Mrs Kelly remonstrating with her for not having notices warning all concerned of the dangers of the wet surface. There was agreement to the fact that the lady did not take kindly to his protestation and that she had responded by throwing a dripping, wet cloth at him, whereupon the Personnel Manager was summoned and he in turn instructed her to re-wash the floor. When by 10.15 he had ascertained that she had done so and done it satisfactorily, he rewarded her by sacking her and telling her to collect her belongings and depart – never to return!

When Annie claimed her Unemployment Benefit the staff at the Employment Exchange wrote to the firm on the prescribed form and asked why the claimant had been released. The firm reported that she had been dismissed for gross industrial misconduct in that she had thrown a wet cloth at a senior executive. Mrs Kelly was given a copy of this statement and invited to comment. Her reply was succinct and direct.

To her credit Mrs Kelly readily admitted that she had done what had been alleged. 'Yes,' she wrote, 'I threw the wet cloot at him. I am sorry. I missed him.' It was not clear, however, whether her regret was directed at having thrown the missile or at herself for having failed to hit her target. This matter was not investigated by the Insurance Officer to whom her case was sent for his decision. So far as he was concerned, the lady had conceded that she had tried to hit the member of the Executive Staff and accordingly he disqualified her: he decided she should be denied her benefit for the maximum period of six weeks and this on the grounds that she had lost her employment as a result of her industrial misconduct.

A copy of his decision was sent to Mrs Kelly who was advised that she had the right of appeal. She was, however, inclined to do no more. As she remarked to her friend and neighbour, Mrs McGrory: 'Efter a', Ah did try tae hit him, so Ah did.'

And that could have been the end of the affair and the end of the case.

But that was not to be. Mrs McGrory told her married daughter, who told her husband, who told his brother, who told his pal who told his father who was very active in the Labour Party, who told Bailie Patrick J. Timmons who was a lawyer specialising in Employment Law and who on being told what had happened looked thoughtful and said that it was all very interesting and who then sent word back along the contact trail that the lady should come and see him in his 'surgery' to see what they could do about it.

So it was that, in due course, Mrs Kelly lodged an appeal to have the case heard by the Local Appeal Tribunal.

Some four to five weeks passed between the lodging of the appeal and the time of it being heard and considered by the Local Appeal Tribunal. Pat Timmons set about using the time effectively. Firstly, he drew on local knowledge to find out the names and addresses of those who had witnessed the incident or who had overheard what Dobbie had shouted. After some difficulties he had three of them provide him with statements as to what had occurred. They were not as formal as affidavits but they did add to what was known and were to prove effective. Secondly, he reviewed his own position vis-à-vis actually appearing before the Tribunal. He was only too aware that he could not appear as a lawyer though he was entitled to appear as a friend of or spokesman for the appellant. This he had done in other cases but he was not comfortable in that capacity and so after deliberation he asked John Fulton, a full-time officer of a large general trade union to represent Mrs Kelly despite her not being a member of his or any other such union. Fulton having agreed to speak on behalf of the lady, the third aspect of the Timmons campaign was to spend time with Fulton discussing and reviewing the case while the fourth thing he did was to see a friend named Vincent Baldie who owned nearly twenty shops in and around Glasgow and had him agree to engage Mrs Kelly as a cleaner for his offices in the Merchant City district of the town centre.

At the ensuing hearing of the Tribunal, Fulton argued that there seemed to be complete agreement that as Dobbie had stumbled, he had shouted about the need for warning notices and the cleaner's failure to have such notices exhibited but that it was his understanding that this had been prefaced by a personal address to the claimant. He went on to assert that Dobbie had called her 'a Fenian bastard,' and indeed that 'Fenian' had been preceded by a word of Anglo-Saxon origin. The Chairman of the Tribunal observed that he did not approve of such suggestive language in his Tribunal, whereupon Fulton argued that if the Chairman resented such language, then they could take it that the lady was even more hurt and resentful.

In short, he argued, she had been provoked. Enlarging on his argument, Fulton said it was his contention that it was not enough to ascertain that a worker had done something: it was necessary to try to learn why such action had been taken. It could be that a claimant was provoked and this was one such case. Here, he argued, there were points by way of mitigation.

In dealing with the case the Tribunal took longer than usual. Eventually they accepted that there had been provocation. Their decision was that the disqualification period should be reduced from six weeks to three.

On learning the decision Mrs Kelly was delighted but Pat Timmons wanted her to appeal to the National Insurance Commissioner and out of gratitude the lady agreed.

When the case came before the Commissioner in Edinburgh the arguments were repeated. In addition, it was argued that as a cleaner the lady had no jurisdiction on the matter of the exhibition of warning notices, this being the responsibility of the Health and Safety Officer, who, ironically, was a cousin of Mr Dobbie. When the decision was revealed and duly published in the Ministry of Labour Gazette, the disqualification was upheld but the period had been reduced to one week.

In the years which followed 'The case of the wet cloot', as it became known, it was seen as an important item of case law. To establish that misconduct had taken place was not enough. One had to go further and determine, as far as one could, as to why it had happened as it did.

Mrs Kelly was very happy working in Baldie's and for its part that firm was very happy in having her as part of the team. Mrs Kelly's replacement back in Ritchie's never succeeded in having the entrance and foyer area as smart and as clean as it had been in the days of Annie Kelly.

The Mother Of The Bride

The romance started in Jersey, in St. Helier to be more precise. Theresa was a senior receptionist in a rather fine four-star hotel in the town. Jamie was a sous chef in the same establishment, though each was totally unaware of the other's existence until one Sunday morning when she stumbled as she came out of the big Catholic Church at the top of the town at the end of the 6.30 morning mass.

The last time I looked, which was a few years ago now, this large and impressive church offered eight masses for Sunday observance: two on Saturday evening, four on Sunday morning and the final two on the Sunday evening. Of the eight, three were in English, two in French, one in Latin and the remaining two in Portuguese, this last a testimony to the substantial inflow as a result of the European Union arrangements. I fully expect that the offerings now extend to one or two in Polish. Whatever one says for or against this denomination, the Catholic Church is catholic!

The ten-minute walk from the church to the hotel was the beginning of the romance which bounced along at a fine pace. It was a wise man of good counsel who said that young people should marry within their own socio-economic standing, within their own religion and within their own racial and ethnic grouping. The presence at the church had established one of these three conditions and ten minutes of conversation established the fulfilment of the other two.

Within a twelve-month, an engagement ring had been purchased during a holiday back in the west of Scotland and introductions to her mother on the south-side of Glasgow and to his parents in Coatbridge had set the seal of approval and acceptability.

The formal engagement on the quay at a small bay on Jersey was rounded off with a protracted kiss, followed in turn by three noisy, lively, far from sedate engagement parties. The first of these took place in Theresa's mum's flat in a multi-storey tenement block beside St Francis' church in the Gorbals district of Glasgow. The second was held in a parochial church hall in Coatbridge and the third in a Scout Hall adjacent to but totally independent of the hotel.

In the wake of these events the young couple's conversation turned to three questions of import. They were:

When would they get married?

Where would they get married? And

Where would they go for their honeymoon?

Of these the first and last were easily resolved. They decided to marry at the end of the next year's 'season' and since the Church frowned on the solemnisation of marriage in Advent, to go for a Saturday in late October or early November. As for the honeymoon, Jamie wanted London with all the new movies and with an abundance of theatres and a wide choice of fare.

It was to be the middle question which was to prove to be the most intransigent: where were they to be married?

Regrettably, this was to lead to their first disagreement, though, thank God, not their first quarrel. The difficulty was that each had an answer which to each originator seemed compelling. So far as Jamie was concerned the answer was obvious and this for three reasons.

He wanted the big church in St Helier, his first and most important reason being that this was where they met, this was where she stumbled and he saved her from falling.

His second reason was that it would mean that neither family would feel slighted that it was not on their tribal territory.

His third reason was that by having it in Jersey some of their friends from the hotel would manage to attend the wedding and both the families could have a wee holiday on the island.

But Theresa was for none of it. Her mother was a widow and in recent years her life had been gey drab; she needed a bit of colour in it. The actual day would be Theresa's big day but it could and should be an even bigger day for her mother. To Theresa there was no question about it: they should be married in the large and impressive church of St Francis in Cumberland Street in Glasgow.

And of course she won. She won because Jamie was astute enough to realise that on such a matter the only course open to the young man is total capitulation to the wishes of his beloved – be her arguments rational or irrational.

So it was in late October of the following year the marriage took place in Glasgow. A lot of folk had gathered outside the church to see the principals arrive. When the car with the bride's mother and the two bridesmaids arrived the mature lady let the youngsters descend first. Then and only then did she choose to emerge. She was magnificent in an outfit of organdie and lace lemon and orange. She and her ensemble won gasps of approval and not a little cheering and applause. Her fellow-cleaners from the local school were well to the fore and the supervisor, who was also the union shop steward, raised her arms and pushed her troops back a little while she stepped forward to pronounce what was a half-way house between a verdict and an acclamation.

'Exquisite! Excellent and exquisite,' she declared and raced on to add: 'Elegant, Esther, 'elluva elegant.' Whereupon Esther with a slight bow of the head acknowledged the approval and swept on into the church. As she did so the supervisor turned and addressed her lieges thus:

'Aye, but she'll no' be a' that smart on Monday moarnin' when she's daein' ra boys' lavvies.'

184

Monsignor Francis Duffy

When Frank Duffy was a boy of thirteen going on fourteen, he announced to his parents and the rest of the family that he wanted to become a priest. His mother was delighted and his father not displeased. So it was that he applied to his own local diocese which was the Archdiocese of St. Andrews and Edinburgh.

He was rejected. To his credit, he was not unduly put out by this decision and he chose to attribute it to his being rather young. He applied again the following year and again he was unsuccessful.

Undaunted, he applied yet again the following spring and this time he was bitterly disappointed to be turned down for a third time. No explanation was forthcoming. All of this gave rise to considerable discussion and speculation within the family which prevailed until an uncle, who was a much respected priest within the Archdiocese, offered to go and see the Vocations Director in an attempt to learn what - if anything - was amiss.

The Director was a formidable man called Graham, who had been a Church of Scotland minister but who had converted to Rome and then entered the priesthood. He was very learned and in later years was to become a bishop. To his credit, he did not muck about. In answer to the uncle's query he pointed out they already had the uncle and two of his nephews: they had no intention of creating a dynasty. The young man could go, should go elsewhere.

When the uncle reported back to Frank and the family, the reactions were gey varied and ranged from mild resentment to quiet resignation. In speaking to Frank, the uncle was anxious to stress that all was not lost: for example, there was a plethora of religious orders and he was confident that many of them would be delighted to have him. Frank was for none of it and made it very clear that he wanted to become an 'ordinary' diocesan priest like his uncle and two cousins. The uncle acknowledged that this was both honourable and understandable, but to which diocese did Frank aspire? Frank admitted he did not know and asked which diocese his uncle recommended, but the uncle made it clear he had neither the desire nor the intention of recommendation. It was, he insisted, for Frank to decide.

Frank took this remarkably well and said he would pick another diocese in Scotland in much the same way as his Gran picked horses for the Derby and the Grand National. So he fetched his school bag and extracted his atlas which he opened at the map of Scotland. He also extracted the dividers from his geometry set. He laid it down, said some prayers, blessed himself, lifted the dividers, shut his eyes and plunged the pointed instrument into the map of Scotland. The pointer went through the map at the town of Auchinleck.

'What diocese is that?' he asked.

'Dumfries and Galloway,' replied the uncle.

'Is that a good diocese?' the boy enquired.

The uncle smiled: 'So far as you are concerned, it is a great diocese and with the Grace of God you will help make it even better,' he replied.

I did not know Frank Duffy when he was a young priest in the diocese of Dumfries and Galloway but by all accounts he soon established himself as a good, reliable, hard-working curate and partly because of his attributes and partly because of the nature of that diocese, he was soon appointed parish priest in a large village/small town in the mining airt to the south of Kilmarnock. As the years went by, he was entrusted with bigger and more demanding parishes while, at the same time being sucked more and more into the administrative work of the diocese. In addition to all this, he found himself being appointed to a wide variety of bodies outside the Church. In all of these he served with distinction but the one in which he excelled was the Religious Advisory Committee of Scottish Television. Both the high-command of the company and the Scottish officers of the Independent Broadcasting Authority were delighted with his wise and perceptive contributions to the meetings of the Committee. Truth to tell, the Company should have appointed him as Chairman of the Committee but for what the senior executives saw as good and compelling reasons, they looked elsewhere.

As the years passed and retirement loomed, he was elevated to the rank of Monsignor and, sometime later, moved from demanding duties in Ayr to the somewhat less demanding post of parish priest in the magnificent church of St. Meddan's in Troon.

I could be mistaken but as I recall it, it was while he was based at Troon that he was involved in the matter of a certain dinner. The dinner was to mark the sixtieth anniversary of the ordination of an elderly and much beloved priest.

Monsignor Duffy was the principal celebrant at the concelebrated mass which preceded the meal. He was also to be the Chairman at the dinner and as though all that was not enough, he was to round off the evening by making the presentation to the hero of the day. All of this he did splendidly. His speech at the presentation was recalled by many as having been quite brilliant. It was and is also remembered that when he appeared to finish he announced that he was about to add an addendum to what he had said. Some might regard it as a sour note, but it was not intended as such – nor was it to be seen as in any way detracting in any way from what he had said earlier.

The issue, he explained, was that as he saw it, whoever was to be the main celebrant at the mass, whoever was to be the Chairman at the dinner, whoever was to make the presentation should have had three to six months' notice. He had not had such notice. On the contrary, he had not much more than 48 hours. 'This is dreadful,' he said. 'I sometimes despair of the Church. I wonder how we survived for nearly two thousand years. Clearly, the Holy Spirit is protecting us from our own maladministration.'

He paused and then said: 'I sometimes think that when Christ and His Apostles were climbing the stairs to the room for the Last Supper, Peter elbowed his way up through the others, caught our Blessed Saviour by the fore-arm and said, 'By the way, boss, the boys and me were thinking: would you say a few words?'

The Horrors Of Eastchurch

During my four and a half years in the Royal Air Force I was on sixteen 'stations' which varied considerably in style and acceptability. The first was a one-time luxury flat in Prince Albert Road at the north end of Regent's Park, my colleagues and I having reported earlier that day to Lord's Cricket ground which was the Aircrew Reception Centre. A confiscated public school in Scarborough was very good and two camps in South Africa were most enjoyable while R.A.F. Kinloss was very congenial. By 1947 I was working 24 hours on duty and 24 hours off with the result that I seemed to work and sleep and my recreation consisted of coffee and chess with two friends and a very infrequent expedition to Elgin or Forres, or - and this was very rare - Inverness.

Of all my stations, the worst, by far, was Eastchurch in the middle of the Isle of Sheppey in the Thames Estuary. It had only one redeeming feature: it was proof positive of the existence of Purgatory.

On arrival at this dreadful station in 1945 we were informed that Sheppey was the only place in Britain where one could get malaria. We learned that it had been a Royal Flying Corps station in the First World War. Remarkably, it appeared that many of the senior non-commissioned officers were Londoners, mainly from the East End and around the Elephant and Castle and Clapham Junction. It was said that most of them had been at that station for years, some apparently since the Twenties. The atmosphere of the place left those of us whose spell there was mercifully temporary with the conclusion that some of these NCOs acted as though they believed the station was really theirs.

Those of us who were temporarily there belonged to two miserable groups. The bigger of these two groups consisted of aircrew cadets and the recently qualified who with the end of hostilities in sight had been declared redundant so far as aircrew duties were concerned. The second group, although less numerous, was markedly more tragic. It consisted of experienced airmen, mainly but not exclusively from Bomber Command who, despite being decorated, had been stood down on the grounds that they were now exhibiting 'lack of moral fibre'. In other words they were brave men whose nerves had been shot to pieces, but instead of being treated with compassion were, in effect, being treated as though they were cowards.

It was our surmise that - so far as the High Command at the Air Ministry was concerned - some of them did not know about Eastchurch and what it was like, while those who did know not unnaturally assumed that the 'quasi-permanent' staff consisting of senior medics, psychiatrists, psychologists and competent academics representing a variety of disciplines all supported by a reasonably efficient admin. team of clerks and secretaries were all working hard with a view to directing the woebegone former aircrew personnel to new, useful and appropriate duties almost exclusively as ground staff.

By and large, this is what happened. The difficulty was that there was another element from the ranks of the team of mainly long-serving non-commissioned officers who seemed to take a delight in humiliating and embarrassing those of us who were there to be re-assessed and directed to other duties. Not all of the NCOs perpetrated this unbecoming and occasionally cruel treatment. But some did and sadly it was more prevalent than one could readily forgive. Those of us who had been mere cadets were from to time at the receiving end of this sadistic behaviour but it was apparent to all of us that the most vindictive treatment was directed at those who had been engaged in combat duties with horrendous casualty rates. It was doubly maddening to note that this was being done by men who, it seemed, had never heard or confronted a gun fired in anger.

Anyone interested in this aspect of life at Eastchurch should try to read the research thesis on Eastchurch which was written for a post-graduate degree of the University of Glasgow by Alex Dickson, the one-time senior executive of, and presenter at, Radio Clyde.

There were two incidents to which I was a witness and which, each in its own way, indicated the desperate malaise at this station.

The first of these occurred in the morning of a dreadful, wet and windy day in late February of 1945. There were fifty men to a flight, as it was called, and each flight was supervised or controlled by a sergeant. All fifty-one of us were on a corner of the parade ground. The sergeant had on him a copy of a well-designed information sheet which was frequently up-dated and which provided all the information which could possibly be wanted on all of us who were there for re-allocation. From time to time the sergeant could be seen consulting this document.

In due course he announced his assignment of duties for the day. As he proceeded with his allocations, some of us to quite pleasant tasks, some to duties less congenial, he announced that six of us were to report to another sergeant who would put us to cleaning latrines. He then went on to call out the names. The announcement of the first five names went without event. When, however, he called the sixth name the man concerned proceeded to move from the 'at ease' position to the rigid stance of the 'at attention' position, calling out 'Sergeant' as he did so. The sergeant adopted the tired and tried demeanour of a man who was weary of the pathetic attempts at avoiding distasteful jobs which had to be done and for which he had to find the workers.

'What's wrong, lad?' he asked. 'Do you think that job is beneath you or do you have some medical condition which should exclude you from such essential work?'

'No, none of that, Sergeant,' the airman replied. 'It is just that I am not qualified for these duties. The others all have Honours degrees, but my degree is just an Ordinary!' The man concerned knew that the sergeant delighted in assigning the cleverest men to the worst jobs: indeed, as the sergeant saw it, the more rotten their tasks, the better pleased he was.

This little episode cost our colleague fourteen days confined to barracks (which on its own was no great hardship as the local environs had little to offer). Nevertheless, another aspect of his sentence was that he had to report each night, in full webbing, to undertake guard duties which operated on a 'two hours on' and 'four hours off' arrangement throughout the night from 8pm to 8am.

The second event or incident was again one where I was a witness. It occurred one evening in the spring and took place in the station cinema. The cinema was the sole place of relaxation I can recall in the whole camp. There might have been a NAAFI or a Salvation Army canteen but I have no recollection of such basic facilities. I was never a man for pubs and so the nearby village had nothing to lure or attract me. I did go frequently to the cinema and my only other form of commercialised relaxation was that on most Saturdays a Fife lad, called Kinnimonth, and I went into Sheerness for a meal - usually either sausage and mash or rabbit pie and chips. Following the meal we would go either to the pictures or to the dancing in the Wheatsheaf Hall, which as those of us who knew our Labour Movement realised, was a Co-operative Hall. The difficulty, whatever our choice, was that we had to catch the nine o'clock bus back to Eastchurch. There were two later buses but one needed a special ticket to travel on them and not surprisingly, such passes or tickets were never available to us. That said, a few half-crowns were spent in enjoying a modern waltz, a slow fox-trot and two quicksteps before a rush to catch the nine o'clock bus.

On the evening of our incident the station cinema was virtually full, with the main feature being an attractive American production. The incident occurred as the ten-minute newsreel was coming to a close. The specific item related to our present Queen who at that time was a lieutenant or a captain in the A.T.S. She was the officer in a squad of young women repairing and servicing motor vehicles. We saw the girls working on the cars and then we saw the Princess going under a car to ensure that the job had been done properly. The unctuous, sycophantic, sanctimonious voice of a commentator told us: '.....and so we say 'Thank You and Good-bye' to Her Royal Highness' and with this he stopped and we were given a close-up view of the Princess who, as I recall it, was wearing two medal ribbons – those of her grandfather's Silver Jubilee medal and the other of her father's coronation medal. There was a moment or two of silence which was broken by the loud raucous voice of what was clearly a West of Scotland WAAF shouting: 'Aye, an' who gied ye yer F.F.I?', a remark that gave rise to very loud storms of laughter.

To explain: F.F.I. or 'Free from Infection' was the Service nomenclature for the inspections to which all 'other ranks' were submitted to ensure they were not carrying sexual diseases. Anyone found to have any such disease was immediately withdrawn and transferred to hospital. Every camp or station had horrendous stories about the pre-penicillin treatment imposed on these unfortunates.

As the laughter subsided a voice could be heard calling for lights. The projectionist stopped the film and a blank screen confronted us. A senior N.C.O. rose from the front row of the circle. He demanded silence and went on to say that the Commanding Officer, who was in attendance, wanted to know which air-woman had shouted this foul and obscene remark. This merely provoked more shouting. Fellow Scots could be heard shouting 'Don't dae it, hen. Jist sit whaur ye ur' while other voices, mainly female, could be heard asking why, if it was all that foul, they were submitted to it at frequent intervals.

Eventually quiet of a kind was restored and the N.C.O. who had spoken earlier announced that, if she who had first shouted did not own up, the entire camp personnel would be confined for 48 hours. Once again there were shouts of support for the initiator. The N.C.O. then announced that the show was over, whereupon we all trachled back to our huts.

Two parts of this memoir of Eastchurch have yet to be related. The first and longer of the two is to report on what happened to me while the second will consist of a short and romantic addendum.

The first attempt to set me on a new career path was a suggestion that I agree to becoming an air-gunner. Foolishly, I accepted this proposal: I say foolishly because whereas the overall casualties in Bomber Command were high, the casualty rate for air-gunners was very high. When I agreed to switch to that activity, I was re-issued with flying kit whereupon I was posted to an air-gunnery school at a station outside Inverness. Come the day, however, I did not get north of Euston Station, where I was stopped by the Military Police and told to return to the delights of Eastchurch. The next day I was told that even new air-gunners were no longer required and that the rest of my R.A.F. career would have to be earth-bound.

The second attempt to re-classify me started when I was interviewed by a very attractive and sympathetic WAAF officer who in introducing herself revealed that she too was from Glasgow and as the interview proceeded, I gleaned that she was a graduate in Psychology of the University of Glasgow.

Her suggestion was that I should become a radar mechanic. I observed that I was not at all mechanical. This she dismissed and went on to point out that the training course lasted ten months. More, she argued, one of the training centres was the Royal Technical College in Glasgow and it was within her jurisdiction to ensure that I was sent there. It was, she suggested, even better in that my mother was now a widow and living on her own, so I could be billeted on my mother who would then be paid a lodging and food allowance for agreeing to my sleeping in my own bed and in the morning having breakfast at my usual place at the table.

It was abundantly clear that the lady was of good intent. She was anxious to find me something which would be respectable, interesting and rewarding. Her kindness was apparent – so much so that I succumbed: I agreed to take the trade test. But even as I agreed I knew I had made a mistake.

The following morning when we were on parade at 9 a.m. I was directed by the sergeant to proceed to a prescribed building to take 'some test or other'. It was a WAAF sergeant who was in charge of the examination. She explained there would be two papers, with 90 minutes for each. The first would be on Mathematics, the second on Mechanics and elementary electricity and electronics. There would be a ten-minute comfort break between the papers. For the maths a slide rule and logarithmic tables would be provided. One of her colleagues, a WAAF corporal, would be the invigilator although it was clear there was no way one could cheat.

I found the maths paper which ran to Trigonometry, Dynamics and the foothills of Calculus to be interesting and within my competence. On completion, with some five minutes or so to go, I felt I had done quite well.

Not so with the second paper, some of which I found unintelligible. I remember that there were three pages on the engines of motor-cars. I wrote: 'I have never owned a car. I do not think I shall ever own a car. I am proceeding to the next section.' Yet when I turned to the next section I found it equally perplexing. Eventually the WAAF corporal said 'Time up,' but I had already stopped. She collected the papers and left. For quite some time I was left on my own. Eventually an airman corporal looked in.

'Are you Carbery?' he asked. I confirmed that I was.

In due course another head and arm came round the door. This was a Flight Sergeant. He too wanted to know who I was. He satisfied himself that I was indeed the man he expected to be there. Shortly thereafter a corporal took me through the same procedure.

There then followed a spell of twenty minutes or so wherein nothing happened. That was broken when the corporal reappeared. 'You should go to the lavatory,' he said in a tone half-way between a suggestion and an order. I did as I was told.

After a further ten to fifteen minutes, the door flew open and the Flight Sergeant reappeared. 'Right then! You, lad,' he bellowed. 'Out here.' I obeyed, of course, and went out to the corridor. Suddenly two men appeared, one stood in front of me and one behind me. No sooner had they done so than the Flight Sergeant roared 'Left right, left right,' and we proceeded on our way. It was clear the man at the front knew where he was going. Moving quickly the Flight Sergeant raced ahead of us, knocked a door, swept it open and raced ahead of us again. As I went into the room he swiped my forage cap off my head. He then ordered us to stop marching and to do a left turn. By this time I knew what to expect.

The Commanding Officer was seated at his desk. Some WAAF NCOs were seated at the side of the room. The Flight Sergeant ordered the escort to fall out, whereupon they came smartly to attention, saluted, turned 'about face' and left.

The C.O. shuffled some papers.

'You are Carbery!' he half-asked, half declared.

'Yes, Sir,' I replied.

'Right then, lad,' he said and went on. 'How do you plead?' Keeping myself as erect as I could, I half-coughed.

'Excuse me, Sir,' I said. 'But am I to take it that I am on a charge?'

At this he was very angry. 'Don't you dare to be difficult,' he half-snarled. 'You know damn well that you are on a charge!'

I paused. 'I am obliged to point out, Sir, that I have not been charged.'

'Of course you have been charged,' he responded.

'No, Sir, I have not been charged: no-one charged me, Sir.'

Again there was a pause. He then turned to one of the WAAFs.

'Fetch the Flight Sergeant,' he ordered.

The girl left and returned, accompanied by the Flight Sergeant.

'You wanted me, Sir?' he said.

'Yes,' said the C.O. 'Did you charge Carbery?'

'No, Sir,' said the Flight Sergeant. 'My understanding was that Sergeant Entwistle had charged him.'

Turning again to the WAAF the C.O. said: 'Fetch Sergeant Entwhistle'. Again the girl left and returned with the Sergeant.

'Entwhistle,' said the C.O. 'Did you charge this man?' and he nodded towards me.

Entwhistle was not at all put out. 'No, Sir. As I understood it, Corporal Havering attended to the matter of the charge.'

'And did he?' queried the C.O.

'I do not know, Sir. As I took it, the Flight Sergeant was in command of the matter.'

'Get out!!' said the C.O. and the Sergeant saluted and left. 'Find Corporal Havering and bring him here.'

For the third time the WAAF left the room and returned with a male NCO. This one was a corporal. I took it he was Havering and so too did the C.O.

Struggling to control himself and keep command of himself the C.O. said: 'Corporal Havering, did you charge this airman?'

'No, Sir,' said the Corporal. 'I have not charged anyone for quite some time,' he paused and then went on. 'I took it that either Sergeant Entwistle or Flight-Sergeant Hardcastle was making the charge and ensuring that everything was tickety-boo, so to speak, Sir!' he declared.

The C.O. was very angry. Very, very angry!

'Everyone out – no, not you, Carbery – everyone else out, out now, the whole lot of you.'

The C.O. shook his head.

'Alright, Carbery, stand at ease.' He waited a while.

'Well, lad, it is your lucky day. I could charge you myself and have another senior officer hear the case. But it has been such a mess, such a balls-up, that I am going to let you away with it. But you really must start to appreciate that you and your friends must stop playing tricks on us. I take it you did set out to fail that test. As I said, you are off the hook – but you will admit that, will you not?'

'I am afraid not, Sir,' I declared. 'It is true I did not expect to do well in the Mechanics and Electricity Paper, but I did not set out to fail. I did my best, Sir. I can assure you of that.'

'No, I am not having that,' he said, but by now was far more calm than he had been. 'Damn it, man, you got the best Maths score since last summer and you got the worst mark we have ever had in the other section. That is impossible. We are assured that those who are good in one section will do well – at least get a pass – in the other section. As it is, we are told there is ....' he stopped, fumbling for the word.

'Correlation,' I dared venture.

'Exactly! That is the word. You see, you understand these things.'

'Yes, I can see there would be correlation, maybe even fairly strong correlation in the marks for the papers – but I am afraid, Sir, that I am the exception to the rule. I am akin to the French irregular verb which by its rarity virtually proves the rule. More, Sir, I believe I could prove it!'

'Oh, you do, do you?' said the C.O. 'How do you propose to do that?'

'By your sending for the papers relating to my aircrew training. Were you to do that, Sir, you would find that in mathematical subjects such as navigation I have done rather well; whereas in Engines you will find that I was given 50% at best, and I suspect it was not deserved but was dragged up from the low forties if not the thirties to throw me over the wall onto the next phase of the training.'

So he phoned for my aircrew file and in due course a WAAF knocked on the door and came in.

'You sent for this file, Sir,' she declared and hovering over his in-tray, she added: 'Shall I leave them here, Sir?'

'No, no, I'll take them here. Thank You.' I sensed that the 'Thank you' was indicative of a cooling. Slowly he thumbed his way through the file.

'By God, man, you are right!' he muttered. 'High 80s and 90s in some subjects and 50% for engines, not once but twice.'

Eventually he gave voice to a great sigh. 'Alright, Carbery, you may go but we shall go through the file again. Maybe we have not paid sufficient attention to these aircrew training files.'

I paused – and then decided to push my luck.

'I am sure your colleagues would find them useful. We, that is the former aircrew cadets, are not one homogeneous lump. We vary quite considerably, you know, Sir!'

He smiled – a rueful, thoughtful smile.

'On you go, Carbery. On you go. We'll find something for you.'

I came to attention. I could not salute – I did not have my forage cap. But I did say, 'Thank you, Sir, thank you very much.' Then I turned and left, shutting the door very quietly. It took me half-an-hour to retrieve my cap.

A week later I was posted as a meteorologist to Ternhill in middle England and served the following two years in that capacity – and loved it.

There remains the addendum which primarily concerns Kinnimonth.

One Saturday when we were in Sheerness and having sausages and chips I wanted to see a movie but he didn't fancy it and anyway, he observed, his feet were itching to dance. When we parted I made for the cinema but he observed it was too early to go to the Wheatsheaf so he would go for a wee walk. Going down a side-street he came to a tennis club with dance music coming from the hall. He assumed the club was having a fund-raising dance in their pavilion. So he went in. A girl took his greatcoat and gave him a token but no-one asked him for money. Undaunted, he proceeded to the dance area. He spotted a very attractive girl dancing with a middle-aged man, so when the music started again with a slow foxtrot he swept across the floor and asked her to dance. Twice round the floor he learned he had stumbled into a wedding reception and that his attractive partner had been one of the two bridesmaids.

It was the start of a romance. In late 1946 they married – in Sheerness. Sadly, I lost track of him, I hope they were happy and that he had the foresight to leave the mining industry before Thatcher and Scargill did for it.

Eastchurch, scene of horrors then, is now an open prison.

Jimmy Hughes

We all liked Jimmy Hughes. 'We' in this instance constituted a group of junior Executive Officers in the Ministry of Labour who worked either in Glasgow Central Employment Exchange or in one of the Department's specialist offices scattered over the Inner Glasgow Area and who availed themselves of the inexpensive lunches which were to be had in the Post Office canteen on the top floor of the Wellington Street Post Office building. The spacious lift which took us to the top floor had a notice, which, as I recall it, read: 'This lift is for a maximum of 12 persons or 8 postmen with loaded wallets.' This gave rise to ribald remarks about inflation and trade union power. To their credit, the P.O. staff did not bridle at these supposedly witty remarks: they had heard it all before.

There were eight of us in this coterie but there were very few days when all eight of us were in attendance. Illness, temporary transfers to out of town offices, training courses and generous annual leave – we were all entitled to six weeks of paid leave each year – all had an effect on our being present.

In one sense we all liked one another which was why we met as a group, but one or two guys tried to be superior, one guy aye grumbled, another was not slow to name-drop and yet another claimed to have contacts at Scottish Headquarters in Edinburgh and therefore had 'foreknowledge' of Departmental affairs.

Jimmy Hughes had no such disconcerting feature. The worst that could be – and was – said about him was that he was no 'Stakhanovite', he was not one of those workers in the Soviet Union who were given extra holidays and the like because they were very hard-working and worked all the hours the Good Lord sent.

It was not that Jimmy dodged work: it was just that he looked to do no more than what he had seen assigned. We knew that he lived in North Lanarkshire and that prior to his promotion had been a Clerical Officer in both Coatbridge and Airdrie employment exchanges. We knew too that he and his wife, who had been a piper in the Dagenham Girls' Pipe Band, and their family (they ended up with 11 children) lived in a 'pre-fab', until modest affluence enabled them to escape to a more commodious house, but still in North Lanarkshire.

The other non-department matter we knew about Jimmy was that during the war he had been an air-gunner in the Fleet Air Arm. It was seen as somehow in character that he should volunteer for a post that was markedly more dangerous than being a private in the Royal Army Pay Corps, yet was an occupation where 99% of his duty was to sit in an air-turret inspecting the waves while on the lookout for the tell-tale signs of a U-boat's periscope.

For his training he had been sent to the United States. His batch of Fleet Air Arm personnel, together with a very large band of R.A.F. potential aircrew, crossed the Atlantic, like St. Brendan, hopping from island to island. When they reached Nova Scotia, some of the R.A.F. personnel disembarked, but the rest, plus all the Fleet Air Arm men, went to New York. From that city they were transplanted in truck-loads to a very big transit camp in up-state New Jersey. There, they were assimilated into living 'State-side'. In short, they were told what and what not to do while they were in the U.S.A. After four weeks of this it was reckoned they could safely be let loose on the American population.

They were told that over the forthcoming weekend they would all be given a 72-hours pass. There were, however, strict conditions. They had a choice – either to go to New York or to go to Newark, New Jersey. Those who chose to go to New York had to stay in a hostel run by a 'voluntary' association – the Daughters of the American Revolution, the Salvation Army, the Union of Catholic Mothers, the Episcopal Church, and so it went on. The alternative to this rather paternalistic approach was to go to Newark where the men concerned would be assigned to private houses.

Of the 2000+ concerned all but six chose to go to New York. James was one of the six. Relating this experience over sausages and chips in the Post Office canteen, Jimmy explained his reasoning. Those who went to New York would have to buy all their meals, they would have to pay for public transport and for their entertainment in cinemas, dance halls, pubs, baseball matches and the like, whereas those who went to the private houses would sleep in proper beds, probably eat very well and not pay for anything.

To Jimmy the choice was obvious, even though only five others agreed with him.

When the train arrived at Newark the platform was 'manned' by 20 or so ladies, who were clearly distressed when only six young men alighted from the train. One bossy, proprietorial lady, by running, shouting and pushing some others away, managed to gather all six and in due course shove them into a large estate car. With a whirl and a flourish she swept out of the station and raced towards suburbia.

As she drove she started her questioning.

'Are any of you from London?' she wanted to know and then after a question about Yorkshire she asked: 'Is there anyone from Scotland?' Jimmy claimed the honour.

'Oh, great,' she exclaimed. 'Are you from Coalburn?'

'No,' said Jimmy. 'But I have been there on my bike!'

'Great,' roared the driver. 'That will do just fine. Your lady, in the house, wanted someone from Coalburn!'

In due course she stopped outside a house. 'Right, Scotty, this is you. Out you go, young man. Have a lovely time!'

When Jimmy was walking up the slightly sloped path which led to the steps outside the house, a lady, probably in her early thirties, opened the door and looked down at him in his navy-blue uniform with its 'bell-bottom' trousers.

'Well, well, well,' she pronounced, 'a sailor!'

It was there that Jimmy pushed his luck.

'Perceptive!' he declared and raced on. 'What's more, I am not from Coalburn.'

The lady laughed. 'Come on in,' she smiled, opening the door further in a gesture of welcome.

Once James was in the house the lady, still smiling and laughing, asked where he was from. 'Coatbridge,' he declared with perhaps a shade more aggression than was prudent.

'And what gives with this Coalburn issue?' she asked.

'That woman, that lady, who dropped me said you wanted somebody from Coalburn,' James explained.

'Oh, her,' said the lady. 'Don't mind her. She means well but she is not the brightest star in the galaxy. What's your name?' she asked.

'Hughes, James, but most folk say Jimmy Hughes.'

'Hmm,' mused the lady of the house. 'Stand over there,' she declared. Jimmy did not demur. He did as he was told! As he stood 'still' if not quite 'at attention', the lady of the house looked at him with intensity.

Eventually, her face broke into a broad smile.

'Is your Aunt Delia a cashier in the Co-op?' she asked with a smile.

'Yes,' gulped Jimmy.

'And did your grandfather work at No. 3 pit?'

'Aye,' said James, with another gulp.

'And did he go for a drink with Charlie McCrystal?' she asked.

'Aye, yes, he did,' replied the still-startled James.

This time the lady's smile broadened visibly.

'I used to take you in your pram for walks,' she declared.

The Commanding Headmaster

His name was Brady, John Brady.

No, that is untrue! It is untrue, because there are good and compelling reasons why his true name should not be used, or not at least at this juncture.

He was the headmaster of a large and very successful Catholic Comprehensive school in industrial Lanarkshire and a great deal of that success was due to him, to his personality and his drive. In particular, he looked the part: he was tall and well-built and carried himself well. He struck me as being of the same mould as Charles de Gaulle and Ireland's De Valera.

His school was akin in many ways to the equally well-known and respected St. Patrick's High in Coatbridge which had the formidable distinction of having been the first Local Authority school in the United Kingdom to have two former pupils in the Cabinet at the same time, this being achieved when Helen Liddell and John Reid were Cabinet colleagues.

Our hero was renowned and acknowledged throughout the county. Stories about him abounded, though no doubt some were apocryphal. It was observed that on one occasion, while addressing the school assembly, he had been heard to say '..and as our Blessed Lord has said, and rightly so, I think…'

Not that he always won in his exchanges with others. An illustration of this occurred on an occasion when on one of the Feast Days of the Church, the entire school had attended Mass in the nearby church. It was reported that as the Mass ended he positioned himself at the back of the central aisle. From this viewpoint he checked to ensure that everyone genuflected properly and that knees touched the tiles. At one point, however, he body-checked a wee Geography teacher as he made his way towards the exit. 'Ah, Mr. Murphy,' said Brady. 'I could not help but notice that you did not go to Holy Communion.'

Murphy, it is said, looked him in the eye.

'State of Mortal Sin, Headmaster, state of Mortal Sin!' And having made that declaration he went on: 'And now if you will excuse me, Headmaster, I need to catch Mr. Hepburn about room allocation!'

The general view was that on that occasion it was a case of 'game, set and match' to Mr. Murphy.

Sometime in the middle sixties I picked up a tale about John Brady which, as I saw it, illustrated the considerable mettle of the man. It concerned the annual prize-giving and key-note address. Hitherto, his predecessors and until the year in question, Brady himself had taken an 'unco safe' approach to the selection of the speaker. The invitations to be the prize-giver and speaker had been confined to members of the hierarchy, distinguished Catholic lay-men, Provosts of Lanarkshire burghs and fellow head-teachers. The break-through came with Brady choosing to be markedly more adventurous: he asked the Area Manager of a leading Scottish bank to undertake the task. The gentleman accepted.

Come the night, Brady hit all the right notes. He had a space reserved in the car park and had the School Captain welcome the guest and escort him to the Headmaster's room. There the guest was treated to coffee and cake and offered a dram or two which he declined. Two minutes before the kick-off time they went downstairs and walked on to the stage to rapturous and well-planned applause.

In the course of his speech the speaker urged the pupils to stay on at school beyond the minimum school-leaving age and to strive to obtain good qualifications as there were many organisations in both the public and private sectors extremely anxious to recruit such talented young people.

When the thanks had been expressed and the formal proceedings closed, the two men returned to the Headmaster's study. This time the whisky bottle was opened. As they drank their malt, Brady looked his guest straight in the eye and asked whether he had really meant what he had said about aspirations and recruitment. The banker assured him that he did.

'Why, then,' asked Brady, 'does your bank, and most of the other Scottish banks, decline to recruit young men from this and other Catholic schools?'

We do not know whether the gentleman squirmed. Only the two of them were present and although Brady leaked his question he said nothing about the response.

What we do know is that in the following autumn four boys from Brady's school and two from another such school were recruited by the speaker's bank. It was no surprise that they were allocated to branches in Coatbridge and Mossend.

There were many other stories concerning Brady and his reign as Headmaster and I reckoned I knew most of them, but there was one which perhaps was the most revealing of them all and yet I did not know about it until the late eighties.

It happened on a Friday towards the end of the academic year. It was nearly two o'clock and I was sitting in the lounge of the University Staff Club. A cup of cold coffee and an unread copy of the *Financial Times* lay unattended on the table in front of me. I was feeling rather sorry for myself.

As I sat with my glum face, a Civil Engineer with whom I was moderately friendly came up, sat down beside me and told me I looked like the principal mourner at a funeral. He asked what was amiss, and I explained that at 4.30 p.m. I was due to make a presentation to a female member of my Department who was retiring. My difficulty, however, was that I could not think of anything good to say about her.

Thereupon my friend told me to be more cheerful as, after all, I knew of John Brady and his colourful and illustrious career. I explained that I did not see the connection. The engineer told me to recall the McFie story and I, in turn, explained that I did not know it. So he told it.

As my engineering colleague reported it, Brady had been very pleased – and proud – to be appointed in his early to middle forties to the headmastership at what he came to regard at 'his' school. That said, he was more than a little dismayed that the teaching staff at his disposal included one Ian McFie, who was regarded by his peers as the worst teacher in Scotland. Having made his own assessment of the man, Brady sadly found himself agreeing with the broad sweep of the profession and thereupon set about trying to get rid of him.

This was to prove much harder and much more protracted than he had thought. McFie's union or staff association fought a magnificent rear-guard action. Recourse was made to every possible escape clause in the Conditions of Service. Meetings were postponed for an endless range of reasons, including funerals which just had to be attended by the association's officials who had been briefed to attend and speak on behalf of the beleaguered McFie.

Eventually a decision was reached. It was, of course, a compromise. The Local Authority would allow the gentleman to retire prematurely on the grounds of ill-health. An assistant headmaster was heard to comment: 'This, surely, is the first time incompetence has appeared as a medical condition.'

Arrangements were made for the retirement and for a dinner in a local hotel to mark the occasion. The place was agog. 'What,' everyone asked, 'would Brady say about McFie?' He would not say anything detrimental. To do so would be uncharitable. But then he would not say anything good about him as a teacher, as to do so would be a lie. So what would, what could he say? Everyone wanted to be there on the night.

Normally the take-up rate within the school for domestic events of this nature oscillated between seventy and eighty per cent but on this occasion it was total: it hit the hundred. So far as adjoining local schools were concerned, they usually took a few tickets, doing so as a sort of gesture. This time they were fighting to obtain tickets. The district was buzzing with excitement.

Come the night of the presentation dinner, Brady was, of course, the Chairman for the occasion. He sat in the middle seat at the top table. McFie was sitting on his right and beyond him was the local Bishop. Mrs McFie was on Brady's left and beyond her was the Director of Education for the county. He did not normally attend such events; on the contrary, he tended studiously to avoid them. He too, however, was bubbling with curiosity to see how Brady would handle it.

When the coffee cups had been cleared away, Brady surveyed the room, apparently concluded that order prevailed, whereupon he rose, used a pen to tap a wine glass and started to speak.

'My Lord' - and there he paused, nodded, partly in acknowledgement, partly in salutation – 'Right Reverend and Very Reverend Monsignors and Canons, Reverend Fathers, Reverend Mother Superior, Reverend Sisters, distinguished guests, ladies and gentleman and colleagues: we are all gathered here this evening to mark the retirement of, and to wish a long and happy retirement to, our colleague Mr Ian McFie. This we do most readily.'

Here there was a ripple, a mild but discernible ripple of applause. He went on. 'Mr McFie has a house in Elie. I am told he intends going frequently to that retreat. We trust all goes well for him when he is in the Kingdom of Fife.'

Again there was some applause – but not much.

Nevertheless, Brady acknowledged it and returned to his speech. 'Mr McFie has been employed as a teacher by the Education Department of the County for almost forty years. He has been on the staff of our school for 22 years of which I have been Headmaster for seven years and I can readily testify that he always, indeed invariably, had his registers promptly marked and submitted in time. I now call on Mrs McBride to make the presentation.'

He sat down to rapturous applause. Brady had done it: he had neither lied nor condemned.

The ensuing presentation was an anti-climax.

The Best Of Advice

Many of those who were aged between twelve and eighteen in the Thirties, in the years leading up to the Second World War, through the War years themselves and into the continuing frugality of the post-war period, will no doubt recall being sent by grandmothers, maiden aunts, neighbours and others to change or extend the loan of library books.

There were in those days two kinds of libraries. First, there were public libraries which were managed by enthusiastic and dedicated staff on behalf of Local Authorities. The Glasgow libraries were particularly good. The second group were operated through shops. The most prestigious of these were operated by Harrods and other impressive stores of that kind, catering for a fairly affluent middle-class. A notch or two down that ladder were those operating through retail outlets throughout the country, and of those Boots the Chemist was the best-known and best supported. Some small shops tried to cash in on this economic activity but most of them were gey pathetic and some downright seedy.

The young people who were sent to the respectable end of this market and in particular the public libraries will no doubt recall two names – Maurice Walsh and Annie S. Swan.

This story concerns both of these successful authors.

Walsh was the more colourful and the livelier of the two. He was an Irishman who, as a young man, entered the Customs service and spent his early years of the service in the Moray and Speyside parts of Scotland where he worked at different distilleries. He had a yen for young women with red hair and duly married one of that ilk. And but for a dramatic political event, there in Scotland he would have remained.

The dramatic event of the early twenties was the division or partition of Ireland and the creation of the Irish Free State. Thereupon, Irishmen such as Walsh were given the opportunity of remaining in the British Civil Service or electing to return to Ireland, to what became known as the 26 Counties, and work for the new Irish State governed from Dublin.

Happy with his wife and family in the north of Scotland, Walsh was expected to opt for remaining there but to the dismay of his wife and some of his colleagues he chose to leave the British Customs service and to leave his wife and family with her father, at least until he was settled in Ireland.

So it was he was assigned to a desk job in Dublin where he found himself in the middle of a bitter and bloody Civil War.

It was said in the West of Scotland that A. J. Cronin's literary career was triggered by an exceptionally wet holiday in Argyll. Bored and inactive, he drove from his holiday cottage to the nearest town where he purchased some jotters and a box of pencils. Having written his first novel he gave it to his niece to type, the publishers accepted it and that was him up and running. He never looked back and as I recall it at least three of his books were turned into films.

The entry of Walsh to the world of authorship was not dissimilar in that having worked by day in his Dublin office he found that his evenings saw him virtually imprisoned in his digs as the streets of the city were too dangerous for normal movement. So he started to write. By the time the twenties were out he was established as an acceptable and popular author. His first two books – *The Key above the Door* and *The Small Dark Man* – sold particularly well. Many gey douce parents saw his work as a suitable introduction to somewhat more mature reading for their late teenage children.

Walsh prospered but not as well as one would have expected. Thus, for the first six months of 1942, when he had eight books available in the shops, his royalties amounted to just over £1000.

His business affairs were not well handled. One example of this arose from John Ford, the film director, reading 'The Quiet Man', in *The Saturday Evening Post* in 1933. Sometime later, apparently towards the end of a drinking session, Ford bought the film rights of that tale for ten dollars. As Steve Matheson brings out in his biography of Walsh, later payments raised this to 6,200 dollars but this was still a derisory sum for the authorship rights of a movie that in time would make millions.

It is, however, high time that Miss Swan played a bigger role in this story.

When I was a boy, Annie S. Swan was a well-established Scottish writer. Her numerous books were much admired and greatly respected across the broad sweep of the community. Her readers were mainly women but many folk noted and commended her success. My two grandmothers, one Irish-Catholic and the other of Ulster-Presbyterian supplanter stock, loved Annie S. Swan novels, lavish quantities of butter on their toast, strong tea and me – their only mutual grandchild.

In the late twenties, Walsh decided to return to Scotland to attend a P.E.N. conference and the accompanying dinner. Some mischievous soul entrusted with drawing up the seating plan apparently thought it would be fun to put together Walsh, an extrovert, occasionally loud, not infrequently drink-taken Papist, and Miss Swan, a somewhat unbending extremely douce and stern Presbyterian. This mischief-maker clearly looked forward to the sparks flying. With luck, the dinner would be remembered for the noisy acrimony between the two writers.

He was bitterly disappointed. They got on famously and a friendship developed. To some extent this could and should have been foreseen, because they wrote the same sort of books in which holding hands in the dark was the high-watermark of pre-marital passion. More, Walsh was to